Advance Praise for
Trump's Ten Commandments by Jeffrey Sonnenfeld

"Only the nation's preeminent scholar on leadership could look across a lifetime of disparate behaviors, actions, and impulses and discern clear principles and patterns that explain the inexplicable. In this masterful work, Jeffrey Sonnenfeld provides the definitive blueprint for understanding what animates the most complicated and consequential president in memory. *Trump's Ten Commandments* is a must-read for those seeking to understand the past and hoping to chart the future."

—Brad S. Karp, Chairman of Paul, Weiss, Rifkind, Wharton & Garrison LLP

"Bringing his unique understanding of leadership styles and management techniques to bear as only he can, Jeffrey Sonnenfeld brilliantly decodes the ten-part method in what others see only as Donald Trump's madness. No one who hopes to understand what makes Trump tick can afford to leave this decathlon of a book unread."

—Laurence Tribe, University Professor, Harvard Law School

"I spent over a decade at Donald Trump's side—through victories, scandals, and self-inflicted disasters. No one understands the mechanics of his chaos better than I do. In this remarkable work, Jeffrey Sonnenfeld dissects Trump's leadership through a lens of truth and experience, translating what most see as disorder into the studied, intentional strategy I recognize as distinctly Trump's. This is a master class in decoding power, ego, and manipulation—essential reading for anyone seeking to understand how Trump truly operates."

—Michael Cohen, Former Personal Attorney to President Donald J. Trump

"I was charmed by Donald Trump, worked for him, and then also saw his dangerous flaws. Some treat him as the village idiot or a madman because of his unorthodox impulses. Sure, he may not have been the top finance, econ, or history student at Wharton, but critics are as wrong to discount his communication genius and street savvy as others are to deify him. Sonnenfeld is the first scholar to reveal just how Trump operates, the method behind the magic and malice—important and timely lessons needed to protect our nation."

—Anthony Scaramucci, CEO of SkyBridge Capital and Former White House Communications Director in the First Trump Administration

"Donald Trump is such a polarizing figure that no author has attempted to analyze his unique skills and failings in a nonpartisan way. Sonnenfeld has done us all the great favor of capturing Trump's nontraditional leadership traits, distilling them into the Ten Commandments that make up his power politics, and presenting them in an insightful, personal, and engaging book."

—Tom Glocer, Former CEO of Thomson Reuters;
Lead Director of Morgan Stanley & Merck

"The crazy, unpredictable, chaotic behavior of Donald Trump has a pattern! Who knew! Jeffrey Sonnenfeld combines his deep knowledge of Trump along with a rigorous analysis and examples of his actions to decode the 'how' of Trump's unique leadership. For all of us scratching our heads, this book provides a lens into patterns of his leadership that have not been previously recognized."

—Anne Mulcahy, Former CEO of Xerox; Former Director,
Johnson & Johnson, Citigroup, and Target

"With *Trump's Ten Commandments*, Jeffrey Sonnenfeld has written an essential and riveting book. He's brought his deep knowledge of leadership as the nation's preeminent leadership scholar to one of the critical questions of our era: How does President Donald Trump actually think, how does he lead, and how does he wield power? In this book, Sonnenfeld provides a persuasive lens through which he argues that Trump is far more intentional, and as a result more predictable, than most of us might believe."

—Bethany McLean, *Washington Post* Columnist,
Author of *Smartest Guys in the Room*

"On the whole, there are few groups more negatively disposed to the personal traits of Donald Trump than the CEOs of large US companies. That's because the CEOs have almost universally risen through the ranks of their organizations through inspiring leadership characteristics such as integrity, team building, diversity of thought, transparency, and positive motivation. Trump's leadership playbook tends to draw from a very different set of characteristics. Unfortunately, CEOs can't speak candidly for fear of retribution, but Jeff Sonnenfeld speaks for them in this book by outlining ten traits that make Trump's leadership style unique. This must-read guide helps business leaders prepare for dealing with an official like Trump without having to learn the hard way."

—Doug Parker, Former CEO, American Airlines

"Jeff Sonnenfeld's *Trump's Ten Commandments* frames usefully and convincingly Trump's leadership style, methods, and motivations for them. It draws great strength from his personal contacts with Trump, with Trump's family, with many of his advisors, and with business leaders. It also draws strength from Sonnenfeld's reference to a wide range of academics who have studied leadership methods. The leadership styles attributed to Trump, while uniquely Trump's in their totality, also apply to other leaders. Understanding them through the lens that Sonnenfeld provides can be very useful both in understanding the other person and being able to relate constructively with them."

—John Pepper, Former CEO, Procter & Gamble;
Former Chairman, The Walt Disney Company

"Jeffrey Sonnenfeld is, first and foremost, a consummate leadership scholar and has been for decades. In this book, he turns his attention to analyzing the leadership strategies of Donald Trump. Neither screed nor apologia, this book explains not only *what* Trump does but, more importantly, *how* and *why* it is so often effective. In a word (or two), amazingly insightful."

—Jeffrey Pfeffer, Thomas D. Dee II Professor of
Organizational Behavior, Graduate School of Business,
Stanford University and Author of *7 Rules of Power*

"Jeff Sonnenfeld has known and counseled presidents and CEOs for decades. Having a long relationship with our current president, Jeff is uniquely able to explain Donald Trump's motivations and methods. Those who reflexively support the president and those who viscerally oppose him have one thing in common: They both think they understand what he's doing and why. Sonnenfeld reveals how they are often both wrong."

—Jeff Bewkes, Former CEO of Time Warner

"Sonnenfeld shows that many of Trump's sharpest critics continue to be conned (or 'fooled,' if you prefer) by the president's ability to brazenly exploit any situation. This book explains how Trump's 'Wall of Sound' approach to leadership has been so powerful, and so dangerous for our democracy."

—Michael S. Roth, President of Wesleyan University

"When I asked Henry Kissinger, my lifelong mentor and confidant, after their first meeting following Trump's election what kind of president he thought Trump would be, he used exactly the same word Jeff Sonnenfeld used in his introduction to this book—'consequential.' He said he would leave it to historians to write about how and why.

"Now we don't have to wait. Jeff's book delves deeply and insightfully into both the how and why. It is unique among all books written so far in the approach he takes to addressing these issues. He does so from a freshly unconventional perspective. But then again, the subject of this book is highly unconventional as a president and as a person.

"To understand how unconventional he is and how this affects his policy, our country, and the world, this book is essential and highly thought-provoking—for those who passionately love Trump, who passionately dislike him, who have not made up their minds, and who are still trying to understand him. Those in the latter category, especially, need to read and study this enormously penetrating work. It is brilliantly written, deeply insightful, filled with rich and unique anecdotes that only Jeff Sonnenfeld with his experience and relationship with Trump could provide, and dazzlingly colorful in his portrayal of Trump and the world around him."

—Robert Hormats, Former US Under Secretary of State for Economic Affairs and Top Advisor to Five US Presidents Across Parties

"Some people see chaos. Sonnenfeld sees the playbook. *Trump's Ten Commandments* is the sharpest decoding of Trump's leadership I've seen, and having lived it in the White House during his first presidency, I can tell you: this book is essential for anyone who wants to understand how power truly operates today. A consequential guide for leaders—and a sanity check for the rest of us. No matter your view of Trump—pro, anti, or just trying to survive the turbulence—this book gives you the tools to understand the moment."

—Olivia Troye, Trump/Pence White House Homeland Security and Counterterrorism Advisor

"In reading Jeff Sonnenfeld's insightful and personal account of what makes Donald Trump "tick," his Ten Commandments, I not only gained a far better perspective on our current president's beliefs, behaviors, and results, but a much stronger realization that we all live in a hub-and-spokes model of relationships to others, one that we impact with our own perceptual reality, behavioral choices, and outcomes, both good and bad. This leads me to question and reflect on the commandments that have shaped my own network of relationships and their consequences on my life. Similar to my many years of learning from Jeff's academic insights and caring friendship, reading *Trump's Ten Commandments* has not only led me to greater knowledge of Trump but also a much deeper understanding of self."

—Thomas Cummings, Professor of Management and Organization, University of Southern California, former President Academy of Management

Trump's Ten Commandments

Trump's Ten Commandments

Strategic Lessons from the Trump Leadership Toolbox

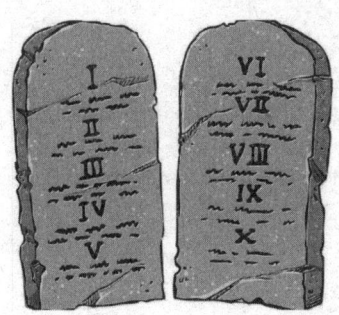

By Jeffrey Sonnenfeld

Trump's Ten Commandments: Strategic Lessons from the Trump Leadership Toolbox

Copyright © 2026 by Jeffrey Sonnenfeld

All rights reserved. No part of this publication may be reproduced, stored in a retrieval system, or transmitted in any form by any means, electronic, mechanical, photocopy, recording, or otherwise, without the prior permission of the publisher, except as provided by USA copyright law.

No patent liability is assumed with respect to the use of the information contained herein. Although every precaution has been taken in the preparation of this book, the publisher and author assume no responsibility for errors or omissions. Neither is any liability assumed for damages resulting from the use of the information contained herein.

Published by Worth Books, an imprint of Forefront Books, Nashville, Tennessee. Distributed by Simon & Schuster.

Library of Congress Control Number: 2025927158

Print ISBN: 978-1-63763-556-8
E-book ISBN: 978-1-63763-557-5

Cover Design by George Stevens, G Sharp Design LLC

Printed in the United States of America
26 27 28 29 30 31 RR4 10 9 8 7 6 5 4 3 2 1

DEDICATION

This book is dedicated to my lovely, loving, brilliant, and bold daughters, Sophie and Lauren. They are the light of my life—the purpose and joy of each day since they were each born. They channel perfectly the spirit and inspiration of my selfless, courageous, patriotic, departed parents, Rochelle and Burton Sonnenfeld, and that of the continued presence of my "big" brother Marc, and of their mother, Clarky, who has been my best friend for twenty-seven years.

CONTENTS

Introduction... 13

Background.. 23

Chapter 1: Trump's Hub-and-Spokes Model of Leadership
Centralizing All Power in Your Own Hands................. 33

Chapter 2: The Real Art of Trump's Deal
Maximizing Leverage by Starting with a Punch in the Face Versus Building Trust.. 55

Chapter 3: Divide and Conquer
Build Walls, Not Bridges............................... 79

Chapter 4: How Trump Makes Money
The Art of Stealing the Deal—Heads I Win, Tails You Lose...... 105

Chapter 5: Trump Behind Closed Doors One-on-One
The Fluidity of Friends, Foils, and Foes.................. 135

Chapter 6: The Wall of Sound
Trump's Perpetual Noise Machine of Constant, Overwhelming Distractions................................ 151

Chapter 7: Trump's World of Winners and Losers
Class for the Masses, Avoiding Losers like the Plague, and Selective Retribution............................. 165

Chapter 8: Rewriting History Through the Sleeper Effect
When Relentless Repetition Becomes Truth 183

Chapter 9: Sultan of Insult
Reducing Complexity to Simplicity 199

Chapter 10: Donald the Great
The Role of Grandeur, Image, and Heroic Aura 211

Conclusion 233
Notes 243
Acknowledgments 263
About the Author 269

INTRODUCTION

President Donald Trump dominates the headlines—with a smorgasbord of books written about him. So why would anyone want to read another Trump book?

No one, neither supporters nor adversaries, has analyzed how he actually leads, and his strategic playbook. The simple truth is that Trump has only a handful of tricks up his sleeve. We have clustered those into ten categories: Trump's Ten Commandments. They are not Moses's laws from Sinai governing ethical conduct; they are Trump's own rules for gaining, wielding, and keeping power, politically incorrect and often uninformed by societal norms, conventional wisdom, or prevailing groupthink, yet startlingly effective and street-savvy. These are the stratagems he returns to time and time again, no matter the context, that comprise his rules of thumb for navigating just about any and every situation.

In his 1964 book *The Conduct of Inquiry*, the philosopher Abraham Kaplan coined the term "the law of instrument,"[1] referring to the paradox of success where a tool that works in one circumstance becomes generalized to be overused for all situations. In short, if you give a young child a hammer, everything will look to him or her like a nail, yet the use of a saw or screwdriver or even a gentle hand gesture might be the more appropriate action. Trump's favorite tactics are similarly blunt tools, and Trump reverts repeatedly to these same Ten Commandments to great effect, regardless of the context. For all his supposed unpredictability, the reality is Trump's rawest impulses in wielding power are often surprisingly predictable. This is obvious to those who have worked with and followed Trump closely for decades—but that is a surprisingly small, and rapidly dwindling, group of people.

Though Trump is surrounded by thousands, if not millions, of self-anointed pals, clingers-on, rotating sycophants, devoted cultists, and partisan loyalists who claim to know him well, the truth is he has had few, if any, genuine, sustained lifelong "intimates." Consider this: For all the mythology about Trump as the supposed "playboy," have you ever heard of any former Trump girlfriends with anything particularly insightful to say about the man on a personal basis?

Even more importantly, most of the loyalists currently surrounding Trump came into his orbit only after he entered politics. Few of Trump's genuine, oldest, closest acquaintances have been able to keep up with his head-spinning, vertiginous, singular career, spanning real estate to entertainment and media and then, finally, to politics.[2] Most were left behind, cowed, or chose to tap out long ago, disoriented by Trump's dizzying metamorphoses and constant reinventions or intimidated into silence.

Those who saw Trump the most clearly and incisively are virtually all dead—not only his parents and his mentors but also most of his contemporaries and three of his four siblings, including his sister, Judge Maryanne Trump Barry, the last person living whom Trump truly feared.[3] In their place, a younger generation of admiring, obsequious yes-men and yes-women have stepped in, to whom Trump is practically a deity and can do no wrong. Likewise, the media—however well-intentioned—has also been of little help in shedding light on Donald Trump, the person, and his strategic playbook.

Instead, they provide breathless yet superficial coverage of the breaking news crises du jour, playing into Trump's hands exactly as he intended. Steeped in the insular world of Washington, political journalists lack the necessary fluency in arenas outside of politics, like business, entertainment, and society, to truly understand how Trump thinks. For these correspondents, the world of New York real estate and Studio 54 are as foreign a universe as Mars, and they had barely heard of the man before he descended Trump Tower's golden escalator in 2015, knowing little about his prior metamorphoses and the ups and downs of his pre-political life.[4] Meanwhile, biographers often get caught up in the quotidian minutiae and material artifices of Trump's life, underestimating, if not downright failing to capture, his strategic savvy. Similarly, the legions of critics who flock to condemn his every move often fail to understand his most basic instincts and thought patterns. However one feels about Trump, chalking it all up to being "lucky" hardly does justice to his methods.

By contrast, I have known and worked closely with Donald Trump for a quarter century, as an advisor, friend, critic, adversary, and everything in between. In fact, I encouraged and helped enable Trump's evolution from businessman to media personality and then politician; and I have served as a catalyst for and motivator of significant opposition to Trump's excesses. These vantage points, along with my shared history with Trump, have given me unique insights into how he leads, his strategic playbook, and his bag of tricks.

To those who argue that the words "Trump" and "strategic leadership" should never go in the same sentence, I say, quite simply, you are mistaken. I hear your arguments and know you will say that Trump is so unpredictable, uninformed, impressionable, and impulsive that clearly he has no strategy. You're not *entirely* wrong. Trump is not a strategist in the classic sense of the word. The second coming of Niccolo Machiavelli or Sun Tzu he is certainly not. But to underestimate Trump's strategic acumen and intentionality is a big mistake.

If Trump is dumb, he is dumb as a fox. While he rarely reads and might not pass some college exams were he to take them today,[5] that is all irrelevant, because an indisputable canniness, a shrewd instinct for survival, and a chameleon-like adaptability guide his every move. He is impulsively, even explosively, open with his opinions but keeps his strategic game plans close to his vest. And make no mistake about it: There is a method to the madness, and he knows what he is doing. Where others see chaos and unpredictability, I see Trump getting exactly what he wants by intentional design. And therein lies his secret sauce. Through decades of sheer repetition and fine-tuning, he has developed a set of stratagems and tricks that allow him to get what he wants when he wants it, no matter how crazy it might seem to the uninitiated. By deploying the same tried-and-true stratagems over and over again—some of them crossing the lines of conventionally acceptable behavior—Trump manages to regularly and consistently bluster, bully, cajole, flatter, and slither his way out of jams, and into positions of maximum advantage and leverage for achieving his goals.

The leadership stratagems that Trump has deployed to overcome successive challenges are visible in plain sight to those who have followed his career closely. That's why I'm writing this book: to give you a better understanding of how Donald Trump thinks and how Donald Trump leads, and his strategic playbook. My hope is that you will come away with not only greater clarity about the world we are living in but some strategic lessons about how to lead, as well as how not to lead, in your own life, and what kind of leader you wish and choose to be yourself.

I acknowledge that there are many things this book is not. For one, this book is not a policy treatise or partisan platform, nor is it a comprehensive chronicling of the impact of Trump's decisions. However I feel about many of Trump's policies and their impact on people, the country, and the world—and as a public intellectual, I have a long track record of commentary across many issues—in this book at least, I am focused first and foremost on understanding how Trump sees and uses power. In other words, *how* he makes his decisions. Nor is this a kiss-and-tell-all confessional. Rather, I selectively draw on my personal experiences with Trump across decades of close interaction but also avoid relying exclusively on personal anecdotes by intentionally drawing on other case studies and illustrative examples to inform this analysis of the Ten Commandments that, combined, make Trump a singular, unique figure in his approach and, of course, his impact.

All this is worth chronicling, because escaping analysis is precisely the point of the leadership tactics Trump employs. Too often, the intentionality and craftiness behind his actions are hidden beneath the veneer of bluster and bravado, by design. But it is exactly this intentionality that is worth understanding about one of the most consequential individuals of our era.

Regardless of whether one loves or hates him, there is no denying that Trump stands alone in the annals of history. It is indisputable Donald Trump will be remembered as one of the most controversial and consequential political leaders in American history. Historians measure US presidents with such varied yardsticks as election results, legislative success, integrity in office, government fairness, economic growth, technological advancement, average standard of living, public safety, public health, global stability, diplomatic victories, and domestic harmony. On all these metrics, the nation's self-concept and global image will never be the same, with the historic milestones of Pre-Trump and After Trump punctuating politics. For some Americans, there is a cult-like allegiance and affection for his unorthodox strong authority, while for other Americans there has been daily horror and defiance of his rule. Some will want to pattern their own power and influence on the strengths of his tactics, while others will want to ensure that what they believe to be authoritarian control and demagogic rhetoric never returns.

Donald Trump's career path is not that of a conventional politician, businessman, or media titan, nor that of a scholar, historian, psychologist, global diplomat, military leader, or economist. Yet he disrupted each of these fields, revealing enormous gaps in what the experts presumed to be the realities of their respective domains. His leadership instincts frequently match the research of decades of scholarship and academic theory, which he never needed to read to deftly intuit and deploy. He has challenged and shattered conventional orthodoxies, regardless of whether that was in pursuit of patriotic, unifying, peace-making, deregulatory outcomes as his supporters argue, or for personally enriching, self-aggrandizing, bullying, repressive, divisive, vindictive purposes as his critics argue.

That has always been the case with Trump across his entire life, but now it is especially true—and especially consequential—in his role as president.

Having personally advised five US presidents across parties, I can confidently claim that Donald Trump has no peer in his portfolio of success or setbacks, nor in his modus operandi.

First, in his tenure as president, Donald Trump has violated all the rules and norms of the presidency as laid out by pretty much anyone and everyone imaginable: historians, psychologists, policy experts, journalists, media commentators, political scientists, you name it. In the 1970s, I was a student of the renowned Harvard political scientist Richard Neustadt. His hugely influential 1960 book, *Presidential Power: The Politics of Leadership*, insisted that the essence of presidential strength is the power to persuade rather than to issue decrees. He described the US presidency as a legally weak position. His core thesis was that the president's formal constitutional powers are constrained, with their effectiveness reliant on their ability to bargain and persuade other key political players. This is because the American system is one of "separated institutions sharing power," not concentrated power in the hands of any single individual.

He warned that a president cannot accomplish much by merely barking orders, channeling President Truman's derisive prediction when General Eisenhower was elected president: "Poor Ike, it won't be a bit like the army. He'll sit here, and he'll say, 'Do this! Do that!' And nothing will happen." To Neustadt, a president had to coax others to join him through prestige and reputation rather than issue commands—in other words, the antithesis of Trump's approach.

Clearly, Trump did not get this memo, nor would he have cared much for Neustadt's theories. Since taking office, he has continued to steadily concentrate power in his own hands, legislative and judicial guardrails be darned.

Both Princeton's revered political scholar and psychologist Fred Greenstein and presidential historian Stephen Ambrose challenged Neustadt's view of Eisenhower as inept, instead portraying a crafty leader who masqueraded behind a genial external demeanor to accomplish careful strategic ends. After decades of research on the effectiveness of thirty US presidents, Greenstein developed a checklist of six qualities by which to evaluate success or failure in the Oval Office: public communication, organizational capacity, political skill, vision, cognitive style, and emotional intelligence. In his book *The Presidential Difference: Leadership Style from FDR to Clinton*, Greenstein argued that emotional intelligence was the most important quality. He suggested that emotional intelligence could be measured by "the president's ability to manage his emotions and turn them to constructive purposes, rather than being dominated by them and allowing them to diminish his leadership." Trump's heated rhetoric, seemingly impulsive actions, vindictiveness, and hair-trigger attacks when feeling insulted would not rate well on these scales; yet before his death in 2018, at age eighty-eight, Greenstein reportedly declared Trump's presidency "fascinating to a scholar of leadership because it's so different from anything else"—an expert acknowledging an aberration to all previously held norms, and acknowledging that his own expert theories were obliterated.

Similarly, careful, reverential biographical profiles of prior presidents authored by distinguished presidential historians lavished praise on their subjects, portraying them as near-mythic heroes and lifting them toward a kind of civic apotheosis, airbrushed of their foibles and the complex trade-offs of wielding power. Perhaps that is why many of these same historians hit a wall of bewilderment when trying to explain how Trump functions. Their condemnations capture peccadilloes and shortcomings in his character but failed to shed any light on how he actually thinks and why he does what he does beyond simplistic charges of greed and vanity. There is far more to understanding Trump than merely accusing him of self-aggrandizing motives and throwing up one's hands in frustration.

All this is to say, Trump's singular journey—and how he navigated the manifold challenges and setbacks along the way—is worth understanding from a strategic and leadership perspective. You should understand *how* he has accomplished what he has, regardless of how you feel about what he has done.

There can be no dispute that Trump has charted an unprecedented and singular course in the annals of American history. Richard Nixon's comeback from his 1960 defeat to win the presidency in 1968 was considered a previously unimaginable milestone by historians.[6] However, Trump's transformation from businessman with no political experience to president and his subsequent comeback after his 2020 presidential defeat to Joe Biden following criminal conviction as a thirty-four-count felon,[7] four federal and state prosecutions including for election fraud,[8] and the desertion of most, if not all, of his original political lieutenants,[9] is in a category by itself and makes all prior comebacks pale in comparison. These Ten Commandments explain how Trump builds but also how he sometimes breaks his intended creations. We will examine how he gets into—and out of—trouble.

Surely there has never been a more divisive US president than Donald Trump, and that does not trouble him. This is not an unintended legacy for him. In his office back in 2015, before he was taken seriously as a presidential candidate, he told me that he hoped to tap into populist anger, and mused about going to the left of Senator Bernie Sanders, while simultaneously realizing that tapping into populist anger on the right might be a more realistic and potent route.[10] Indeed, ideology has never been the correct prism through which to understand the notoriously flexible and unideological Trump, with Trump scrambling the conventional dividing lines of left, right, and center.

To understand Trump, it's not enough to rely on overripe ideological explanations, nor is it sufficient to take any of his actions on global and domestic matters individually. Like the old Indian parable of the five blind men and the elephant, you might discern parts of Trump while missing the whole, for he is more than the sum of his parts. Many otherwise insightful observers of Trump often fail to capture that essential truth, revealing illuminating anecdotes about how Trump approached specific decisions while failing to see the broader *patterns* hiding in plain sight. Similarly, many former Trump deputies subsequently wrote books, both supportive and critical, capturing their perspectives on their own individual interactions with Trump, but these Trump lieutenants invariably missed the forest for the trees, for *anecdotes* alone miss the *patterns* of how Trump operates. Trump lets each of his subordinates see a different part of himself while rarely letting anyone see the full picture.

Ultimately, Trump, the leader, is a complex and contradictory blend, exhibiting strokes of genius while also hampered by huge and readily apparent blind spots, producing a man who is at once revered and vilified, seen as a messiah by his most passionate supporters and a dangerous megalomaniac by his most virulent critics. But underneath all of this, there is some discernible, understandable logic to how Trump approaches problems. Shedding light on this logic is the purpose of *Trump's Ten Commandments*.

Regardless of how one might feel about Donald Trump's leadership and his objectives, it is important to document and analyze how he accomplishes his objectives, why he does what he does, when it works for him in achieving his goals, and when it does not.

As his son-in-law Jared Kushner has repeatedly told my Yale CEO Summits, "Before you judge Donald Trump, you have to understand him. He thinks differently than you do."[11]

Here's my firsthand view into Donald Trump's bag of stratagems and his most frequently used, go-to chess moves.

BACKGROUND

I have been a scholar and professor of leadership for five decades, teaching at Harvard, Emory, and Yale. In my research, I study all kinds of leaders, from iconic heroes to failures and frauds, in sectors as diverse as business, entertainment, and politics. I have advised thousands of leaders along the way, including five US presidents from both political parties, countless bipartisan cabinet secretaries, elected officials at every level from mayors to the US Senate, and thousands of Fortune 500 CEOs. I continue to convene gatherings of top leaders frequently at events as varied as my Yale CEO Summits, Yale Mayors Colleges, and Yale Higher Education Leadership Summits.

Having studied social psychology, sociology, economics, history, political science, and anthropology, I have come to realize that these academic disciplines tend to minimize the importance of individual personality traits and differences, instead focusing on economic, national, regional, interest group, and demographic drivers of behavior. Brendan Maher, Harvard's long-serving chairman of psychology and social relations, and a pioneer of the scientific study of psychology, told me that "the study of human behavior approaches personality psychology with enlightened skepticism." John Padgett, the renowned Chicago sociologist and political scientist, told me that personality psychology was "misleadingly and hopelessly reductionist and simplistic," dismissing the need to understand leaders as individuals. Meanwhile, while journalists appropriately focus on the individual personalities of leaders, they often vilify them with reflexive ideological skepticism rather than seek to understand their unique attributes, and they fail to sufficiently contextualize their leadership style on a spectrum of individual values, skills, and motives.

While my lifelong study of leaders across sectors informs this book, it is my unique experiences with Donald Trump across many decades that give me some unique standing to analyze his leadership tool kit. I first became close with Trump when, paradoxically, I was an original critic of his hit TV show *The Apprentice* in the early 2000s, writing scathing critiques of his reality TV stardom. At the time, NBC had asked me to review each episode for the first season to analyze the leadership lessons. Not having tracked Trump as closely as *Spy* magazine—which trailed him religiously and satirically, anointing him "The Donald"—I agreed, figuring it would help me catch up. What I saw horrified me. I thought that it was the exact wrong model of American business leadership for young, ambitious, rising generations of proteges to seek to emulate, or for our global trading partners seeking to understand how to do business in the US. It was the antithesis of all the ideal values of the truly great business leaders I had studied.

In one early critique in the pages of *The Wall Street Journal*, I ridiculed, "[*The Apprentice*] neglects the core functions of leadership, integrity, inspiration, and invention. No business innovation surfaces, no societal problems are solved. Instead, we see people hawking sex, booze, bags of dirt, and more sex, and celebrity access." I likened the elimination game format of the show and the salacious intrigue as "akin to a musical chairs game in a Hooters restaurant."

My vocal, high-profile criticism resulted in Trump and myself being constantly juxtaposed in media narratives about *The Apprentice*, which predictably drove Trump crazy.

In case readers haven't noticed, Trump can be very sensitive to criticism. Less than amused, he lashed out at me on TV, bragging, "Sonnenfeld, this guy, he gets more publicity from this show. . . . The real world has all the things he hates. He says there's too much sex, it doesn't exist. Excuse me, I can tell you it exists, from personal knowledge." Trump then wrote a response in *The Wall Street Journal* blustering, "Sonnenfeld lacks the insight required to understand the architecture of a corporation. Perhaps that's why he's a professor at Yale instead of the Wharton School of Business, my alma mater."

Alas, Trump should have remembered the Streisand effect—where an attempt to censor information backfires, leading to it being seen by a much larger audience—for his attacks on me only poured fuel on the fire. There is nothing the media loves more than a good food fight, as we were subsequently set up as foils on CNN, CNBC, and NBC, on shows like *Kudlow & Cramer*, *The Today Show*, and *Dateline*, and even at in-person and hybrid forums in places as far away as Kuala Lumpur, Malaysia, and São Paulo, Brazil.

Apparently really fed up, Trump started bombarding my phone line, calling me privately at my office at Yale. I knew that he had taken down countless critics through endless, largely frivolous litigation—more on Trump's law-as-warfare, or "lawfare," strategy later—and I wasn't eager to follow that path. Even though his threats were meritless, I religiously avoided his many calls.

Except one day, my administrative assistant, in a devilish mood, put the call through knowingly, warning me in good cheer that it was The Donald just as I picked up, a moment too late for me to hang up. I went, "Oh no," but there he was, his voice booming clearly through the line.

Trump began a blue streak of insults, while I frantically tried (unsuccessfully) to locate Yale's general counsel and get her to join the call. After Trump was through, I calmly replied that I thought we'd covered this ground already in public media forums. "If you're done,

I'm done," I said, and tried to hang up. But Trump responded, "Not so fast," and suddenly pivoted to ask how I might like to become the founding president of Trump University. I'd expected more litigation threats, but I guess he realized that I didn't have much in the way of assets at the time and decided that attempting to drown a squeaky wheel in oil might be the better approach than trying to replace the squeaky wheel.

I told Trump that, while I was flattered, that wasn't the right career move for me. My mother had always wanted me to become a college president, but perhaps not of this specific institution. Then Trump pivoted course again, complimenting me by saying, "Well, you seem like such a bright young man." I bantered back, "Can you repeat that?" He replied, "Which part?" Playing along, I said, "Either part, I don't hear either part so much around here." Trump chuckled and said to somebody sitting with him who hadn't been introduced, "I think we can work with this guy." Then, directing his attention back to me, he asked if I played golf.

I tried to beg off, saying that I was terrible at golf and that it wouldn't be a great experience for either of us. He offered to teach me, and when I still said no, he insisted. Figuring that golf was better than a lawsuit, I agreed but asked to bring some friends. In designing the perfect support crew, I chose a striking lady friend, who is a single-digit handicap golfer, and a brilliant mathematical economist colleague of mine at Yale, who is a genuine negotiation expert and loves to argue playfully but intensely. Both friends were hugely skeptical of Trump and came to our golf game loaded for bear, so I was expecting our first in-person meeting to be feisty, if not outright combative, with hugely divergent personalities and colliding agendas.

To my horror and amazement, my support system collapsed upon meeting Trump, and they gravitated to his aura. Yes, the once deep animosity of both of my friends immediately melted as soon as we arrived as Trump laid on the charm. My lady friend went out and played golf with him; they arrived back shortly thereafter, having played only three holes because she beat him. But he flattered her nevertheless, saying that she reminded him of his then-fiancée, Melania, and giving her clubs and shoes. She had not been a fan of Trump previously; she had joined me in viewing *The Apprentice* outtakes NBC had sent to us a day in advance for *The Wall Street Journal* series I was writing, and she did not find the salacious and unsavory things she saw amusing. But she was plainly charmed by Trump after she met him in person, even claiming to all who would hear her out that his hair was real and that he was a delightful person.

Meanwhile, my brilliant economist colleague was similarly converted, selling Trump on endorsing a litany of entrepreneurial products and businesses he was developing. After a while, Trump turned to me and said, "Look, your friends love me, what does it take to win you over?" I replied that I couldn't be bought and that I saw the premise of the show as the problem, taking engaging, starry-eyed young people and turning them against each other in a vicious, musical chairs, zero-sum game. Trump said don't blame him, blame Jack Welch—the then-head of GE, which owned NBC, which produced *The Apprentice*. According to Trump's retelling, after Welch saw how well CBS's *Survivor* was doing, he told Jeff Zucker, the then-head of NBC Universal, to try to secure *Survivor* for NBC, because reality TV was getting great reviews and was so cheap to produce.

Then, according to Trump, when Zucker couldn't get *Survivor* from CBS, he had Mark Burnett create the same show with the same premise, but instead of throwing contestants off an island, they would fire them from a job, and that became the premise of *The Apprentice*.

After Trump explained his perspective, I replied that while I didn't know about Jack Welch's take on all this, I thought Trump ought to change the show to past-their-prime celebrity "apprentices," like Don Rickles, Joan Rivers, Jackie Mason, and other offensive comedians such as Andrew Dice Clay—all public figures so acerbic toward others that they deserved each other—and let them go at it with each other instead of corrupting starry-eyed young people. As an added bonus, these washed-up comedians would surely be happy to do it for free, for the free publicity. Trump defended the elimination game formula of the show as critical for drama but was intrigued by my counterproposal and asked me to give him a year to figure it out and transition the show toward that model. I trusted him and withheld continued public criticism until he could morph *The Apprentice* into *The Celebrity Apprentice*, and indeed, he delivered on his word. To his credit, I found him genuinely disarming in his candor, charm, and willingness to understand my criticisms, as he clearly wanted to see what he could do to stop me from criticizing him so vocally.

We became friends at that point, and I continued to visit Trump Tower through the years at his invitation, even bringing the CEOs of the largest Chinese state-owned enterprises along to visit with him when they came to Yale for an executive program I was teaching in. That mutually amicable relationship continued up through Trump's pivot into politics and the 2016 presidential election. In fact, in the earliest days of Trump's bid in 2015, when virtually the entire political establishment refused to take him seriously, I was one of the first media commentators to grasp the serious potential of a Trump candidacy, writing some of the first objective profiles on him in a set of *Fortune* magazine columns.

Although I was a Hillary Clinton friend and supporter, at one salon-style dinner for wealthy GOP donors hosted by Larry Kudlow in August 2015 at his Redding, Connecticut, home, I ruffled some feathers when I cited Trump as the front-runner and expressed my belief that he could really win. The fifty attendees had all spoken in favor of their own favorite GOP primary contenders, from Jeb Bush to Marco Rubio to Ted Cruz to Carly Fiorina; they all offered strong endorsements of virtually anyone but Trump—except Roger Stone, who refused to endorse anyone, having just left the Trump campaign

Trump repeatedly called me to Trump Tower to offer advice, and I often brought along a diverse set of voices whose insights I thought might benefit him.

abruptly. I questioned whether the group might be overlooking the credibility of Trump's candidacy as the elephant in the room, thinking that the GOP elephant mascot would be a popular symbol. The group, however, burst into laughter. Mary Kissel of *The Wall Street Journal* told me I was unfair to Carly Fiorina, as she was far superior to Trump. Another attendee, Kellyanne Conway, stood up to scold me, saying that as a schoolteacher, I lacked her political savvy. She said to the group, "As an expert on the psychographics of Republican women voters, I can tell you Trump will never get 10 percent of GOP women voters, and that is why I am helping lead the Cruz super PAC." Ironically, both Kellyanne Conway and Mary Kissel would later join the Trump administration and become true believers.

Trump repeatedly called me to Trump Tower to offer advice during his early candidacy, and I often brought along a diverse set of voices whose insights I thought might benefit him. For example, I brought one liberal political scientist from Yale who was originally highly skeptical of Trump but, to his own amazement, became cautiously intrigued by Trump's curious mind after a spirited discussion on varied topics ranging from health-care reform to gerrymandering. As another example, after hearing Trump's hardline perspective on China, I brought to his attention a book written by my old Harvard friend, the controversial, virulently anti-China economist Peter Navarro. Before I knew it, Peter had landed on the Trump campaign, writing economic and trade policy memos. To my surprise, Trump often cited me by name in his early campaign speeches in 2015 and even in a GOP presidential debate, accurately capturing my perspectives but botching my title, promoting me several rungs up the ladder to the dean of all of Yale! After he was elected in 2016, he suggested to me a senior position in his government that I declined, as I had his offer of the presidency of Trump University so many years earlier.

Trump continued calling for advice throughout his first term, and I became friendly with many of his most trusted lieutenants, including his son-in-law Jared Kushner and a dozen or so of his cabinet members such as Elaine Chao, Wilbur Ross, and Linda McMahon as well as advisors and officials such as Peter Navarro, Larry Kudlow, Robert Lighthizer, Tom Bossert, and Anthony Scaramucci. In fact, I even introduced several of these officials to Trump. Candidly, knowing he generally supported Democratic candidates throughout his career and that he was not driven by ideology, I thought he had the potential to surprise many by drawing disparate parts of the nation together. Okay, I admit I got that wrong. So now I will share what I have learned about Trump since. Before closing, however, I must admit that despite having written dozens of high-profile critiques of the Trump administration, and despite catalyzing CEOs to walk off his Presidential Business Advisory Councils in 2017 following his failure to forcefully condemn white supremacists in Charlottesville, and despite my role catalyzing one hundred major company CEOs to instantly certify the Biden victory in the 2020 elections, he never has attacked me. In fact, I was still invited to join the administration in the earliest days of Jared Kushner's brilliant, historic Abraham Accords, and Trump has never rebuked me or threatened me for voicing prominent criticism of some of his actions.

CHAPTER 1

Trump's Hub-and-Spokes Model of Leadership

Centralizing All Power in Your Own Hands

You can't understand Donald Trump unless you understand a fundamental truth about how he sees the world: Everything—everything—is about Donald Trump, and Donald Trump only.

This isn't a value judgment, and it's not to say whether this is good or bad. It's just a cold, hard, indisputable fact. Trump isn't very motivated by anyone or anything except himself, plain and simple. He is interested in external things, events, and people but largely in relation to himself—and how they can be leveraged to serve his own interests.

He is the center of the Trump universe. In the Trump solar system, everything revolves around Trump.

Even when he's on his best behavior and lays on the charm—and nobody lays it on thicker and smoother than Trump when he so chooses—it's often because he sees a self-interested reason to win you over. While he does truly like some people, admiring them in their own right, nevertheless, you can be assured that even when he is laying it on thick, he's already brainstorming how to exploit and manipulate the situation to his personal advantage, even if that means potentially double-crossing you down the line. Perhaps all that's no surprise, given his upbringing in the competitive, street-savvy culture of New York real estate development,[1] which forced Trump to navigate the world through audacious, aggressive, unrelenting self-focus rather than altruism.

Critics looking in hastily from the outside have long diminished Trump by attacking him as chaotic, unpredictable, impulsive, childish, and disorderly.[2] Even if not entirely inaccurate, those labels obscure a hugely underappreciated truth about Trump's leadership. He is far more deliberate and strategic than his reactive, temperamental-seeming actions convey. In particular, he has consistently, intentionally managed to create, cultivate, and sustain systems where, in every situation and every interaction, Trump becomes the sun around which everything else revolves.

For Trump, every new day, every new situation, is another opportunity to insert himself into the middle of what is going on, giving himself maximum leverage. It can be something as weighty as global diplomatic negotiations between countries or something as trivial as internecine squabbles between staffers. For Trump, it's all one and the same—extensions of the Trump show, for and by Donald Trump and nobody else, with Trump as star, director, producer, and puppeteer, all in one.

It's no coincidence that he has long expressed a fascination and affinity for strongman leaders, as evidenced by his well-documented bromances with Russia's Vladimir Putin, Hungary's Viktor Orbán, China's Xi Jinping, North Korea's Kim Jong Un, and others of that ilk.[3] For Trump, these strongmen represent an idealized if exaggerated version of his perfect world, one in which everyone answers submissively at his beck and call, his word is the last word, and his whims are your commands. That's the world Trump wants to live in, and that's the world Trump has consistently tried to create around himself.

Consider Trump's "dear leader" cabinet meetings brimming with effusive, obsequious puffery.[4] The setup, with cabinet secretaries taking turns prostrating themselves in front of the almighty Donald, seeking to one-up each other in singing his praises in front of TV cameras, bears an uncanny resemblance to carefully stage-managed "leadership meetings" more befitting of, say, Putin's Russia than historic US cabinet meetings.[5]

But even Trump doesn't always get what he wants, and there are times when he actually doesn't want to be seen as too overbearing. In such cases, he is capable of surprising subtlety, resorting to seductive guile, deception, and outright trickery to nudge events toward his preferred outcome and avoid coming across as too despotic, while also giving himself plausible deniability.

In this exploration of the Trump leadership toolbox, it's only natural that we start by examining how Trump leads his own subordinates—where his subtle, wily ploys and schemes are on fullest display.

HOW TRUMP MANAGES DOWN: THE TRIBAL CHIEFTAIN

The biggest misunderstanding about Trump's leadership of subordinates is that he is somehow hugely impressionable and manipulable, a blank canvas without his own ideas willing to listen to the last person with whom he talks. "A sophisticated parrot," in the memorable words of some critics.[6]

In reality, those claims largely reflect the delusions of naïve, disgruntled, self-important cast-offs and political adversaries who never fully understood Trump. Nothing could be further from the truth.

The reality? Most of the time, Trump is the manipulator, not the manipulated. As Trump memorably clapped back at Hillary Clinton, "I'm not a puppet. You're the puppet."[7] Fearful of being "managed" by deputies and resentful of being "cornered" by his own subordinates, Trump has knowingly, intentionally created and cultivated organizational systems where everyone exists to please and serve him, reporting to him directly, free of the layers of rigid bureaucracy that dilute and distort his will.

Instead of conventional organizational charts or hierarchical pyramidal structures with clear, linear chains of command, Trump's organizations inevitably function as a "hub and spoke" model—where Trump is the central authority, all power derives from him, and all primary subordinates report in to him directly.[8] Weary of turf wars and empire-building by power-hungry lieutenants within his team, Trump will intentionally pit rival subordinates against each other to prevent his subordinates from ganging up to box him in. As a result, Trump becomes the sole arbiter of competing interests and factions within his team, an all-powerful tribal chieftain who centralizes power in his own hands. This is the space where he is most comfortable, cocooned in a comfortable, insulated world of his own creation where everyone exists to serve him.[9]

Trump is far from the first leader, across sectors and throughout history, to pit rival subordinates against each other and set themselves up as the central force from which all authority flows.

Interestingly, at one of our Yale CEO Summits in 2002, Martha Stewart drew an organizational chart of Martha Stewart Living Omnimedia—and it, too, was an overt solar system with herself at the center. Having spent time visiting her in person at both her enterprises, I saw firsthand there is surprising loyalty and long service at these businesses, despite the external aura of presumed capriciousness and grandiosity, not unlike the Trump Organization. With some common worldviews, it was no surprise when Trump generously

Trump exemplifies the hub-and-spokes model of leadership with no conventional hierarchical chain of command. He has centralized power in himself with all his deputies reporting directly to him. Trump is the sun around which everything else must revolve.

backed her for a cooking show with a premise like that of *The Apprentice* upon her prison release, but also no surprise when these two had a falling out, different worlds colliding.

Many Trump admirers and critics alike share misguided pronouncements that Trump modeled his management of cabinet lieutenants and personal advisors on the renowned "team of rivals" model of Abraham Lincoln. As presidential historian Doris Kearns Goodwin chronicled in her best-selling 2005 book, it was almost unimaginable that Lincoln was able to keep his fractious, strong-willed team together. Lincoln's team included powerful factional leaders who had competed against him for the presidential nomination and who held not just disdainful views of each other but similarly disdainful private assessments of Lincoln. Rivals such as Secretary of State William Seward, Secretary of the Treasury Salmon P. Chase, Attorney General Edward Bates, and Secretary of War Edwin Stanton each commanded deeply anchored pockets of popularity and influence independent of Lincoln. Lincoln's genius was in transcending the trading of insults and slights, and unifying such forceful, complementary personalities across petty rivalries to get the best out of each of them in their respective domains, drawing on the unique strengths and experiences of each while tapping into their diverse constituencies. Seward focused on foreign affairs, Stanton focused on the war effort, Chase focused on financing the war, and so forth.

That Lincoln "team of rivals" model, with clear delineation of responsibilities based on the strengths and experiences of each team member, is not at all like Trump's hub-and-spokes model. By design, Trump's lieutenants lack dazzling credentials anchored in expertise and independent power bases, and they are pitted against each other with overlapping jurisdiction and ambiguous demarcations of authority. As a result, they are beholden to Trump entirely, as their influence, both against internal rivals and externally, emanates from his blessing and reflected glory. Rather than seek private harmony between them, Trump stokes the tensions. That can often lead to dramatic WWE-style verbal slap-downs both publicly and privately, sometimes even erupting into near fistfights.

I studied this leadership style extensively in my 1988 book *The Hero's Farewell*. In that book, I identified categories of CEOs who defy limits on their terms of office, sabotaging succession efforts, that I labeled as either "Monarchs" or "Generals," depending on whether they left office and returned or whether they left office feet-first. Both categories were prone to schemes to retain power and maximize their own leverage by cultivating the intramural animosity of rival warlords within their organization. It was believed that only the incumbent leader could transcend these differences, emerging triumphantly on top of the pile every time. Historical examples of such CEOs whom Trump would have known of included William Paley, the founder of CBS; Juan Trippe, the founder of Pan-American World Airlines; Harold Geneen of ITT; and Robert Woodruff, the long-standing patriarch of Coca-Cola. Similarly, examples of transformational heads of state who fortified their power by bridging warring fiefdoms include France's Charles de Gaulle, Yugoslavia's Josip Broz Tito, and Ethiopia's Haile Selassie.

But the success of these examples tend to be the exception, not the norm. Many leaders who attempt the hub-and-spokes model collapse under the weight of their own shortcomings—devoured by factional infighting, cast as petty tin-pot dictators, or, most often, succeeding only in uniting the entire organization against themselves.

Few leaders can pull off the hub-and-spokes model with the flair, relish, and authenticity needed to make it work.[10] Where lesser leaders come across as inauthentic panderers, cruel soul crushers, or indecisive weaklings, at its best, Trump's hub-and-spokes model allows him to develop and nurture contradictory ideas and proposals, drawing out divergent but genuine sides of himself through his own warring subordinates, which then allows him to comfortably weigh contradictory trade-offs while still coming across as authentic. Such contradictions might disorient most people, but not Trump.

F. Scott Fitzgerald's quip that "the mark of a first-rate intelligence is the ability to hold two opposed ideas in the mind at the same time and still retain the ability to function"[11] reads as if he anticipated

Trump. A complex man with many paradoxical sides to himself—aided by the fact that he is an opportunist of the highest degree, virtually completely untethered by any ideology whatsoever[12]—Trump is a master of selectively revealing different versions of himself depending on his audience and, crucially, having the audience actually believe him. After all, when was the last time you witnessed a political rally where an orthodox rabbi promised Trump would be the most pro-Israel president in history, after a conservative Muslim imam voiced the claim that Trump would be the most pro-Arab president in history amid a wildly cheering audience without anyone batting an eye?[13]

There are many additional benefits, for Trump at least, of this hub-and-spokes leadership model. It allows him to comfortably defer action—an underestimated but powerful Trump signature move. While many conventional leaders attempt to show strength through prompt decisiveness (cue George W. Bush's memorable declaration, "I'm the decider"),[14] Trump often relishes refusing to take any options off the table until the last possible moment, plodding, dithering, refusing to constrain the freedom to navigate and provide himself maximum leverage. In the interim, while waiting to see how things unfold, Trump is content to let rival subordinates fight it out, secure in the knowledge that he can subsequently reverse course and go any direction he sees fit, overriding his own people and contradicting his own prior decisions if necessary.

This centralized leadership approach works beautifully for Trump—but not nearly as well for his overworked subordinates.[15] In Trump's hub-and-spokes model, subordinates are deluded into thinking that they are crucial, irreplaceable advisors who hold the ear of the boss, and indeed they do enjoy greater entrepreneurial freedom and more direct access to the top than in virtually any other structure. This, however, masks a sad truth. At the end of the day, they are effectively little more than disposable, interchangeable widgets completely beholden to and dependent on Trump—and are nothing without his

Loyalty is a one-way street in Trump world, as countless disgruntled staffers have found out the hard way.

favor. In Trump-land, nobody is indispensable except Trump, and anyone who thinks they are becomes immediately dispensable.

The wry observation that "no man can argue on his knees" was attributed to an anonymous source by the British political journalist Walter Bagehot in his 1867 book *The English Constitution*. Bagehot used it to illustrate that subservient posture fortifies conformity and obedience among members of the king's inner circle.

One favorite device Trump uses to keep subordinates off-balance and beholden to him is to overload deputies with a vast, even overwhelming, array of responsibilities. For example, consider how "Lil Marco" Rubio is now working four cabinet-level and cabinet-adjacent jobs: as secretary of state, national security advisor, USAID administrator, and national archivist.[16] This strategy of overloading deputies with overwhelming responsibilities, which *The Atlantic* derisively calls "The Mad-Dual Hatter,"[17] is actually anything but mad by Trump. Rather, it reflects his intentional strategy.

Underqualified, overworked deputies who don't always know exactly what they're doing, with huge job definitions and many different fields reporting into them outside of their usual expertise, is precisely what Trump wants because it neutralizes any independent sources of power within his own team outside of himself. These overwhelmed amateurs are operating outside of their lanes of professional competence, without expertise or qualifications, so they don't have professional networks to draw on, nor the technical language and knowledge to do an end-run around their boss.

Contrast that with someone like, say, General James Mattis, from Trump's first cabinet.[18] Instead of swearing filial piety and professing gratitude to Donald Trump, he would simply state that it was a great honor to serve the country. A renowned war hero, Mattis was a four-star Marine Corps general who commanded forces across multiple wars. Described by detractors and admirers alike as urbane, polished, and intellectual, he had independent stature, accomplishments, relationships, and authority outside of his position in Trump's cabinet.

That independence made him a threat to Trump, which is why the two fell out fast.[19] Trump doesn't want General Mattis types who can challenge him publicly, drawing on their own independent stature, expertise, and perspective; he wants loyal, dependent subordinates who rely completely on him for their positions, their prominence, and whatever authority they hold. If such deputies possess great independent stature and expertise, they not only are privy to information that Trump doesn't know, something he dislikes, but they also have the authority to counter him publicly, which he cannot stand.

That is where Mattis and Trump's relationship flew off the rails. In private, Trump is far more open to disagreement and divergent advice than he ever permits himself to be in public; but he bristles at anything that feels like a lecture or even a hint of condescension. The one thing he finds completely intolerable is any public challenge to his authority, much less from a nominal subordinate.

This explains why Trump grew so disillusioned with "his generals" so quickly during his first term. While he was initially enamored by their gravitas and independent stature, he quickly turned against them once he realized those same qualities empowered them to question his judgment—drawing on their own professional expertise, credibility, and standing independent of their roles with Trump—and to constrain his authority. Being chaperoned by the "adults in the room," as they became known, was anathema to Trump.

Thus, instead of four-star general and renowned war hero General Mattis running the Pentagon, we now have Pete Hegseth, who topped out at major and never led any organization larger than his own nonprofit, which, incidentally, he largely ran into the ground.[20] Simply put, it neutralizes the defense chief as an independent power center. The examples are manifold of how Trump neutralizes independent power centers. That's why we have Tulsi Gabbard, with little intelligence background, serving as director of national intelligence, largely neutralizing the intelligence community as an independent power center.[21] That's why we have my charismatic but often incoherent Harvard classmate Bobby Kennedy, with little credible public health background, running Health and Human Services, largely neutralizing the public health community as an independent power center.[22] And so on and so forth.

Trump's penchant for appointing "acting" agency heads in lieu of putting up nominees for Senate confirmation is drawn from the same playbook.[23] Once an appointee is confirmed by the Senate, Trump has very little leverage with which to push and nudge them, short of firing them or icing them out. By contrast, interim appointees are much more subject to his whims and must continually strive to remain in his favor as they pursue the elusive, tantalizing prize of a potential formal appointment—the proverbial pot of gold at the end of the rainbow—with Trump maintaining maximum leverage over them every step of the way.

Trump needs to maintain this level of dominion over his deputies because, almost akin to a mafioso boss or a Mafia don, there are a lot of subtle cues, ambiguous nudges, and sometimes even overt "suggestions" rather than direct, clear orders. This secret, shared language of silences, nods, and signals by which he governs is virtually imperceptible to outsiders but familiar to those within his circle.[24] It's an approach that evokes the famous tale of the four knights who assassinated the Archbishop of Canterbury ostensibly on their own initiative, hoping to prove their loyalty to King Henry II of England after he "merely" asked, "Will no one rid me of this meddlesome priest?"[25] Trump has a long pattern of achieving plausible deniability for himself by subtly encouraging risk-taking and rash action by his deputies without directly ordering it, substantively offloading the resulting risk and reputational damage onto them, then cutting them loose as liabilities afterward while he emerges clean as a whistle.

Just consider how mercilessly Trump seemed to drop his personal attorney, Rudy Giuliani, reportedly declining to pay not only Giuliani's legal bills but also the money he owed Giuliani personally, after Giuliani went full throttle defending Trump's attempts to overturn the election results.[26] Trump continued to keep Giuliani at arm's

With Trump, there is a lot of "will no one rid me of this meddlesome priest," with suggestive musings almost akin to a Mafia don.

length as Giuliani's standing in MAGA circles plummeted, ultimately granting him a pardon nearly a year into his return to office only after repeated entreaties from allies. Similarly, Trump's trade advisor, Peter Navarro, went to jail for four months for refusing to testify against Trump on his role in the January 6 riot—an ordeal Navarro might have possibly avoided had Trump bothered to formally involve executive privilege on his behalf. The court found that Trump never did, leaving Navarro to face the consequences alone.[27]

Of course, with Trump, loyalty tends to be a one-way street—and not always a winning proposition even for staunch loyalists who have done little to cross him. His first vice president, Mike Pence, was rewarded for four years of loyal service with calls of "Hang Mike Pence" after he refused to validate Trump's denial of legitimate election results,[28] while other loyalists from his first term, such as Secretary of State Mike Pompeo and foreign policy advisor Brian Hook, were abruptly excommunicated and humiliated for no discernible reason, their security details inexplicably stripped despite the real threat of Iranian assassinations.[29] Similarly, when his ally in the House, Kevin McCarthy, faced an attempted coup led by Matt Gaetz, Trump refused to lift a finger to save his longtime ally, leading to McCarthy's unceremonious, abject ouster.[30]

At least those deputies survived for years before learning how fickle Trump can be. Notoriously, New York hedge fund tycoon Anthony Scaramucci was tossed aside eleven days after his anointment as Trump's new communications director, a reminder that it can be merely hours or days, rather than months or years, before Trump turns on you.[31] Scaramucci's brash New York persona shone too brightly, for Trump can tolerate no competitors to himself on his own team. Trump staffers with strong personalities who are too independent, such as Elon Musk and Steve Bannon, are always, inevitably, quickly shown the door. Not only were they presumptuously speaking for Trump without being dispatched to do so, melding their own agendas with Trump's, but even more importantly, their independent prominence, crowding Trump's spotlight, made them threats to Trump's unrivaled, unquestioned standing as the boss.

Indeed, Trump has always been highly touchy about subordinates commandeering opportunities he sees as his own, to the point where it can be difficult for them to make a living after their employment with him ends. In some cases, his reasons may be valid, but the sheer number of ex-employees unceremoniously excommunicated after a trivial fissure with nothing to show for their years of effort helps explain why so many disgruntled, desperate former staffers eventually end up becoming his most vocal, public critics.

As the all-powerful tribal chieftain, there is no space in Trump's universe for ex-deputies who turn against him. If anything, Trump targets these former allies-turned-critics with a vengeance with which even his political adversaries are rarely subjected. The unfortunate fate of his first attorney general, Jeff Sessions, stands as a stark reminder of Trump's wrath. After drawing Trump's ire by recusing himself from the Russia investigations, opening the door for the appointment of Special Counsel Robert Mueller by Deputy Attorney General Rod Rosenstein, Sessions attempted a political comeback by running for Senate in Alabama. Trump responded by attacking Sessions with such gusto that he finished last in the GOP primary, losing to the Trump-endorsed Tommy Tuberville by double digits.[32] Then there's the sad case of Chris Krebs, Trump's first cybersecurity agency director, who was fired after Krebs contradicted his claims of election fraud and whom Trump is now investigating.[33] Such cases serve as potent reminders that when Trump taunts former deputies turned critics, such as when he mused about executing General Mark Milley for treason,[34] he is not entirely joking, as there is a special kind of animus he reserves for staffers-turned-critics. Former National Security Advisor John Bolton got a stark reminder of that when the FBI showed up to raid his home in August 2025, resuscitating what seemed to be a long-dormant, closed probe started during the first Trump administration into whether Bolton transmitted, retained, and published classified information in his book, and leading to his criminal indictment.[35]

These disgruntled deputies may have thought that Trump didn't listen to them, but that is an unfair assessment which underestimates Trump. It's more likely Trump listened but plain disagreed with their recommendations. These deputies subsequently burned whatever relationship they had left with him when they went public with their disagreements, which is a cardinal sin in Trump-land. Trump often asks naïve questions of his deputies, because he is truly interested in various alternative, fresh approaches and loves to challenge orthodoxy. He is prone to believing that he is smarter than the experts and thus isn't afraid to ask the naïve questions others might shy away from asking. These naïve questions become misinterpreted by overconfident expert advisors as signs of Trump's ignorance or stupidity when, in fact, they reflect how he thinks through potential alternatives and trade-offs. As unique as his approach may be, that is Trump's tried-and-true way of making sense of things. He is no scholar, but he is a quick learner. Once he has heard and weighed potential alternatives, he makes a decision. Once he goes public with that decision through announcements, it is nearly impossible to change his position unless there is overwhelming external pressure. Those who want to influence him through constructive engagement are most successful when they reach him at an early, private formative time, when he is still learning about the issue and weighing his options.

When it comes to staffing, Trump has his share of idiosyncratic peccadilloes, chief among them a well-documented proclivity for hiring staffers "straight out of central casting"[36] and nixing otherwise well-qualified candidates on the basis of physical appearance. Physical attributes seem to take on a particularly outsized focus with female candidates, with some astute Trump observers commenting on the "look-alike women in Donald Trump's orbit."[37] If Roger Ailes was notorious for prioritizing a certain look in minting Fox News anchors,[38] Trump's tastes take the practice to a whole new level—some say almost Hugh Hefner-esque. Observers note that Trump is almost always surrounded by a coterie of pretty, young female staffers in his inner circle, and that he often seems to treat his young and pretty female staffers as interchangeable accessories the way others might treat luxury handbags.[39] In fact, much ink has been spilled about the seemingly endless stream of ever-younger, ever-prettier women who bear an uncanny resemblance to Melania Trump who appear at his side. Think Madeleine Westerhout, Hope Hicks, Cassidy

Conjuring up the ghost of Hugh Hefner?

Hutchinson, Molly Michael, Margo Martin, Natalie Harp, and so forth. Even his wife is not immune to Trump's peccadilloes. Supposedly, Trump believes Melania is dispensable as well, allegedly musing that if she were to leave him, he would just get another wife.[40]

Despite how terribly Trump sometimes treats them and the locker room macho bravado that permeates his conversations and interactions with women, female staffers sometimes indulge his demands, literally changing their looks to appeal to Trump's whims. *The New York Times* pointed out that Secretary of Homeland Security Kristi Noem traded her "all-business layered bob" for the classic MAGA hairdo, complete with new teeth and what some allege to be a new facial structure,[41] and female ex-staffers have been vocal about how Trump would sometimes suggest they change their physical appearance while making snide comments about their looks.[42]

Observers note that Trump is almost always surrounded by a coterie of pretty, young female staffers in his inner circle and that it can be hard to keep track of the look-alike women in Trump's orbit.

Whether Trump treats the women in his employ worse than he does the men is hard to say, because at the end of the day, he is rather tough and demanding with virtually all of his staffers. Though capable of acts of warmth, Trump's managerial style is all about keeping subordinates off-balance, shunted from disadvantage to disadvantage while remaining entirely subservient and dependent on him. Acts of apparent generosity or kindness are often aimed at pulling you closer into his flytrap.

Even the process of being chosen as a Trump staffer comes straight from reality television, with candidates pitted against one another as Trump publicly auditions them one by one. Nothing exemplifies that Trump-driven process of paranoia, backstabbing, and insecurity more than his vice presidential selection processes. Instead of the practice virtually every other president followed in picking their running mate—methodical, careful vetting—Trump fostered *Apprentice*-style auditions and smackdowns, dragging out the process as long as possible while keeping potential candidates entirely in the dark, akin to a street knife fight played out behind the scenes and in the media. Poor Mike Pence was kept waiting in a hotel for days after being summoned, not knowing whether or not he'd actually get the vice presidency, while Trump publicly toyed with installing New Jersey Governor Chris Christie in his place.[43] Similarly, JD Vance suffered through weeks of fierce competition with Florida Senator Marco Rubio and North Dakota Governor Doug Burgum in a battle notable for leaked opposition research dossiers and media hatchet jobs. Meanwhile, Trump reveled in the feeding frenzy he'd created.[44]

Subordinates who prevail in such contests and rise up must twist in the wind, continually trying to please their almighty leader, lest Trump decide they've become too big for their britches and need to be cut down. That is the fate invariably suffered by any deputies who delude themselves into believing they have any independent power. In Trump-land, there can be only one decision-maker—Trump himself.

Trump's habit of cutting deputies down to size can take the form of subtle, or not so subtle, cues.

A frequent target is his own vice president, JD Vance, whom he has repeatedly ribbed for being too big for his britches, barbs delivered with a veneer of humor. For example, after riffing about how Chinese President Xi Jinping's deputies are uniformly deferential to their leader, Trump turned to Vance and asked, "Why don't you behave like that? JD doesn't behave like that! JD butts into conversations! I want to have that for at least a couple of days. Okay, JD? We'll keep you long term, but a couple of days of that would be very, very nice." While Vance reacted to the joke in good humor, he surely could not have missed the underlying message. A similar moment came during the middle of an otherwise entirely unrelated speech announcing tariffs on Liberation Day, when Trump abruptly pointed to his vice president and remarked, "JD, he's gaining a lot of confidence nowadays, isn't he?"—a seemingly offhand aside, but one freighted with meaning. At least these warnings to Vance are softened by jocularity; sometimes Trump resorts to far more overt insults, such as his once-routine public ridicule of his sons, Don Jr. and Eric Trump.[45]

Trump can get away with such brutish behavior because of who his staffers are: As noted earlier, he populates his team with staffers who are completely dependent on him and who, absent his favor, will turn back into nobodies. It's no coincidence that few alums of Trump world have successfully moved on to build second acts of tremendous influence or affluence on their own, since few have the professional experience, credentials, and expertise to succeed on their own merits. That's why MAGA world clingers-on, such as Corey Lewandowski and Reince Priebus, remain pathetically loyal to Trump, continually trying to work their way back into his good graces despite being abjectly fired and publicly humiliated.[46] With little in the way of non-Trump professional networks, credentials, or expertise to fall back on, their only hope and pathway is filial piety to Trump—which is exactly what Trump wants.[47]

While many critique what they see as the vanity and narcissism of Trump's hub-and-spokes model, where he is the center of the Trump solar system, his unconventional style is rooted in anthropological and strategic anchoring, which he intuits instinctively. Trump abhors the traditional model of bureaucracy of large enterprises. Both his celebrated leadership successes and his highly public setbacks stem from following an intrinsic model of the foundations of authority of a tribal chieftain blended with the necessary fluidity and creative chaos of a business entrepreneur.

The solar system model, or hub-and-spokes model, where all authority emanates from Trump, is not unique to his micromanaging proclivities and limited trust in others, nor is it unique to the prior generation of monarchical CEOs I documented in *The Hero's Farewell*. Rather, it is well-documented as the instinctive leadership style business historians like Alfred Chandler and management scholars like Larry Greiner identified a half century ago as being typical of early stage business builders, for whom retaining entrepreneurial dynamism and maximum flexibility are paramount objectives. While this style is common to entrepreneurs and certain types of business leaders; there are also certain advantages when applied to the political arena, and Trump is hardly the first politician to adopt such a management style. Robert Woodward's *The Agenda*, a study of the early days of the Clinton White House, depicted his White House staff as chaotic, drawing on the analogy of a kids' soccer team with everyone chasing the ball all over the field. When I asked Bill Clinton, on a January 1, 1995, New Year private morning run at Renaissance Weekend while he was president, if he was offended by such a description, he stopped running and started to shout at me—to the alarm of the Secret Service detail jogging with us. "NO! That image is correct and appropriate, Jeff. You can't get things done in government by filling out forms and holding committee meetings." He was conveying that following a normal chain of command, bureaucratic process would have stifled his ability to accomplish his goals. The challenge inherent to an improvisational approach, however, is to recognize when the dynamism of creation must sometimes yield to a more institutionalized system of governance—requiring more formal roles, functional specialized expertise, and the delegation of real authority. That is a discipline Trump has neither embraced nor attempted to master, leading to the often accurate observation that he runs everything—whether it is the White House or weighty global diplomacy—as if it were a family business, with Trump the sun around which the rest of the solar system must revolve.

CHAPTER 2

The Real Art of Trump's Deal

Maximizing Leverage by Starting with a Punch in the Face Versus Building Trust

It's hardly surprising that the man who wrote *The Art of the Deal* (though Trump's coauthor, Tony Schwartz, claims he authored most of it) has a unique approach to negotiations.

START WITH BLOOD

For most people, negotiations start with building trust incrementally, almost like building a fire. You might start by throwing in the kindling and then smaller branches to build up the fire before tossing in the big logs.

Trump doesn't do any of that. He starts by taking the biggest log he can find and whacking you in the face with it, striking the first blow and staking out the most maximalist stance before you can even get your bearings.

That's Trump's way of creating maximal leverage for himself and seizing the momentum—manners and custom be darned. By

Trump's negotiating style is distinctly not based on building mutual trust. He starts most negotiations by striking the first blow and staking out the maximalist stance, creating maximum leverage right off the bat.

inflicting maximal pain right away, anything that comes afterward will seem mild in comparison, which is how Trump gets away with asking for things he never would have gotten otherwise. His bloodied and disoriented opponents emerge from the onslaught all but dying to find a solution. It is a brute force, blunt trauma approach to negotiation, almost akin to ripping people's arms off in the hope, often realized, that they will emerge grateful to have escaped with their lives, having lost only an arm.

Trump's almost-predatory approach to negotiations—bite first, talk later—is fundamentally a reflection of his zero-sum worldview. Somebody must always lose for him to win, because in Trump's world, win-wins don't exist. If the other guy is getting something good, that's a dollar left on the table that you should have seized. There is no such thing as trust-building, reciprocal gratitude, or long-term relationship nurturing with Trump. Everything is in-the-moment, transactional: What can I get from you right now?

This is the opposite of how most people approach negotiations, harmonizing through challenges to find common ground, mutual interests, and shared values. Much of that prevailing orthodoxy can be traced back to the popularization of a model of conflict resolution that preaches de-escalatory tenets such as trust-building, emotional

President Zelenskyy of Ukraine and President Ramaphosa of South Africa were not expecting to be ambushed in their White House sit-downs with President Trump, but it was par for the course with Trump's negotiating style.

decompressing, and analytic calm, which emerged from Harvard when I was there. In 1981, soon after I became a professor at the Harvard Business School, two of my friends and colleagues, Roger Fisher, a political scientist, and Bill Ury, an anthropologist, wrote the book *Getting to Yes: Negotiating Agreement Without Giving In*. It forced us to all rewrite our teaching notes on conflict resolution.[1] Their pathbreaking approach to principled negotiation techniques emphasized the importance of detaching emotion and personality, with analytic techniques such as "separate the people from the problem," "focus on interests, not positions," "invent options for mutual gain," and "insist on using objective criteria." One of the top all-time nonfiction bestsellers across fields, this book has received criticism from other political scientists, such as Gerald Steinberg in the *Naval War College Review*, for advising conflicting parties on how the world should be versus the way it is.

Trump surely never read the book or its criticisms. He did not need to do so, and he would have dismissed its precepts as idealistic and impractical anyway. Trump's approach is the diametric opposite: Escalate first, ask questions later—becoming, when necessary, a one-man incendiary force willing to scorch the earth before negotiations even begin. There are no sacred cows, as Trump relishes challenges to precedent and orthodoxy, with flagrant disregard for the notion of common values, norms, or conventionally acceptable behavior.

Furthermore, Trump's approach flouts trite conventional orthodoxies by purposefully jumbling together the issues, the positions, and the people in every confrontation. There is no separating the people from the issues. If there is any disagreement with Trump on an issue, no matter how legitimate a disagreement, he will treat it as a personal grudge match. That pairs with his preferred tactic of disproportionate escalation: When someone dares so much as poke at Trump, he will immediately bring out the heavy artillery, so brutalizing his opponents that they are cowed into surrender.

Trump has pulled off some real victories with this approach, particularly during his real estate career, when adversaries were so battered by his brute force and sheer power they all but unconditionally capitulated to his demands.

Take, for example, the story of his acquisition of Trump Winery in Charlottesville, Virginia. The previous owner, Patricia Kluge, fell on hard times and was running short on cash. The ex-wife of John Kluge, once the richest person in the US, she blew through her divorce settlement at record speed and found herself unable to pay the bills during the 2008 financial crisis, declaring bankruptcy and staring down aggrieved lenders by the dozen.

Kluge, naïvely, approached Trump for help trying to sell her house and vineyard for $100 million. Believing him to be her friend, she visited him at Trump Tower in 2011. Of course, Trump's world has no room for the kind of altruistic friendship Kluge thought they shared, and his instinct for the jugular immediately kicked in when he grasped Kluge's precarious finances. The solution he devised was pure Trump.[2]

Discovering that the land adjacent to the Kluges' estate was held in a trust for her only son, Trump bought the right of first refusal to acquire the land for a measly $500,000. Then Trump turned his attention to Bank of America, which held the Kluge estate through foreclosure. Using his control over the adjacent land, he threatened to build an ugly, twenty-foot concrete wall with "TRUMP" painted in massive letters directly in front of the house, rendering it virtually unsaleable. As Jason Greenblatt, executive vice president of the Trump Organization, quipped at the time, "We'll be happy on the front lawn . . . who is going to pay for a house with no front yard?"[3]

By taking the most maximalist position up front, Trump had the bank exactly where he wanted them: in his crosshairs and at his mercy, with little leverage to push back against unreasonable demands. Not only was Trump, by default, the only viable bidder for the house, he was hell-bent on paying as little as possible. After prolonged knock-down, drag-out negotiations, the bank was surely finally relieved when Trump offered to purchase the estate for $13 million—a tiny fraction of the estate's $100 million asking price and less than the amount Bank of America paid at a foreclosure auction to acquire the property. Ironically, the house had what some said to be $25 million of high-quality wines sitting in the basement, meaning Trump not only engineered acquiring the property at a massive discount through his imaginative ploys but got $25 million in free wine thrown in as a kicker.[4]

Amazingly, that transaction wasn't the first time Trump successfully pulled off the same ploy. It was almost an exact duplicate of the steps he followed years before in acquiring Mar-a-Lago. Former owner Marjorie Post had bequeathed her prized Palm Beach estate to the US government for use as a winter White House, but when the Carter administration refused the gift, intimidated by the potential property maintenance costs, Post's disenchanted descendants put the property up for sale.

Nearly immediately, Trump offered $15 million. When the offer was turned down, he bought the beach in front of Mar-a-Lago and threatened to build a monstrosity that would block the oceanfront views. As in Charlottesville, Post's descendants were faced with a lose-lose proposition: They could either spend years and millions trying to fight Trump in court with little likelihood of success, or they could try to reach a deal with Trump, who had turned himself into their only viable bidder through his machinations. Ultimately, after years of haggling, Trump finally agreed to buy the estate for a modest $5 million plus $3 million for the lavish antique furnishings within its mansion—a fraction of its original asking price and fair market value. Today, the property brings in over $50 million every year. Not a bad rate of return![5]

Clearly, from the prism of achieving his objectives, it's evident from Trump's approach to negotiations that there is a method to the madness, with savvy, even if ruthlessly manipulative, stratagems.

That's how and why Trump negotiates the way he does—to stake out a maximalist position up front, throw the first punch, and knock the opposition right out of the ring.

PUNCH THEM IN THE FACE FIRST, THEN TRY TO CUT A DEAL

Of course, there are times when Trump realizes that even if he can throw the first punch, he can't knock the opposition right out of the ring from the outset. That's when Trump's pragmatic streak kicks in. The core of Trump's dealmaking approach is a fundamental, instinctive belief that he can make a deal with anyone over anything. To Trump, there are no obstacles that can't be negotiated away, at least in his own head. That holds true for challenges small and large. That's why, when it comes to weighty global diplomacy issues, Trump takes the same approach: a trenchant, sometimes overconfident faith in his ability to strike personal rapports and negotiate deals personally with any global leader, no matter how improbable or unlikely. This extends to Xi Jinping of China on trade imbalances, Kim Jong Un of North Korea on denuclearization, and Vladimir Putin on ending the Ukraine invasion, to name just a few examples where Trump believes that he can strike a deal where others have failed.

FORGING THROUGH THE FOG OF NEGOTIATIONS WITH SHEER WILL

In addition to starting with a punch to the face and staking out the most maximal position, another of Trump's favorite negotiation tactics is to simply cut through the fog by announcing a deal has been forged, even when no such deal exists. Catching everyone by surprise, he essentially muscles the negotiations toward a deal through sheer force of will.

When he uses this tactic, Trump is often lambasted by critics for putting the cart before the horse, and indeed, there are many times when Trump's declarations of "deals" are comically premature and fall through, such as his premature declaration of trade deals with China and India or his infamous declaration that North Korea is "no longer a nuclear threat," which did not age well.[6]

However, there are times when this method pays dividends, with Trump successfully forcing negotiators to solve seemingly intractable problems by muscling them into the same room to resolve their differences with the pressure of a ticking clock in the background. (Trump loves to set deadlines to create that manufactured sense of urgency.)

Consider the improbable path Trump traveled to achieve a deal to secure the release of the remaining Israeli hostages from Hamas and a cessation of hostilities between Israel and Hamas in the Mideast, however precarious. First, he publicly declared and then subsequently repeated that the war between Israel and Hamas was over, although the two sides had yet to reach a deal. He combined this public pressure with intense private pressure behind the scenes on all participants, including Israeli Prime Minister Netanyahu as well as neighboring Arab nations, seeking to forge a resolution through seemingly intractable disagreements such as the release of the hostages, the governance of Gaza, Israeli troop withdrawals from Gaza, the disarmament of Hamas, and the reconstruction of Gaza. Trump further pressured participants by staking highly unusual negotiating positions, such as floating the idea of the US taking over Gaza and building Trump hotels, musings that were widely lampooned as ridiculous but that nevertheless lit a fire under the participants to forge a deal before Trump imposed an unfavorable deal on them.[7]

At least partly due to Trump's unorthodox negotiating tactics, Egypt, Qatar, and Turkey joined with United Arab Emirates, Morocco, Bahrain, and Sudan in pushing Hamas toward mediation and acceptance, with a summit at Sharm El Sheikh, Egypt, bringing more than twenty Arab leaders to lend legitimacy and diplomatic momentum to the budding peace accords. Trump directly muscled the key participants into acceding, even traveling to the Israeli Knesset to make a speech declaring the dawn of a new Middle East, while signing individual declarations with the leaders of states such as Egypt, Qatar, and Turkey to fortify their resolve.

WHEN TRUMP OVERPLAYS HIS NEGOTIATING HAND

The problem, however, is that despite Trump's faith in his negotiating ability, he doesn't always get it right and has a tendency to overplay his hand. Sometimes, by coming out swinging so hard right off the bat, he poisons the well so much that trying to drown the squeaky wheel in oil no longer works, rendering later conciliatory efforts ineffective. Rather than being primed to make concessions, his adversaries are instead emboldened and driven to counterattack.

That's when Trump's most pugnacious instincts kick in: Always escalate, always stay on the offensive; when they punch back, you punch harder. That was perhaps the most enduring, foundational lesson Trump learned from his early mentor, the notorious Roy Cohn. Trump first engaged the legendary fixer in the early 1970s, when the Trump Organization was staring down a Department of Justice investigation for alleged racial discrimination at Trump housing developments, due to having only a handful of Black tenants across thousands of buildings. Instead of persuading Trump to settle for a nominal sum as most would have done, Cohn encouraged him to fight the lawsuit in court, in the media, and in the political arena, sparing no expense to attack the DOJ and to claim he was the victim of unfair persecution.[8] Ironically, Cohn and Trump's scheming went for naught, as ultimately they realized the futility of their case and settled with the DOJ—which is what many had advised doing from the outset.

Nevertheless, Trump settled with an agreement that did not admit guilt, allowing him to declare victory, however nominal. As one astute observer noted, "Cohn's playbook for the race discrimination suit became an enduring guide for Trump in handling future crises: deny everything, fight back, and go on the offensive to declare victory."[9]

However, as we saw from the examples above, the "punch harder" strategy is not without merit. By beating up on opponents, Trump can pull some surprising, improbable rabbits out of the hat. After

Since the passing of his once-fixer Roy Cohn, whom Trump dropped like a hot potato toward the end of his life, Trump has been casting around for "where's my Roy Cohn?" with a rotating cast of loyalists aspiring to fill the role but largely failing to live up to Trump's expectations.

all, as George Washington noted in 1799, the best defense is a strong offense. But, Trump sometimes does that to excess. When he continuously escalates, he can overreach dramatically, backing himself into a corner. To use a boxing analogy he would appreciate: Though Trump thinks of himself as the Mike Tyson of big fights, biting off the ears of his opponents, there were times when even Tyson ended up punching in the air to the point of exhaustion.

Perhaps not coincidentally, it is noteworthy that Tyson and Trump are friends, and the parallels are uncanny. Tyson is legendary for having bit off a portion of Evander Holyfield's ear in the third round of their 1997 heavyweight championship rematch. Initially, referees allowed the fight to continue. Yet moments later, an unrepentant Tyson bit Holyfield's other ear and was disqualified as well as fined.

Trump tends to be similarly unrepentant when a rough opening technique has failed. Consider, for example, his unorthodox approach to tariffs. Virtually everyone—including 90 percent of major CEOs per our proprietary Yale CEO Summit polling—agrees that we need at least some tariffs on certain strategic sectors where there are genuine trade imbalances, such as steel and aluminum, where there has been ample documentation of foreign entities subverting US producers. But there's a difference between selective tariffs on strategic sectors and the approach Trump decided to take: indiscriminate bludgeoning with all tariffs, all the time. True to form, Trump ignored nearly universal warnings, including from many pro-tariff allies, that he was dangerously overplaying his hand and risked taking the tariff tool way too far.

In announcing Liberation Day, a package of disproportionately massive and unprecedented "reciprocal" tariffs on April 2, 2025, Trump ended up inadvertently tanking financial markets, sending stocks plummeting nearly 20 percent and causing the cost of debt to soar over the course of five days, while global commerce and trade came to a near standstill.[10] Recognizing that perhaps the warnings he had ignored were actually right and he might well have inadvertently set off economic Armageddon, Trump then quickly reversed course, announcing a ninety-day halt to his reciprocal tariffs to allow for further negotiations—the strategy he probably should have started with. As one extra kicker, Trump announced 145 percent tariffs on China, whose leadership had retaliated against Trump's original announcement.

But then Trump quickly realized he had accidentally set off a total trade embargo and economic decoupling with China, since a 145 percent tariff is basically enough to stifle all trade. Trump put out olive branches to Chinese president Xi Jinping, going so far as to claim he would be talking with China shortly. The Chinese were quick to respond that there was no such call planned, a public slap to the face to Trump.

Boxed into a corner, Trump desperately threw ideas against the wall to see what would stick in a head-spinning series of flip-flops: announcing a suspension of Chinese tariffs, then the reimposition of fentanyl-specific tariffs, then exempting certain sectors from those China-specific tariffs, then un-exempting those same sectors from China-specific tariffs. Next, after settling on an adjusted 30 percent rate for China, Trump imposed 50 percent tariffs on the EU, only to suspend them for ninety days a mere two days later.

I carefully combed through Trump's tariff announcements and documented 150 instances of tariff flip-flops within the span of his first one hundred days, with constant flipping of his tariff positions not week by week or day by day, but often hour by hour. Little wonder that foreign leaders' heads were spinning. Who could keep track of such dizzying reversals? As Trump continually reversed himself, some analysts came up with the acronym TACO to describe the madness: Trump Always Chickens Out.[11] To foreign leaders, once it was apparent that Trump would eventually back down from his bluffs if you let him wear himself out, why would they budge first? Similarly, Wall Street traders and investors began discounting Trump's tariff announcements, dismissing them as empty threats Trump would inevitably back down from. When CNBC reporter Megan Cassella asked Trump what he thought about the TACO acronym at one of his daily press conferences, Trump lost his temper, tearing into Cassella as a "nasty journalist" and warning her menacingly, "Do not ever say that again."[12]

Naturally, Trump would justify his flip-flops as a part of his strategic genius, touting his flexibility and painting them as part of a strategy to catch his adversaries by surprise. And to Trump's credit, by staking out the most maximal position on Liberation Day, the subsequent tariffs that actually stuck became acceptable by comparison, even if they would likely have been viewed as unacceptable prior to Liberation Day. After all, consider the fact that the US now has what is essentially a universal 10 percent tariff on all goods coming into the nation, minus some carveouts, such as USMCA-compliant goods. If Trump had tried to implement a 10 percent universal tariff from the start, the outcry would have been tremendous. After the triple-digit numbers thrown out on Liberation Day, however, the relatively tame 10 percent universal tariff came to be seen as a relative reprieve and a palatable middle ground. Indeed, by staking out the most extreme initial stance, Trump ensured that the tariff policies he ultimately enacted were met with relief instead of revulsion.

Nevertheless, Trump's reversals do come at a cost, with credibility fading with each about-face. Critics observe that each time after Trump overplays his hand in negotiations and "chickens out," afterward, his preferred face-saving exit is often a big, gaudy announcement of some deal or accord, sometimes blatantly exaggerated and often amounting to very little at all. Consider, for example, the supposed "trillions" in foreign investment Trump brags about having secured for the US from foreign countries. These numbers are often squishier than he likes to admit. For example, in 2017, Trump boasted about securing $450 billion in investments during his first trip to Saudi Arabia, a jaunt replete with awkward Saudi sword dances and bizarre orbs of light. But the export of American goods and services from 2017 to 2020 totaled only $92 billion, less than a quarter of the promised amount and even lower than the amount exported during President Obama's second term.[13] Similarly, in his second term, Trump appears to be using fuzzy math to get to the gaudy $600 billion investment commitment from the Saudis, double-counting many of the same deals already in effect from his first administration as well as other projects already in progress—not genuinely "new" investments. At least some of those deals actually did materialize; other promised investments from foreign companies and countries, such as Foxconn's planned $10 billion electronics factory in Wisconsin, simply faded away as the company pulled back on expansion plans, abandoning its promised infrastructure projects no matter the initial hype.[14]

Thus, the reality is that the veneer of glitz and glamour and fawning Oval Office press conferences announcing new investments hides a much more complicated reality. Announcements of "big investments" are sometimes merely existing and preplanned capital expenditure spending repackaged as gauzy, headline-drawing "foreign investments" in the US. This smoke-and-mirrors trick generates lots of noise but few tangible wins.

Sometimes, much-hyped negotiations fizzle out so badly that it is difficult to save face with even some cursory "win"—in which case Trump quickly moves on.[15]

For example, Trump's attempts to reach a nuclear disarmament deal with Kim Jong Un of North Korea were also much hyped. But when a deal remained elusive after their intense courtship, Trump largely lost personal interest and simply moved on to the next issue du jour.

These are some of the many tangible downsides to Trump's tendency to overplay his hand and subsequently "chicken out," as well as his highly personalized style of negotiating. Trump believes he can look anyone in the eye and make a deal. Thus, for him, every deal becomes a personal negotiation. When he fails, he is left with little choice but to manufacture some flimsy pretext for declaring victory and swiftly moving on, while the real issues remain unaddressed.

Furthermore, once a negotiated agreement is reached, Trump frequently loses personal interest. What energizes him the most is the chase—the drama of reaching a deal—not the painstaking work of implementation and execution. As a result, mechanisms to ensure that commitments are honored are frequently minimal or nonexistent. That is due in part to Trump's belief that no deal is ever truly permanent; he is always prepared to reopen negotiations whenever it suits his purposes or he senses he has stronger leverage. Indeed, his own record reflects this fluid approach, such as when he expressed his eagerness to renegotiate the signature trade deal made during his first term, the painstakingly negotiated Trump USMCA, believing it to be too soft.

In his negotiations, Trump also sometimes aims so high that he simply runs out of time, with his opponents finding it easier to run down the clock rather than make a concession. For example, he has repeatedly expressed disappointment that a grand bargain he sought with China during his first administration, which he claims would have fully opened up Chinese markets to US companies, never materialized. With China running out the clock and stalling, he had to settle for a US-China trade deal containing only a fraction of what Trump originally envisioned. (And even then, China didn't stick to the lesser deal terms, blatantly failing to meet the trade targets set by stalling and running out the clock on Trump's term.) Similarly, the team negotiating the Abraham Accords, despite their heroic and valiant efforts, simply ran out of time to secure additional agreements from key Middle Eastern countries such as Saudi Arabia as Trump's first term drew to a close. That proved to be historically tragic, for if Saudi Arabia had joined the Abraham Accords as Jared Kushner originally intended, then the attack of October 7, 2023, might never have happened, saving countless lives in the Middle East, Arabs and Jews alike.

Trump likes to think he has time on his side in every negotiation, but in many instances that proves not to be the case. His habit of seeking to create an artificial sense of urgency with invented deadlines can sometimes backfire, such as when his self-imposed tariff-negotiating deadlines for several sectors came and went with no movement and no apparent penalty. This, in turn, led many companies to conclude that the best course when staring down a Trump tariff tantrum was to take no action at all, letting deadlines expire and treating the threats as largely ignorable unless circumstances forced otherwise.

TRUMP THE STREET SAVVY KNIFE-FIGHTER

Trump, the street-savvy knife-fighter, has a few favorite tricks he pulls out of his sleeve time and time again in creating maximum negotiating leverage for himself. Chief among these is his unparalleled use of lawfare—the law as warfare—meaning his unabashed, career-long habit of weaponizing the legal system to go after adversaries, wearing them down to the point where they all but beg for a solution, no matter how unfavorable the terms.

Perhaps Trump was influenced in this by his early fixer, Roy Cohn. At a minimum, Cohn certainly got Trump started, thanks to his litigious response to the DOJ's housing suit, as documented earlier. But in the subsequent decades, Trump made the lawfare strategy

Trump is a master of lawfare—using the legal system to wear down opponents.

entirely his own, through the sheer, unprecedented breadth of his frenetic legal activity and the depths to which he is willing to go.

The factual record shows that perhaps no other American businessman is as adept at weaponizing the legal system as Donald Trump, and that was even before he ever pivoted to politics. Up until his first presidential election, by some counts, Donald Trump and Trump-affiliated businesses were involved in more than four thousand lawsuits as either plaintiff or defendant, an unparalleled, staggering number, more than fellow real estate tycoons Sam Zell, Steve Schwarzman, Stephen Ross, Edward DeBartolo Jr., Donald Bren, and Larry Silverstein combined.[16]

A vast majority of those cases were either settled out of court, dismissed, or decided against Trump, but no matter, because Trump didn't have to win in court for him to win, period. Even obviously frivolous lawsuits that were ultimately tossed out served his immediate purpose: weaponizing the legal system to intimidate, bully, bankrupt, and harass adversaries, compelling them to change their behavior regardless of the formal legal outcome.

A classic example of how lawfare, Trump style, works was when Trump filed a $5 billion defamation lawsuit against his biographer, Timothy O'Brien, who reported in his book that Trump had inflated his net worth, based on corroboration from three well-placed, independent sources. Despite knowing that O'Brien's assertion was factually sound, Trump filed suit against O'Brien, claiming that O'Brien was motivated by malice and had cost Trump business deals and damaged his reputation. Although those claims were laughable under the circumstances, Trump asked for punitive damages of $5 billion, knowing full well not only that O'Brien did not have $5 billion but that the author could ill afford the costly legal fees such protracted litigation would entail. The suit was ultimately thrown out of court, but not before O'Brien incurred the equivalent of millions in legal fees.[17] Trump later admitted that the suit was nonsensical but confessed his true purpose: "I spent a couple of bucks on legal fees, and they spent a whole lot more. I did it to make his life miserable, which I'm happy about." One has to wonder why O'Brien didn't countersue Trump for vexatious litigation, given Trump's braggadocio.[18]

Filing apparently frivolous lawsuits in an attempt to wear down and bankrupt adversaries has become a Trump signature move, because it's effective. In fact, even the mere threat of lawsuits can be enough for adversaries to preemptively surrender, thanks to what Trump has always understood better than anyone else: Lawfare can double as PR warfare, and vice versa.

One illustrative example vividly demonstrates the potency of legal threats amplified by Trump's PR machine. When Trump was renovating the Doral resort, he did what Trump allegedly always does—cut corners—insisting on using the cheapest paint he could find, the notoriously poor-quality Benjamin Moore Super Hide paint, instead of the typical commercial-quality paint everyone recommended. Predictably, the paint started peeling off walls, but instead of blaming himself, the Trump Organization threatened Benjamin Moore with not only litigation but also the inevitable bad press that would result. After Michael Cohen put through several bellicose calls to Benjamin Moore, unsurprisingly, the company quickly folded and provided Trump with thousands of gallons of free paint, despite having done absolutely nothing wrong.[19]

There is Trump's lawfare strategy in a nutshell: Start by drawing blood even when sitting on a terrible hand, even if that's nothing more than an empty bluff. Sometimes that tactic alone so disorients and wears down his adversaries that it succeeds. One remarkable example was during the Great Recession, when Deutsche Bank attempted to collect $40 million that Trump personally guaranteed for the Trump International Hotel and Tower in Chicago. Instead of paying the debt, Trump seized the offensive, preemptively suing Deutsche Bank for a whopping $3 billion for undermining the project and for damage to his reputation. Despite the ludicrous nature of Trump's accusations, Deutsche Bank was forced into a defensive position, countersuing to obtain the comparatively measly $40 million, while defending against a fusillade of Trump's attacks in court and in the media, which battered the bank's reputation at a time it could ill afford any reputational damage. Ultimately, despite having essentially zero leverage from a financial perspective, Trump was able to win a concession from Deutsche Bank to extend the loan term through his savvy use of lawfare, with a dose of PR pressure.[20]

Trump may not have loved having to sit in a courtroom during his criminal trials, but he has used lawfare to his advantage repeatedly, having initiated thousands of civil cases over the years, effectively wielding the legal system as a cudgel to get his way.

There is seemingly no amount too small for Trump's lawfare. In 2016, he filed five lawsuits against eight neighbors of the Doral golf club, seeking to recoup a comparatively puny $15,000 in damages for supposed "vandalization" of plants his groundkeepers installed on the property line. For virtually anyone else, the legal fees would far outweigh $15,000 in damages; but for Trump, apparently, trying to recoup the $15,000 was worth the months of time and effort.[21]

When Trump is on the receiving end of lawsuits as the defendant, his strategy is even simpler: Never settle and fight to the end, stalling, delaying, and evading along the way, to try to outlast and wear down the plaintiff. The same Doral incident above offers a telling example. After the fiasco with Super Hide paint, the contractor on the Doral project quit, and a local paint supplier named The Paint Spot sued after its bills went unpaid. Trump's litigators in Florida fought the case vigorously, throwing up all kinds of procedural obstacles and hurdles and even filing for the small-business plaintiff to cover billionaire Trump's legal bills, to the point where The Paint Spot owed

$300,000 in legal bills over an unpaid paint bill of $32,000. Trump gave up only after exhausting several layers of appeals—and even after an appeals court definitively decided against him, he still refused to convey payment to the proprietor of The Paint Spot, forcing him to go to the media in an effort to shame Trump into payment.[22]

Trump's lawfare flies in the face of conventionally accepted legal norms and behavior, which may explain why prosecutors and judges are routinely surprised by his open defiance. In particular, the process-oriented, bipartisan, experienced officials of the Justice Department during his first administration and into the Biden era, ranging from Robert Mueller to Jack Smith to Merrick Garland, never really understood the efficacy of Trump's consistent practice of bending the law to his favor with distortions of protocol and acts of plain bad faith. These legal veterans have a quasi-religious belief in the traditions, norms, and sanctity of the legal system, but Trump doesn't play by the same rules, and he certainly doesn't ascribe to the same norms. He subverts and bends institutions for his own advantage. For Trump, the legal system is just one more institution to subvert from within. For all these legal veterans' years of prosecutorial success and litigation experience, they had never experienced a wily nonlawyer who could run circles around them the way Trump does, with nothing off the table, not even cheap gimmicks—endless delays, procedural stalling, frivolous motions, and manufactured and outrageous calls of bias, both inside and outside the courtroom. This willingness if not even enthusiasm to go where few others can or would explains why Trump's lawfare strategy is so effective for him.

Even when Trump seems to be committing legal suicide in the eyes of conventional legal pundits, there is generally a method to his lawfare madness. He thinks outside the bounds of the law and colors outside the lines, focusing on how he can redraw the lines while most lawyers obsess about merely staying within them. Just consider how he took on the presiding judge, Juan Merchan, in his

2024 New York State criminal trial. He launched merciless attacks on the judge, his family, and his staff, while intentionally flouting legal niceties and even legal necessities with a slapdash defense team of obscure, little-known lawyers who regularly screwed up even the most basic legal procedures. While pundits mused that Trump was blowing his own case in court, the reality was that Trump wasn't fighting it out in court so much as playing to the cameras and the American people. Perhaps Alina Habba was not one of the better known criminal defense attorneys in the nation, but she looked good on television defending him and attacking the rigged system, or so Trump's thinking would have gone.[23]

As president now, Trump's lawfare has taken on an additional dimension, as litigation has become another way for him to line his own pockets, most blatantly by suing media companies he doesn't like and by suing his own DOJ for damages. He's already made quite a bit of money this way. Elon Musk and X settled with Trump for $10 million; ABC/Disney settled with Trump for $15 million; and Paramount/CBS is settling with Trump for $16 million, not to mention a $230 million DOJ settlement bid.[24] These are not payments due to Trump's campaign but to Trump's library and foundation—almost akin to Trump personally—and to whatever Trump-aligned causes and organizations he often steers money toward. There is no precedent in American political history.

PROJECTING HIS OWN ATTRIBUTES PREEMPTIVELY ONTO OTHERS: "LOOK THERE WHILE I'M DOING THIS OVER HERE"

Ironically, Trump perennially attacks the media for fake news even as critics allege he is an inimitable fountain of misinformation and disinformation. That's reflective of a broader pattern and a key part of Trump's negotiating toolkit: He preemptively accuses others of what others accuse him of doing. This projection is an effective negotiating tactic for him because it scrambles the narrative, muddies the evidentiary waters, and forces opponents onto the defensive before they even realize what is happening. As such, although Trump is often the initiator of aggressive tactics, his projection allows him to claim to be the aggrieved victim in virtually every situation, always claiming that he is the one being wronged and that he is merely defending himself against a bigger bully.

This projection takes many forms, well beyond the well-worn "fake news" attacks with which we are all by now familiar. We've documented that Trump is an aggressive perpetrator of lawfare, far exceeding his tycoon peers' use of legal systems as a tool in handling disputes, yet Trump routinely accuses opposing lawyers and prosecutors, and judges others for using the same lawfare tactics he consistently practices, casting doubt on every prosecution and investigation by labeling them a witch hunt or a politicization and miscarriage of justice, and claiming that his own lawsuits are merely corrective defenses against the overreach of his adversaries.

It's all part of Trump's tried-and-true negotiating playbook, used over and over again. No wonder several people have suggested that when it comes to understanding Trump's negotiating style, the art of the deal is all about starting with a punch to the face rather than building trust.

CHAPTER 3

Divide and Conquer

Build Walls, Not Bridges

In chapter 1, we discussed Trump's use of a hub-and-spokes model to manage his people, akin to a tribal chieftain who centralizes all power in his own hands. That approach extends to the way Trump seeks to lead outside his organization. Whether driving wedges between creditors during his real estate career or between adversarial institutions or foreign countries now as president, Trump consistently resorts to what may well be his favorite tactic: divide and conquer.

Trump learned during his first administration that many of his initiatives were blocked by collective action, whether by the business community, Congress, his own Republican Party, US trading partners, or other pillars of society. Across history, strongmen have always realized that their efforts to intimidate can be countered by effective collective action.

To Trump, groups such as NAFTA, NATO, the old Republican Party, and the Business Roundtable resemble the dangerous unified effort of tiny Lilliputians binding the great giant Gulliver with paralyzing strings in Jonathan Swift's 1726 saga, *Gulliver's Travels.* While

Trump probably hasn't read this work of eighteenth-century English satirical literature, I don't doubt that his imagined parallel to Gulliver's travails is what propels him to fight such unified action of perceived adversaries.

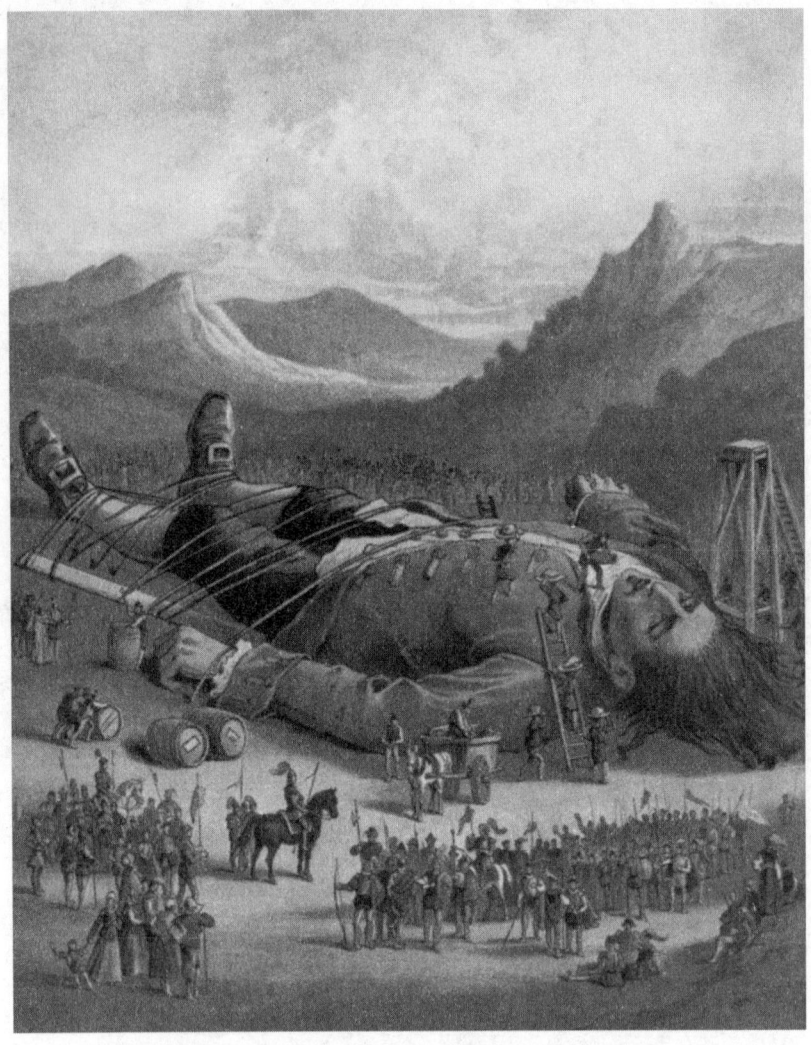

To Trump, his resistance to unified action by perceived adversaries is essentially equivalent to Gulliver resisting the efforts of the tiny Lilliputians to bind and blind him in the famous 1726 book Gulliver's Travels.

By pitting others against each other, shunting them from one disadvantage to the next and keeping them embroiled in draining, internecine squabbles—Trump, and Trump alone, can rise above the chaos he creates as the all-powerful arbiter and decider navigating deftly between warring parties fighting for his attention and blessing.

TRUMP'S ATTACKS ON LAW FIRMS, UNIVERSITIES, COMPANIES, AND INSTITUTIONS REFLECT THE SAME FUNDAMENTAL DIVIDE-AND-CONQUER IMPULSE

Trump uses "divide and conquer" as an intentional strategy to weaken his targets and to bring them to heel. Consider the methodical way in which he attacked our nation's most well-known law firms, issuing executive orders seeking to strangle the business of several big law firms that represented or hired those who had challenged his actions in courts and forcing them to come to the negotiating table, hat in hand. This was classic divide and conquer. Trump knew that if he took on the entire legal profession at once, he might end up coalescing and uniting all the big law firms against him—which would be a nightmare scenario. However, by throwing carrots at certain law firms—such as Trump-friendly firms like Jones Day, Quinn Emanuel, and Sullivan & Cromwell—and sticks at others, Trump created the division and dissent necessary to weaken law firms he attacked and prevent collective action from forming to resist those attacks.

That disunity was manifest in how different law firms responded to Trump's executive orders targeting them. In early March 2025, The Trump administration issued an executive order against the venerable Paul, Weiss law firm, allegedly for its role in investigating the Trump administration during Trump's first term. While that investigation was legal and appropriate, the investigator in question had previously long departed from Paul, Weiss. I was told the true impetus behind the attack on Paul, Weiss was retaliation for the firm's courageous campaign to rally support for peer law firms facing political reprisals—with executive orders that would have barred them from federal buildings, stripped them of government contracts, and jeopardized the security clearances essential to representing their clients. By standing up to Trump in an effort to heroically defend peer firms being targeted, Paul, Weiss found itself in the crosshairs.[1]

With the legal community splintered, and firms adopting an every-firm-for-itself stance, there was no unified support for Paul, Weiss. Faced with the inherently perishable nature of client relationships and legal talent, Chairman Brad Karp was compelled to prioritize his fiduciary duty to his partners. At that point, Karp understood he had little choice but to meet with Trump and attempt to secure a resolution, ultimately spending three hours at the White House negotiating a settlement. Remarkably, one of the advisors Trump consulted during those negotiations was the cochair of a Paul, Weiss rival—Sullivan & Cromwell—who was simultaneously serving as Trump's personal attorney in the appeal of his conviction on thirty-four counts of falsifying business records. That conflicted Sullivan & Cromwell chairman even joined the meeting by phone as one of Karp's principal interlocutors throughout the three-hour session, all while Trump himself greeted Karp with an almost jocular warmth.[2]

That anecdote illustrates the essence of divide and conquer: Draw one rival closer while striking at another, ensuring they never have the chance or inclination to unite against you. That dynamic persisted even after Karp reached his agreement. Other law firms continued circling, eager to exploit what they saw as Paul, Weiss' moment of weakness. In a remarkable episode, the chairman of one rival firm inadvertently copied Karp in a private, surreptitious 4 a.m. email to his partners, outlining a scheme to capitalize on the vulnerability of Paul, Weiss by poaching senior partners and clients from the firm.³ Adding to the fire, the press coverage in *The New York Times* continued to blame Karp for cutting a deal to save his firm, as though he were duty-bound to become a martyr, rather than spotlighting the venality of his attackers or the cowardice of his peers in the legal community.

That divided response, with internecine warfare and finger-pointing hopelessly pitting different law firms against each other, reflected exactly the response Trump was hoping to elicit. The lack of collective action from the outset resulted in each law firm having to navigate its own way, as Trump methodically picked them off one by one. While three of the targeted firms—Jenner & Block,

Trump is a master at using divide and conquer to ensure his adversaries cannot unite against him.

WilmerHale, and Perkins Coie—eventually challenged the president in court and won, obtaining restraining orders against their respective executive orders, far more law firms found themselves isolated on precarious terrain and rushed to settle before things turned worse for them. Only months later did several hundred mid-sized law firms jump in to support those firms targeted by Trump that chose to fight in a long-overdue demonstration of collective resistance to the campaign against law firms.

Trump's use of divide and conquer tends to follow that familiar script. What looks to outsiders like callous, childish tantrums is often calculated coercive pressure—and brutally effective in enabling him to get what he wants. First, he beats up on a sacrificial lamb, cowing peers into silence, if not abject fear. Should anyone dare to have the courage to push back, he pivots instantly, directing his fiercest fire at them. Simultaneously, in the classic prisoner's dilemma setup of offering both "carrots and sticks," he dangles prospective rewards and promises leniency for early capitulators who strike a deal with him, while threatening harsher punishment for anyone holding out.

That is the very playbook Trump is now applying to America's universities, especially the Ivy League. In the spring of 2025, he abruptly canceled $400 million in federal funding owed to Columbia University, leading its then-president, Katrina Armstrong, to accept a series of demands from his administration. After a firestorm of backlash on campus, Armstrong resigned. However, Trump's success in getting Columbia to fold only emboldened him to take his attacks on higher education even further, freezing $2.2 billion of federal research funds due to Harvard while issuing an even more sweeping set of onerous, and at times ludicrous, demands on its leadership.

Realizing that the demands issued to Harvard University in a notoriously absurd April 11 letter were untenable, Harvard President Alan Garber, with the full backing of the board—which included luminaries like former Commerce Secretary Penny Pritzker, former Merck CEO Ken Frazier, and former American Express CEO Ken Chenault—rejected those demands.[4]

Enraged by Harvard's refusal to acquiesce, Trump aimed the full fusillade of his anger squarely at the university, threatening to revoke its tax-exempt status, canceling billions in federal funding, and stripping its ability to host and enroll foreign students, among other attacks clearly intended to debilitate the school.

While he battered Harvard, hewing to Trump's classic prisoner's dilemma setup, the Trump administration simultaneously encouraged other Ivy League universities to reach a quick settlement to avoid Harvard's fate, the classic "carrots" complement to the "sticks" Harvard was experiencing. Meanwhile, the Trump administration also continued to heap unsolicited praise on peer universities, such as Dartmouth, in an attempt to drive a wedge between institutions of higher education and isolate Harvard.[5]

Unlike the law firm community, which quickly fragmented, Trump's inducements largely failed to succeed in breaking the collective resolve of universities in standing together. Despite the cowardice of certain college boards of trustees in hiding under statements of "institutional neutrality," nevertheless, universities largely held their ground and stood together in the face of these attacks. I helped catalyze the resolve of higher education to stand together, convening one hundred current and former university presidents to publish multiple collective letters in support of Harvard and condemning Trump's overreach in *Fortune* magazine.[6] At one such gathering, the revered former president of the University of Pennsylvania, Amy Gutmann, cited Benjamin Franklin's admonition, "We must hang together or we will surely hang separately," as a poignant reminder that the only way to stand up to divide and conquer is to stand together in unity.

University presidents joining forces demonstrates the power of collective opposition to Trump's favorite tactic of divide and conquer, and other sectors have similarly found collective action effective when Trump has come after them—including the CEOs of our nation's largest companies.

TRUMP AND THE BUSINESS COMMUNITY: THE POWER OF COLLECTIVE ACTION

Trump, who considers himself a businessman first and craves the support of business titans, has long sought to bring the CEOs of America's largest companies to heel by dominating them through divide and conquer. His carrots-and-stick measures aimed at CEOs have been extreme, even by Trump's standards. Unafraid to cast fortune and favor on business allies in good standing, his interventions in private markets have been drastic. There are no parallels in history for measures such as directly brokering the talks that brought TikTok into the hands of his longtime friend Larry Ellison of Oracle or staging what amounted to a promotional stunt for his then-friend Elon Musk by purchasing a Tesla in front of the White House.[7]

Those are the kinds of carrots Trump dangles, but the sticks he wields are just as stark. Trump shows no compunction about wielding the levers of government and regulatory power to go after businesses he doesn't like directly and unabashedly, leading critics to accuse him of being anti-capitalist with the taunt of "MAGA Maoism." For example, during his first term, AT&T tried to buy Time Warner, which owned CNN, in an $85 billion transaction. Pressure was building for AT&T CEO Randall Stephenson and Time Warner CEO Jeff Bewkes to fire the CEO of CNN, Jeff Zucker, and change CNN's coverage to make it more like that of Fox News. When Stephenson and Bewkes stood up for Zucker and defended journalistic integrity, the DOJ Antitrust Division abruptly sued to block the deal on rather frivolous legal grounds, despite the chief of that division having previously publicly supported the merger a few months earlier.

In fact, that antitrust head, Makan Delrahim, had even appeared on TV stating, "I don't see this as a major antitrust problem," right before Trump apparently nudged a change of legal opinion.[8]

Even though AT&T and Time Warner ultimately prevailed in court, the Trump administration dragged the case through a grueling eighteen months of appeals, with the merger finally cleared only after the administration exhausted every appeal and avenue of potential leverage. I learned from those directly involved in the deal that top leadership at both companies considered this unfortunate two-year delay the primary catalyst for its epic failure, which nearly wrecked two iconic American enterprises, with thousands of employees losing their jobs and hundreds of billions in lost shareholder wealth.

Thus, unlike the EU, NAFTA trading partners, the GOP congressional leaders, and others, business leaders quickly figured out the power of collective action early on in Trump 1.0 and learned that collective action was necessary to stand up to some of Trump's excesses. Contrary to what many think, prior to his presidential candidacies, Trump was not tight with many fellow CEOs, despite his own media image as a businessman. The leaders of the US business community, bona fide CEOs of Fortune 500 companies, were largely unknown to Trump, and in turn, they were skeptical of what they knew about him, given his flamboyant reputation and offensive rhetoric. Many CEOs were aware that his real estate enterprise was not considered a peer in size or scale, nor was he considered an easy business partner to deal with, as many of his bankers, lawyers, and business partners over the years could attest to. When, in 2005, I welcomed Trump to our December CEO Summit at the Waldorf Astoria, the crowd was wowed and appreciative, but many of the top tier CEOs walked out with disapproval. In his 2016 candidacy, not a single Fortune 100 CEO donated to Trump.[9]

All that changed after the election. Trump called to tell me, "Jeff, your CEO friends are all coming by here now." And he was correct.

Just as CEOs flocked to Trump in late 2024 after Trump returned to office, CEOs in late 2016 traveled to meet with Trump in waves and eagerly joined his Presidential Business Advisory Councils in early 2017. The CEOs told me in varied ways, "President Trump is now our nation's president, and we want to help him to be the most successful leader he can be."

However, these business leaders were soon in for a rude awakening. Two to three months after assuming office, Trump hosted sequential small group meetings at Mar-a-Lago and the White House with business leaders, which proved less constructive than they had wished. At many of those sessions, he hosted direct competitors such as Boeing and Lockheed; Merck, Pfizer, and Johnson & Johnson; and GM and Ford, where they were set up to be in combative exchanges, *Apprentice* style. They soon grew weary of being set up in such intrigue; they also resented being used as potted plants in photo ops regarding controversial social issues, such as the Muslim travel ban when the announced agenda was on a very different topic, such as "Infrastructure Week."

These frustrations came to a boiling point in August of 2017, with disappointment over what were widely seen as Trump's insufficiently condemning remarks following the killing of an innocent young woman rally-goer by a violent white nationalist crowd in Charlottesville, Virginia. That led Ken Frazier, the then-CEO of Merck, to quit these business advisory councils, whereupon Trump attacked his character and that of Merck. Frazier's model of courage had quietly ignited a pent-up revolt in the US business community against Trump.[10] After a delay of just a few hours, a stampede followed, with CEOs of such firms as UPS, Walmart, Intel, PepsiCo, GM, IBM, and BlackRock walking out in solidarity, and these Trump business support groups imploded. This collapse of business support was the first time in US history that the US business community collectively rejected a US president's call to service.[11]

Then, four years later, after Trump challenged the 2020 election results and widespread concern grew that he might refuse to leave office despite dozens of recounts, CEOs again mobilized in defense of democratic norms and the integrity of a peaceful transfer of power. After losing the popular vote, Trump took to the national airwaves to denounce the election as fraudulent, before he was cut off mid-broadcast by major networks who deemed his claims baseless.

As reported widely in the media, several dozen prominent CEOs began calling me immediately, asking if we could convene an urgent, impromptu "pop-up" CEO forum, as we did during the governance failure of 2001, the financial sector collapse of 2008, and other times of national crisis. I contacted one hundred CEOs and, twelve hours later, we catalyzed a swiftly gathered session of ninety-four renowned industrial leaders—CEOs from the largest firms across sectors—from finance to pharma, manufacturing to media, transportation to retail, and consumer goods to consulting.[12]

Calling themselves "Business Leaders for National Unity," this group of largely Republican CEOs condemned Trump and drafted six bullet points of agreement—including expressing pride in encouraging the largest voter participation in US history with paid time off to vote, congratulating Joe Biden and Kamala Harris as the winners, calling on Trump and anyone who disputed the results to take their grievance to the courts, demanding that such complaints reveal any evidence of systematic fraud, acknowledging that they saw no such evidence, and suggesting a speedy, transparent transfer of power.[13]

Midday the next day, when the Pennsylvania election was called by major media outlets, this statement was released. The Business Roundtable, the US Chamber of Commerce, the National Association of Manufacturers, and even world leaders quickly paralleled and echoed these key points in their own instant pronouncements of congratulations to Biden and Harris. The CEOs unraveled Trump's intrigue to undermine the free and fair elections while fortifying American democracy.[14]

At the initiative of these engaged, patriotic, alarmed CEOs, we convened this group for three more impromptu sessions: on January 5, just ahead of the January 6 attack on Congress, while certifying the Electoral College results; a few days later, after the president's near three-hour delay in responding to the riot of January 6; and then again in April, during the proliferation of laws intended to restrict voter access. When Trump/MAGA-inspired boycotts were threatened against a given airline, retailer, or beverage company, their competitors and peer firms across industries came to the rescue of those firms by standing together.[15] Thus, Trump's efforts to intimidate businesses from taking courageous patriotic actions were blunted through effective collective action. It was not the courage of clergy, the unity of universities, the toughness of trade bosses, or other such pillars of society but the voice of business that helped fortify the foundations of American society during that precarious time. It was the voice of business. Thus foiled by the collective action of the business community during his first term, Trump learned he had to address the threat of business collective action differently in his second term.[16]

A DIFFERENT PLAYBOOK FOR HIS SECOND TERM

In his second term, Trump grew more adept at zeroing in on issues that fractured the business community, enabling him to deploy divide-and-conquer tactics with far greater efficiency. He learned to eschew issues that unified business leaders in opposition to him.

Consider, for example, the way in which Trump has handled negotiations with business leaders amid massive frustration over his implementation of tariffs, reflecting his penchant for pitting CEOs against each other—rewarding Trump-friendly CEOs while attacking those he perceives to be less so—to ward off the prospect of collective action.

Contrary to some misguided narratives, CEOs are not all opposed to tariffs. Far from it: At one of my recent Yale CEO Summits, nearly 80 percent of CEOs surveyed agreed that selective tariffs are needed to rectify trade imbalances and protect strategic industries. The key word there, however, is "selective"; few CEOs support the indiscriminate overuse of all tariffs, all the time. As such, a whopping 90 percent of the top CEOs polled at the Yale CEO Summit agreed that they believe Trump's tariffs are backfiring amid rising costs and supply chain pressures. Broader public opinion seems to mirror this tariff angst, with disapproval for Trump's handling of the economy higher than it's ever been, showing approximately three-fourths of the nation believes the economy is in bad shape.

Although companies nearly universally share the common thread of concern over tariffs, some industries have been hit harder than others, while certain industries and companies have even benefited from tariffs, making a collective response highly challenging. Furthermore, key business groups and forums such as the Business Roundtable (BRT) have been all but missing in action on this divisive issue, eschewing any broader response beyond putting out rather cursory statements and supposed behind-the-scenes lobbying.[17]

As a result, the lack of collective action on tariffs has allowed Trump to pick off companies and industries one by one, pitting them against one another in a competition for his favor and for much-needed tariff exemptions. Just as Trump intended, some industries and companies have been more successful than others in securing exemptions. For example, Trump announced scaled back auto tariffs immediately after meeting with the CEOs of leading carmakers. Similarly, Trump backtracked and announced scaled-back tariffs on nearly a thousand food products after leading retail CEOs emphasized affordability concerns amid broad consumer angst. No detail is too small to escape his personal attention—and wrath. After reports that Amazon was planning to list tariff surcharges next to products—despite Commerce Secretary Howard Lutnick saying, "It's nonsense, a 10% tariff is not going to change virtually any price"—Trump officials attacked Amazon for being "hostile and political." Ultimately, it took a heated phone call from Trump for Amazon founder Jeff Bezos to back down, but back down he did.[18]

DRIVING WEDGES IN ALLIANCES NULLIFIES THE POWER OF COLLECTIVE ACTION IN STANDING UP TO TRUMP

The Business Roundtable is merely one of many alliances Trump views with disfavor. In fact, Trump has never, in any sector, met an alliance he particularly liked. One can speculate that the reason is simple: Divide and conquer doesn't work in the face of a strong oppositional alliance. You can see this dynamic play out in decisions large and small. Collective alliances are especially prevalent in the realm of diplomacy and foreign policy, so it's not a coincidence that Trump has routinely attacked NATO, NAFTA, the EU, and every alliance that has underpinned the post-WWII world order. Trump is always lashing out at these alliances, even those composed of the US's historic allies, because they get in the way of his preferred transactional approach, pitting foreign countries against each other in competition for his goodwill. Canada versus Mexico, Justin Trudeau versus Claudia Sheinbaum, France versus Germany, Putin versus Xi all exemplify his practice of battering one party while flattering the other. Dealing with countries in a one-off way is a worldview far more to Trump's liking than a values-based world order built on norms, consensus, mutual respect, and alliances among international organizations and nations. Those constrain Trump in ways he does not appreciate, impeding his ability to bully, cajole, bluster, and divide and conquer his way to domination.

Consider the divergent ways in which Trump slapped tariffs on Canada and Mexico during the earliest days of the trade war, in March 2025. On March 6, the very same day he praised Mexican President Claudia Sheinbaum on Truth Social, he took a jab at Canadian Prime Minister Justin Trudeau. About Sheinbaum, Trump posted, "After speaking with President Claudia Sheinbaum of Mexico, I have agreed that Mexico will not be required to pay tariffs on anything that falls under the USMCA Agreement. This Agreement is until April 2. I did this as an accommodation, and out of respect for, President Sheinbaum. Our relationship has been a very good one, and we are working hard, together, on the Border, both in terms of stopping Illegal Aliens from entering the United States and, likewise, stopping Fentanyl." In stark contrast, on the same day, Trump posted about Trudeau, "Believe it or not, despite the terrible job he's done for Canada, I think that Justin Trudeau is using the Tariff problem, which he has largely caused, in order to run again for Prime Minister."[19]

Leaning into divide and conquer has always been Trump's modus operandi, long before he entered politics and dating back to his earliest days in business. It's not for nothing that some perceptive Trump chroniclers, such as Peter Baker and Susan Glasser, have called Trump "the divider." In fact, divide and conquer was how he finagled his way through several bankruptcies, escaping with minor nicks while largely leaving others holding the bag—but more on that in chapter 4.

Even outside his business and real estate pursuits, pre-politics Trump was a master of divide and conquer in virtually every facet of his life, including his management of the media. Despite his ostensibly adversarial relationship with the press and his loud cries of "fake news," there is no more savvy observer (and manipulator) of the media than Trump, who forged deep relationships across the press

In classic Trumpian divide-and-conquer style, Trump pitted the leaders of Mexico and Canada against each other with vastly divergent tariffs treatment.

long before his plunge into politics and who masterfully dangles both carrots and sticks in managing his own press coverage.

Trump has long believed, not without reason, that he is his own best publicist and PR advisor. He understands that the fundamental currency of journalism is relevance and exclusivity, with every journalist perpetually trying to break hot news stories before their rivals. And Trump was a perpetual gusher of constant breaking news even before he entered politics. Recall that his every date and restaurant outing was covered breathlessly by the New York tabloids in the '90s. He knew better than anyone how to play reporters off each other, giving or withholding exclusive news items as he saw fit and using that leverage to shape coverage of himself. (Of course, he had other levers as well, including taking advantage of reporters' perennial and desperate need for quotes with his now-infamous practice of using the "John Barron" pseudonym to feed them tidbits about himself or his company that he wanted to see in print while maintaining the thinnest veneer of plausible deniability.)[20]

Just as he pummels CEOs who don't play his game and heaps rewards on those who do, Trump has done the same with journalists. With him, that can be two sides of the same coin. It's an approach embodied by the infamous example of *Wall Street Journal* reporter Neil Barsky, who crossed Trump and learned to regret it. In 1991, Barsky accepted a gift from one of Trump's senior executives: tickets to a boxing match featuring Evander Holyfield and George Foreman, which was sponsored by Trump. Reasoning that it was an opportunity to cover Trump in his natural habitat, Barsky sought permission from his higher-ups, and his bosses okayed Barsky getting one ticket. Figuring it would be innocuous to bring his brother and father as well, Barsky accepted two additional tickets from Trump for his family.

Trump loudly and publicly complained about Barsky's "bad ethics," insisting that the reporter had unduly extorted him into giving him three tickets and exaggeratedly claiming that Barsky had also asked for a suite at the Taj. Trump thus claimed that Barsky was tainted and was pursuing a personal vendetta because he had failed to extort more from Trump. Trump's complaints were so loud and the optics were so terrible that the *Wall Street Journal*'s editors ultimately decided that, regardless of the validity of Trump's claims, Barsky should stop covering Trump entirely—a victory that Trump then bragged about for years to come, an implied warning to all future journalists of the fate that awaited those who found themselves on the wrong side of Trump.[21]

The craziest part about the story? It was all a setup. As Trump wrote in his 1997 book, *Trump: The Art of the Comeback*, he ordered his subordinate to give Barsky the tickets, pledging that "the next time he writes anything, I'm going to blast him like he never got blasted before." In that same book, Trump continued, "Of all the writers who have written about me, probably none has been more vicious than Neil Barsky of *The Wall Street Journal*." Left unstated was the implied warning: Look at what I did to Neil Barsky before you even think about writing a bad story about me.

MAGA OR MAO? HOW TRUMP ATTACKS AND WEAKENS INSTITUTIONS BY INVERTING THE HIERARCHY OF AUTHORITY

Trump's attacks on institutions that he views as adversarial to him go much further than divide-and-conquer tactics. With an almost preternatural instinct for weaknesses, he zeroes in on and exploits his adversaries' vulnerabilities with precision, systematically undermining any centers of authority he does not command. In his drive to topple established hierarchies, upend existing systems, and reconstitute them around his own central authority, one could almost say that he resembles history's greatest revolutionaries like Mao, Lenin, and Stalin, much more than any conventional US political leader or corporate leader.

Consider how Trump delights in inverting the rank-based, hierarchical organization that is the military by elevating lower-ranked, obscure junior officers and enlisted military servicemembers into positions of real authority over their nominal superiors. After Trump regretted his pick of James Mattis, a real general, as secretary of defense, he never made the same "mistake" again. His subsequent secretaries of defense have been among the lowest-ranked military men to oversee the Pentagon in history, including Mark Esper, who topped out at lieutenant colonel; Chris Miller, who topped out at colonel; and Pete Hegseth, who topped out at major. And after Trump soured on his pick of Mark Milley, a real four-star general, as chairman of the Joint Chiefs of Staff, he plucked an obscure, retired three-star general, Dan "Raizin" Caine, to serve as his Joint Staff chair in his second term, the first chairman of the Joint Chiefs of Staff in history to have never reached the rank of four-star general or admiral. One has to wonder what all the four-star generals on the Joint Chiefs of Staff thought of a three-star general being picked to oversee them.

Trump's penchant for flipping the tables on authority and inverting the hierarchy of command in the military manifests itself in many more instances than merely nominations of lower ranked officers to oversee their higher-ranking officers. He has long attacked genuine war heroes in ways that were previously thought lethal for any political candidate, taking shots at everyone from John McCain to Gold Star families like the Khan family. However, an even more illustrative episode is Trump's handling of the Eddie Gallagher affair during his first term. In July 2019, an obscure Navy SEAL named Eddie Gallagher was convicted for wrongfully posing for a grotesque, wildly inappropriate picture with a human casualty. He was sentenced to time served and demoted one pay grade. From the beginning, Gallagher and his lawyers sought to portray Gallagher as a heroic, manly man of a soldier who was unfairly targeted and singled out for punishment by Democratic career lawyers. Gallagher's spouse even regularly appeared on Fox News, transforming the Gallagher case into a cause célèbre among certain circles on the right.

These messages evidently resonated with President Trump and parts of his base, and Trump inched toward a full pardon. Sensing danger, the then-Secretary of the Navy Richard Spencer discreetly tried to head off further intervention, repeatedly imploring the president not to get involved. It was no use. Pat Cipollone, the White House counsel, soon called Spencer with Trump's order that Gallagher's punishment be reversed and his rank restored. Furthermore, despite the determination of the commander of the Navy SEALs that Gallagher be stripped of his Trident pin, Trump seemed set on letting Gallagher keep it.[22]

As Spencer noted at the time, "This was a shocking and unprecedented intervention in a low-level review. It was a reminder that the president has very little understanding of what it means to be in the military, to fight ethically or be governed by a uniform set of rules and practices." Rather than carry out Trump's order, Spencer resigned.[23]

Trump is focused on inverting the hierarchy of power in the military because he instinctively dislikes sources of independent legitimacy and authority outside his control. He wants to call all the shots and therefore doesn't want competent professionals who have credibility anchored in expertise and qualifications, professional networks to draw on, and the technical knowledge and language to run circles around him.

Even hierarchies of power of his own creation are not immune to Trump's overriding instinct to invert power structures and turn the high-flying into the downtrodden, and vice versa. An oft-touted accomplishment from his first term was packing the judiciary with conservative judges vetted by the right-wing legal advocacy group the Federalist Society, whose leader, Leonard Leo, was a staunch Trump ally. Yet, in his second term—after falling out with Leo and feeling personally betrayed by conservative judges who ruled against him in his manifold legal challenges—Trump turned on Leonard Leo and the Federalist Society. He blasted Leo on Truth Social as a "real sleazebag" and "bad person who . . . hates America," and vowed not to nominate Federalist Society–approved picks while nurturing a new, parallel universe of Trump-ified legal advocacy groups, such as Mike Davis's Article 3 Project, to rival and challenge the Federalist Society's primacy and authority.[24]

Trump's desire to invert power structures extends beyond these realms—literally as well as metaphorically. Even heavenly matters are hardly daunting for Trump, who, despite leading a political party built on the backs of many devoutly religious evangelicals, has shown a consistent, flagrant disregard for the norms and customs of religions across faiths. Catholics around the world were horrified when Trump flippantly posted a picture on Truth Social depicting himself as pope after the passing of Pope Francis. In private, Trump's derision of the

Almighty runs far deeper, often bordering on the sacrilegious in the eyes of his critics.²⁵

Consider the way Trump treated a group of evangelical pastors who came to meet him at Trump Tower the first time he ran for president in 2015, in the retelling of one of Trump's former lieutenants. Unsurprisingly for a group of conservative family values–focused evangelical pastors, the group focused, with great concern, on such red flags as Trump's three marriages and his ambiguous views on abortion.

Trump posting a picture of himself as pope is only one of many examples of his flagrant, flippant disregard for the norms of organized religion—and any institution or power center outside of his immediate control.

But when Trump made his entrance, he put on a show, telling the group exactly what they wanted to hear—even if it was of dubious truthfulness. He claimed he was against abortion when, in private, for many years, he had often joked about how much he hated condoms and boasted that he had held a personal celebration when abortion became legal in New York in 1970, noting that it ought to have been called "The Trump Law" for how often he would use it.[26] Impressed and convinced by Trump's claims, the evangelicals rallied to his defense, closing the meeting by calling a moment of prayer for Trump. After the meeting ended, Trump looked to his deputy, who recounted how Trump incredulously muttered, "Can you believe that bullshit? Can you believe people actually believe that bullshit?"[27]

It is worth noting, however, that as much as Trump relies on the strategy of divide and conquer, and as much as that tactic can come across as devious, if not ruthless, paradoxically, he is also capable of leveraging it to build common ground by forcing neutral parties to pick a side and by drawing the lines of division cleanly. In this, he is intuiting the research of academic conflict management researchers he surely never heard of but whose theories he has grasped instinctively without ever needing to study them. Conflict management scholars have long built on the scholarship of MIT's Kurt Lewin in the 1940s and Harvard's Herbert Kelman in the 1970s, who advocated the importance of resolving immediate disputes by enlarging the scope of the problem, including imagining a harmonious post-conflict future that would make short-term concessions tolerable. By expanding the scope of the problem and by forcing a reckoning with urgency and clarity, this approach can forge bridges across entrenched divides.

This is the principle that Trump's son-in-law Jared Kushner engineered in the historic Abraham Accords, breaking down once-hostile barriers between Arab countries and Israel. The framework of the Abraham Accords had seemed impossible if not unimaginable to most Mideast experts—until Jared Kushner achieved the impossible.

Trump's divide-and-conquer strategy can, paradoxically, draw the lines of division more clearly and create leverage to build common ground between unlikely allies—as we saw with the Abraham Accords.

Before a political solution could be sold to either Israel or its Arab neighbors through persuasion, all parties had to imagine a highly desirable scenario far better than the status quo, making hard, short-term concessions worth it. While the lasting unity and trust this initiative built may seem like an odd example of divide and conquer, it reflects how the tactic can be used to actually build common ground. With the Abraham Accords, Trump used divide and conquer to draw the lines of demarcation more clearly and starkly than anyone ever had before. On one hand, Trump first isolated Iran, Hamas, Hezbollah, and other bad actors in the region, pummeling them with sticks. On the other hand, Kushner created a far more appealing, attractive pathway for Arab countries and for constituencies within the Palestinian people who did not want to go down the path of Iran. Through Kushner's bold initiatives, for the first time, these groups were able to visualize what a peaceful, prosperous future might look like with stronger diplomatic and economic ties to Israel. This divide-and-conquer process forced the Arab Gulf Coast leaders to pick a side in no uncertain terms, driving the first-ever public vilification of Hamas, Hezbollah, and other bad actors by Arab Gulf Coast leaders alongside breakthrough diplomatic accords for the recognition of Israel—all of which was previously thought impossible.[28]

I worked closely with Kushner on the design and delivery of the initial Bahrain Peace to Prosperity Summit in 2018, which laid the groundwork for the historic Abraham Accords. This conference, hosted by the Trump administration and the crown prince of Bahrain, saw over three hundred top delegates come in from thirty countries, from Australia and Argentina, Dubai and Delhi, Nigeria and Norway, and even such unlikely pairings as Saudi Arabia and Qatar and Greece and Turkey. The explicit purpose was to reverse the sequence of the past fifty years of peace efforts (e.g., Oslo, Paris, Annapolis)—that is, to share an economic vision for what the future could be, enlarging the scope of the problem, before delving into divisive political real estate battles.

Kushner, as senior advisor to Trump, unveiled a $50 billion economic investment plan that was predicated on the soon-to-follow political peace agreement. His plan provided opposing parties a chance to visualize what the quality of life could be like when tensions subside. By enlarging the problem and introducing new challenges, paradoxically, he drew closer to a breakthrough than by rehashing the same ground over and over again. Kushner, with Trump's backing, drew on the remarkable economic-development successes in other countries torn apart by past political violence, including Bangladesh and South Korea. A combination of grants, low-interest loans, and private investment would double the size of the Palestinian economy, create one million new jobs, reduce Palestinian unemployment from 30 percent to single digits, and reduce Palestinian poverty by 50 percent. Drawing on the World Bank and other organizations, this was the first comprehensive economic transformation plan linking private investment to public capital—and to adequately fund the projects under discussion.

Many prominent US business leaders, including Blackstone Group CEO Stephen Schwarzman and AT&T CEO Randall Stephenson, were present to endorse these plans, expressing their enthusiastic support. They and scores of other executives cited the proposals as attractive investment opportunities with very reasonable financial targets, in an environment where the rule of law could help them thrive.

Mohamed Alabbar of the United Arab Emirates, founder of Emaar Properties and one of the world's biggest commercial builders, told the conference, "The younger generation will not let us continue to be trapped by our past. Palestinian people are our people. We get up every morning positive, and we want to do more. . . . By generating jobs, income opportunities and filling gaps in delivering basic services, the private sector can help build momentum behind a fragile economy and instill hope in the people of the region."

The effort stands as a shining example of how, paradoxically, divide and conquer can sometimes create maximum leverage to actually achieve common ground by drawing the lines of demarcation clearly and by forcing neutral observers to pick a side.[29]

In the case of the Abraham Accords, divide and conquer laid the groundwork for enduring trusted bonds, personal friendships, and mutually beneficial relationships. While some complain cynically that the Trump family benefited later from such friendships, the important aspect is that vital cooperative ties were built between cultures that had been at war for hundreds, if not thousands, of years. The events that occurred after Trump left office in 2021, culminating in the tragedy of October 7, 2023, and the ensuing chaos which engulfed the region, were sadly avoidable but for the unfortunate mistakes of certain misguided officials in the subsequent administration.

Nevertheless, with Iran now dramatically weakened and tensions in the Mideast subsiding, the prospect of expanding the Abraham Accords, and advancing peace and prosperity across the region, once again appears within reach, and all that traces back to how Trump and Kushner miraculously performed a divide-and-conquer maneuver for constructive results that virtually no Mideast expert could have predicted would have been possible.

The Abraham Accords were an example of Trump's unconventional style being used for diplomatic harmony and intended peace in the Mideast, reflecting that Trump has always had a keen understanding of the value of dividing prospective adversaries—whether for better or for worse.

CHAPTER 4

How Trump Makes Money

*The Art of Stealing the Deal—
Heads I Win, Tails You Lose*

After I declined Donald Trump's offer of the presidency of Trump University—a tale recounted in the introduction—Trump asked me to help and advise the new president, Mike Sexton. Soon I learned that enrolled students were promised a photo with Trump, which was often obtained by standing next to a cardboard cutout of Trump. An old friend of mine, a Harvard economist, joined me in helping warn Trump of that racket, but he did not seem to lose much sleep over it.

Eastern philosophy often echoes the wisdom of Sun Tzu in *The Art of War* to "leave your adversary a dignified path for retreat." This, however, is not Donald Trump's mantra when it comes to doing deals and making money. Trump does not leave much on the table after a deal and is likely to have even sold the other side's furniture in the negotiation process. The renowned senior economists Robert Frank of Cornell and Phillip Cook of Duke warned of the consequences of such a philosophy in their 1995 book *The Winner-Take-All Society: Why the Few at the Top Get So Much More Than the Rest of Us*. They criticize those who opportunistically seize and exploit small differences in performance that yield enormous differences in rewards. Citing lotteries, sports markets, and the entertainment industry where many compete to be among a small number who achieve extreme success, they complain that superstar tiers have emerged across sectors, with those superstars clearing the deck for themselves. That lament is surely not one that makes Trump lose any sleep at night.

Critics point out that many of Trump's business ventures over the years call to mind P. T. Barnum's infamous quip: "There's a sucker born every minute." As his political nemesis Barack Obama quipped, "There are constant attempts to sell you stuff. Who does that? Selling you gold sneakers and $100,000 watches and most recently, a Trump Bible. You know, he wants you to buy the word of God, Donald Trump edition. Got his name right there, next to Matthew and Luke.

Trump has endorsed an almost comically long list of branded products over the years.

Trump University attendees found themselves posing with a Trump cardboard cutout as a photo with Trump.

You could not make this stuff up. If you saw it on *Saturday Night Live*, you'd say, 'Now, that's going too far.'"[1]

Long before he entered politics, many of Trump's business deals reeked of a certain inimitable yuckiness, a whiff of the style of, say, a used car salesman. His customers, vendors, and others unfortunate enough to have been crossed by Trump find out the hard way, time after time, that his business schemes are rarely as good as they sound, no matter how exorbitant the marketing—akin to the cardboard cutout photos with Trump given to attendees of Trump University.[2]

In chronicling Trump's manifold business activities and exorbitant marketing schemes, it's hard not to see echoes of certain famous fictional caricatures, such as the humorous shady traveling salesman Mr. Haney from the classic 1960s sitcom *Green Acres*, who, with a truckload of scam gadgets, was always ready to sell to the naïve customer Mr. Oliver Douglas something "you can't do without," such as a makeshift washing machine that had a boat motor inside that went haywire, spraying water and clothes. Similarly, it's hard not to see echoes of the humorous Joe Isuzu, the fictional Isuzu spokesman from 1980s television ads who made outrageous and satirically overinflated claims about Isuzu's cars, such as the car being so inexpensive it could be bought with spare change, or that the vehicle had more seats than the Houston Astrodome, or that it could travel three hundred miles per gallon.

For Trump, business—as in most things in life—is a zero-sum game; for him to win, someone else presumably has to lose. And for Trump, it's all about making sure that he's always the winner.

There's a certain savvy logic to how Trump deploys his modus operandi when it comes to making money. He rarely takes on the riskiest parts of any deal himself, preferring to offload risk whenever possible to others while reaping the benefits. It's part of Trump's art of stealing the deal: Heads I win, tails you lose. It's a model Trump has fine-tuned to perfection over his adult life, but it's also how he's always approached business, even his earliest deals.

THE MYTHIC ORIGIN STORY: ONLY A MYTH

In my book *The Hero's Farewell*, I analyzed how many renowned CEOs, such as Henry Ford, Armand Hammer of Occidental Petroleum, and Harry Gray of United Technologies, dramatically reinvented their own biographies. Gray, for example, not only changed his name, which was Harry Grusin, but fabricated his education, which was journalism and not engineering as he claimed. He fabricated his religion of origin, which was Judaism (and he was a bar mitzvah), not Unitarian as he claimed; and he was not born in Milledgeville, Georgia, as he claimed but in Latvia. Even the legendary Horatio Alger, contrary to the popular myth, was a failed journalist who had previously been a defrocked pedophilic preacher and not the rags-to-riches, self-made business success he claimed.[3]

Trump similarly crafted his own origin myth, that of the entirely self-made entrepreneur, a global business tycoon, over many years. He relentlessly pushed that narrative in the media, claiming that he had transcended his father's "tiny" un-prestigious outer-borough operation and parlayed a single $1 million loan from him into a $10 billion empire through nothing but effort and hard work. Sporadic sniping from skeptical journalists and biographers hardly pierced Trump's self-mythologizing.

Of course, this origin story has now been largely debunked, in part due to his niece, Mary Trump, leaking thousands of pages of never-before-seen family financial documents in 2018 to *The New York Times*. These documents revealed definitively that Trump had received a much more massive boost from his father than was previously appreciated, with his father, Fred Trump, the genuine business genius who built a property development empire from scratch. In fact, by age three, Trump was already earning $200,000 a year from his father's businesses, and by age eight he was officially a millionaire. By the time he graduated college, he was drawing over a million dollars from his father's empire every year.[4]

Fred Trump was a witting and willing coconspirator, hiding his own crucial role while leaning into the media feeding frenzy of Donald, the self-made real estate savant. In the very first profile of Donald Trump in 1976 in *The New York Times*, an undertone of skepticism underlies the title, "Donald Trump, Real Estate Promoter, Builds Image." One gets the distinct sense that veteran journalist Judy Klemesrud isn't quite sure whether the younger Trump is a bona fide real estate developer or a scam artist who cares only about PR. Klemesrud began the piece with a portrait of the younger Trump that seems timeless, recognizable, and instantly familiar:[5]

> He is tall, lean and blond, with dazzling white teeth, and he looks ever so much like Robert Redford. He rides around town in a chauffeured silver Cadillac with his initials, DJT, on the plates. He

dates slinky fashion models, belongs to the most elegant clubs and, at only thirty years of age, estimates that he is worth "more than $200 million."

Of course, we now know Trump wasn't worth $200 million then. He apparently claimed the entirety of the Trump Organization's net worth as his own, even though the business was owned by his father. In the same piece, his father meekly leaned into their shared conspiracy, admiringly claiming, "Donald is the smartest person I know," and sitting by idly as the younger Trump ran roughshod over his accomplishments, bragging that his father failed to grow the business because "it was psychology" and portraying himself as the family's savior: "Now, that psychology is ended."

In that same 1976 profile, Trump discussed his quest to diversify his family company's real estate activities, intent on expanding into Manhattan and developing luxury properties rather than the low-income outer-borough developments on which his father had built the company. To that end, he was intent on redirecting the substantial cash flows from Fred Trump's empire to buy low in Manhattan, at a time when the city had sunk to a new low amid fiscal woes, rampant crime, and population exodus.

As Trump predicted, "New York is either going to get much better or much worse, and I think it will get much better. I'm not talking about the South Bronx. I don't know anything about the South Bronx. But in Manhattan, I feel a new convention center will be a turning point for the city. It will get rid of all that pornographic garbage in Times Square. Psychologically, I think if New York City gets a convention center, it will resurge and rejuvenate. . . . There are a lot of good deals around right now."

Trump was intent on capturing one of those "good deals" for himself, and to his credit, he did. At the time, other developers were leaving Manhattan in droves. It was, after all, the era of "Ford to City: Drop Dead," as the infamous *New York Daily News* headline screamed. But Trump took a contrarian stance and bought in. He ended up buying low at exactly the right time, as the city's economic recovery resulted in a rising tide that lifted all boats.

Trump's first big opportunity in Manhattan arose when the Commodore Hotel next to Grand Central station came up for sale, with its owner, the Penn Central Railroad, desperate for funds after declaring bankruptcy. The Commodore needed not only a rescuer with financial largess but also connections in city government to finagle the permits and licenses required for a complete makeover. Nobody would have taken thirty-year-old, relatively unknown Donald Trump seriously for such a deal, since he lacked both the capital and reputation to independently finance and manage a massive real estate development in Midtown Manhattan. Except that he possessed one major advantage: The mayor of New York at that time, Abe Beame, was a longtime friend of Fred Trump, dating back from their youth together in Queens and rise up the local Democratic Party organization.

Leveraging his father's ties to the Democratic mayor closely (Mayor Beame is said to have instructed his underlings, "I support whatever Donald and Fred want"), the younger Trump set about methodically boxing out other potential bidders by securing the support of every agency and corner of the Beame administration.[6] By the end of the process, Trump had secured quite the sweetheart deal, reflecting his "heads I win, tails you lose" approach. Rather than buying the property outright, the state's Urban Development Corporation purchased it directly, then gave Trump a ninety-nine-year lease, saving him money on the front end. Furthermore, Trump negotiated a forty-year property tax exemption, unprecedented at the time and the first ever for a commercial property in NYC. This was a game changer in getting the economics of the project to work, as it reduced the carrying cost to practically zero. Trump argued that the tax exemption would be a worthwhile trade for the city because the Commodore would stimulate economic activity. However, most commentators were convinced that Beame's support had tilted the scales. Ultimately, according to one study, the unprecedented tax exemption cost the city more than $410 million in lost tax revenues.[7]

The structure of the deal Trump negotiated effectively de-risked the entire project for himself. If things went well, he would enjoy all the upside as the operator of the hotel and retain all its earnings; and if things didn't go well, it would be the city stuck with a bad asset on its hands while Trump washed his hands and walked away. But Trump wasn't finished. Once he had secured the property, he again leveraged his father's assets and reputation to secure a $70 million construction loan to renovate the decaying property, with his father as guarantor, and enlisted the Hyatt Corporation, led by the Pritzker family, as his partners.[8] (They would eventually fall out, but that's a separate story.)

Trump's first project was a big hit when it reopened in September 1980 as The Grand Hyatt New York, which still stands next to Grand Central, in largely the same shape. The hotel generated millions for Trump annually until he sold his stake to Hyatt in 1996 for $142 million, ending his direct involvement.

In many ways, his Commodore Hotel transaction embodied the prototypical Trump deal. Already, the contours were taking shape of patterns that Trump would repeatedly deploy to great effect in structuring business deals throughout his career, and a business model for making money that he would come to refine and duplicate over and over and over.

- First, Trump rarely buys anything other than distressed assets, whether in bankruptcy or near bankruptcy, from highly motivated sellers strapped for cash and desperate for relief. His purchase of the Grand Commodore Hotel from its owner, Penn Central Railroad, desperate for cash, would start a pattern that would play out again and again, whether with Trump's acquisition of Mar-a-Lago or the Trump Winery or Trump National Doral.

Trump's first big major transaction, the Commodore Hotel, embodied the prototypical Trump deal of offloading much of the downside while retaining the upside.

- Second, Trump rarely purchases anything at full price or anywhere near top dollar. Buying property from those down on their luck and driving the hardest deal possible became a Trump specialty. Some Trump associates noted that beating down the price and taking advantage of people and organizations who had once been wealthier and more powerful than Trump gives him a thrill. Paying top dollar in frothy markets is never Trump's preferred approach.
- Third, Trump always puts down as little money as possible up front. Whenever possible, he likes to buy things with other people's money. He generally offloads as much downside risk as possible so that his share of the investment carries minimal exposure while retaining maximum upside for himself. Furthermore, he almost always structures deals in such a way that he is relatively unencumbered, enabling him to wash

his hands and walk away if things turn south for whatever reason, while someone else is largely caught holding the bag.

Trump used the momentum from his success with the Commodore to expand his family's burgeoning real estate empire, developing, in rapid succession, Trump Tower in 1983, the signature fifty-eight-story tower on Fifth Avenue that became Trump's headquarters and a symbol of his opulent, gaudy personal branding with gold everywhere and a pink marble atrium; Trump Plaza in 1984, a relatively drab East Side condominium; Trump Parc on Central Park in 1986, which Trump transformed from the dilapidated Barbizon Plaza Hotel; and Trump Palace in 1991, one of the tallest residential towers in NYC at the time. These deals quickly turned to gold for Trump, at least initially, thanks in part to riding the rising tide of a rebounding NYC economy, as the 1970s-era slump faded into history and the 1980s NYC boom times famously memorialized in Tom Wolfe's *Bonfire of the Vanities* took shape.[9]

Despite this favorable macro backdrop, Trump's real estate deals did not always pan out. Around the same time that he acquired the Commodore Hotel, he also purchased an option to acquire two old, derelict Penn Central railyards, undervalued and underutilized real estate on the West Side that extended from Fifty-Ninth to Seventy-Second Street and from Thirtieth to Thirty-Ninth Street. It was "the greatest piece of land in urban America," he bragged. Trump envisioned a grandiose "Television City" mega-development on the fifty-seven-acre site, with sweeping plans for massive skyscrapers, replete with an on-site NBC studio, 2 million square feet of retail storefronts, and 3.6 million square feet of television and movie studio space, as well as eight thousand apartments, ten thousand parking spaces, and twenty thousand condominiums.

On paper, it was a prime opportunity for Trump since, more than anything, the project needed political connections of exactly the type that he had with Abe Beame and that he had used with aplomb on the Commodore Hotel project. In the words of the bankruptcy trustee, the properties needed a developer "who seemed best positioned in the New York market to get rezoning and government financing . . . very, very high in his political position."[10]

In practice, however, it turned into a disaster, Trump's dreams turning to dust. Where he saw grandiose magnificence, others saw a horrific monstrosity, with fervent, spirited opposition arising from local residents and businesses alike. More importantly, after Abe Beame left the mayoralty, Trump lost his strongest political ally, and his successor in city hall, Mayor Ed Koch, proved intractable in his resistance to Trump's bluster, refusing to grant him the necessary tax breaks, zoning, and subsidies he needed to build Television City. Furthermore, Koch provided tax breaks to persuade NBC to stay at Rockefeller Center, undermining Trump's Television City pitch for NBC to become its core anchor tenant. The relationship between Trump and Koch quickly devolved, New York City seeming too small for two titanic egos, neither of whom ever backed down from a fight. Trump called for Koch's resignation, deeming him "a horrible manager" and a "moron," while Koch taunted, "If Donald Trump is squealing like a stuck pig, I must have done something right. Piggy, piggy, piggy!"[11]

Beneath the heated rhetoric and clash of egos, Koch was distinctly unimpressed with Trump's value proposition, with incisive perception regarding what Trump was really after. A senior Koch aide later recounted, "Ed always had this sense that Donald was looking for six quarters for a dollar." Another said Trump "liked to assert that he was going to do this and everybody else was going to go along with it." When Trump's grand plans eventually fizzled out in the '90s, he stopped paying property taxes on the sites, abjectly surrendering control over the properties for a meager sum to a syndicate of foreign investors, who finally began construction on the site three decades after Trump's initial promises. In typical Trump style, he still managed to muck up the waters enough to be able to claim his fumble was actually a victory. While receiving very little financially for surrendering control, Trump pitched himself to his new foreign partners as a branding partner and leveraged his small minority stake to successfully negotiate having his name placed on many of the luxury towers built, creating the false impression that he had built the entire project. Trump's name was stripped from these projects only after he got into politics, when tenants voted to remove it on the basis that it hurt resale values.

As the example of Trump's West Side developments show, with all things Trump, and even in successful projects, often there is less substance than first appears and there remains an inescapable whiff of the used car salesman. Take, as another example, the well-documented saga of the project to rebuild Central Park's Wollman Rink, billed by Trump as an act of beneficent generosity, but more closely resembling a profitable PR ploy than genuine philanthropy.

The story of how Trump got involved with fixing the ice-skating rink in the middle of Central Park has become a foundational myth in Trump world, its flames fanned most avidly by Trump himself. In his retelling, the municipal government, led by Mayor Ed Koch at the time, had spent millions of dollars over half a decade trying to fix the decaying ice skating rink, with little success. Trump, who had been feuding publicly with Koch, saw an opportunity to publicly one-up "Hizzoner" and offered to finish the project within six months "at his expense," on the condition that he would be able to secure from the city, gratis, the operating leases for the rink and a restaurant. Koch foolishly agreed—though he would soon come to regret it.

Trump, naturally, had a field day trampling all over the mayor, holding frequent press conferences trumpeting every increment of progress, plastering his name everywhere and turning the renovation into the Trump show. To Trump's credit, thanks to his jawboning and the outsized public attention generated as a result, the project finished ahead of schedule and nearly a million dollars under budget.

Contrary to his promise to fund the renovation out of pocket, a vast majority of the expenses incurred were subsequently reimbursed by the municipal government, making Trump's actual outlay minimal. Plus, despite Trump's pledge to donate the profits he made from operating the skating rink and restaurant to charity, city audits later found that he significantly underreported revenues, failing to fully include cash receipts, as well as underreporting concession sales and skating admissions fees. Trump was forced to pay $120,000 back to the city, but getting caught for that transgression didn't stop him from continuing to profit from Wollman Rink.[12] Except for a brief interlude, Trump ran the Wollman Rink concession all the way until 2021, when the city finally severed ties after the January 6 attack on the Capitol.[13]

As with all things Trump, these initial successes soon went to his head. He continually pushed the limits and expanded his operating

There was less to Trump's "rescue" of Wollman Rink than met the eye; and later city audits found that he significantly underreported revenues, failing to fully report cash receipts as well as underreporting concession sales and skating admissions fees.

sphere into new business lines far and wide. Throughout the 1980s, he branched out and experimented with investments outside his area of expertise in real estate. The results were a distinctly mixed bag, some scattered wins interspersed with duds.

For a while, Trump joined in the great fad of 1980s financial engineering, "greenmailing," following in the footsteps of other raiders such as Carl Icahn and Boone Pickens. By buying large stakes in publicly traded companies and then threatening a hostile takeover, Trump could pressure those targeted companies, with their boards and executives fearful of losing control, to buy back the shares at a hefty premium, effectively paying him to go away. Trump scored some quick hits as a greenmailer, such as with the 6.5 percent stake in Quaker Oats he purchased in 1986 that he quickly sold back to the company for a $30 million-plus profit, followed by a similar maneuver at Holiday Inn the next year, where he once again made a $30 million-plus profit within weeks.[14] But he soon overreached as target companies began to understand that he was all bark, no bite, and learned to disregard his threats.

In 1989 Trump bought a large stake in the parent company of American Airlines and pulled out the same hostile takeover playbook, threatening to grab enough of a stake to toss out its management. Wise to his ways, and realizing he was all bluster, American Airlines basically ignored the move, all but daring Trump to launch the takeover he threatened. His bluff called, Trump folded and quickly sold his stake at a significant loss.[15] He was apparently burned so badly by this foray into the stock market that, despite remaining an avid watcher of stock market gyrations and tweeting frequently about stock market levels as president, he has rarely held any substantial positions in stocks himself. As Trump later declared, "I don't invest in the stock market. I don't trust it." Expounding, he claimed to prefer real estate: "Real estate is something I can see and touch and control. Stocks go up and down, and you have no control."[16]

Other exotic Trump investments outside of real estate in the 1980s were similarly troubled. In 1989 Trump bought a lower-tier commercial airline, Eastern Air Shuttle, which he promptly, characteristically renamed Trump Shuttle and tried to reposition as a premier luxury service, replete with gold-plated seatbelt buckles and gourmet cuisine. Unsurprisingly, the airline lost money from the outset and collapsed, landing in the hands of angry creditors within two years. Trump's investment in a football team was just as disastrous. In 1983 he purchased the New Jersey Generals football team. The Generals were a part of the United States Football League, a rival upstart competing with the far more powerful and well-known NFL. True to his combative style, Trump leveraged his ownership perch to encourage the USFL to sue the NFL on frivolous grounds. The lawsuit backfired, with the start-up league blowing up and Trump losing virtually the entirety of his investment.[17]

Some Trump ventures were hopeless from the start, particularly those where Trump mixed his commercial interests with personal

Many of Trump's business ventures, such as the ill-fated Trump Shuttle commercial airline, failed to get off the ground, figuratively and literally.

whims. In 1987 Trump purchased a $29 million luxury yacht from a notorious Saudi arms dealer. It was one of the world's largest private yachts at the time, replete with a disco, cinema, heliport, and gold-plated bathrooms. He promptly renamed the yacht *Trump Princess* and sought to monetize his ownership by hosting lavish parties and marketing ploys, or so he claimed. In reality, the yacht became his play toy, more a personal vanity project and promotional vehicle for his brand than a serious business asset.[18]

Continuing to expand his business empire to the point of overreach, Trump expanded into various arenas in which he had little expertise and even less success. The straw that finally broke the camel's back was Trump's ill-fated foray into Atlantic City. For once, even though he managed to pass some of the pain off to his investors, creditors, employees, and partners, the grandmaster was unable to entirely escape the fallout. This unvarnished disaster destroyed Trump's dreams of turbocharging his wealth and firmly establishing his status as one of the richest people in the world. Instead, it plunged six Trump businesses into bankruptcy and wiped out a significant portion of his net worth, resulting in more than $1 billion in documented losses, with approximately $1 billion in business value wiped out, on top of another approximately $1 billion in losses borne by investors, creditors, suppliers, and employees.[19]

It was, in many ways, a classic leveraged buyout gone wrong. Trump, convinced that the boom times of the 1980s would keep on rolling, leveraged himself up to the hilt, taking out a mountain of debt to fund his acquisition spree. Bankers not yet wise to the ways of Trump (how that would change) were charmed by the golden boy of New York real estate, believing him to be a strong, creditworthy borrower, and all too happy to keep supplying low-cost debt, as much as Trump wanted whenever Trump wanted. As all that debt piled up, Trump's buying binge showed no signs of slowing down, funded by more and more loans. By 1990, he had amassed nearly

$4 billion of debt, with Trump personally responsible for close to $1 billion of that.[20]

In any acquisition, debt magnifies the potential upside but also the potential downside. When things turn sour, there's less of a safety cushion to fall back on. As a result, when Trump's bets in Atlantic City started bleeding cash and sinking into the red, he had little margin for error and little recourse. Faced with mounting interest expenses to service his massive debt burden, coupled with declining revenues from his other properties, Trump suddenly faced a classic liquidity squeeze—meaning while he might have been a billionaire on paper, he was cash poor. Things got so bad that his father famously had to help him meet an interest payment by sending a crony to buy $3 million worth of casino chips at one of Trump's properties as a tax-evading gift.[21]

When push came to shove, underneath all the hype and glam and chutzpah, Trump was little more than another over-leveraged, cash-strapped tycoon who had overreached. He joined many other high-flying 1980s tycoons, ranging from Boone Pickens to Saul Steinberg to Robert Maxwell, all masters of the universe who crashed spectacularly under the weight of their own debt-fueled empire building.

Of course, even as everything around him burned, Trump still found ways to shift at least part of the burden onto others in classic Trumpian form, making sure that others went down with him. Nowhere was this more apparent than in his treatment of the banks and other creditors that had put their faith in him, lending him more money than he was able to pay back. Trump repaid their faith by turning on them, methodically pitting his investors against his creditors, and creditors against creditors, in internecine warfare, pitting his common adversaries to fight between themselves rather than target him. That's why, after rushing to throw loans at him throughout the '80s, virtually every major bank except for scandal-ridden, desperate Deutsche Bank refused to do business with him subsequently, a rarity in the upper echelons of American business.[22]

There was a certain method to the madness with how Trump divided and conquered his creditors. The first step was in creating new groups of creditors with very different interests and priorities than his existing creditors, which he accomplished by issuing $775 million worth of junk bonds with 14 percent interest rates, despite explicitly promising to his earliest creditors that he would not need to issue junk bonds. In an ironic, only in Trump world twist, while these new creditors fought it out with the original creditors over who should be first in line to be made whole, more than half of the windfall actually went toward paying off Trump's personal loans rather than into the casinos.[23]

The second step was to bring in additional shareholders to fight it out with the existing investors and get those investors to also start fighting with the creditors over who would get what. This was accomplished with the initial public offering of Trump Hotels and Casinos, in which Trump sold ten million shares for $14 each. Adding insult to injury for his existing creditors, Trump also sold an additional $155 million in junk bonds at an even higher 15.5 percent interest rate. Once again, much of this money went not into the casinos but toward paying off Trump's personal loans and other side projects.[24]

If you are confused by all this financial engineering, don't worry, because that's exactly the point. The endless stream of new, complex layers upon layers of investor and creditor groups with divergently different interests that must then fight among themselves like hyenas was a purposeful creation. Trump's fundraising activities were designed at least in part to line his own pockets, making himself whole while offloading downside risk onto an assortment of new investors and creditors, all of whom would then be so busy fighting among themselves and fighting with prior groups of creditors that they would be unable to form any collective front to gang up on Trump himself. When there wasn't enough internecine warfare between his creditors for Trump's taste, he could solve that by simply going out and bringing in more creditors to stir the pot back to boiling chaos, by issuing new high-yield bonds and bringing in new creditors whose priority was to cut the line of existing creditors in getting paid back. For Trump, it was all about making sure that as much as each creditor came to despise him, they reviled one another far more, enabling him to remain in the pole position while his adversaries were shunted from disadvantage to disadvantage.

It was smart, if somewhat diabolical, financial strategy: He was constantly playing different groups of bondholders against one another, knowing that each feared being squeezed out by others. It was a classic prisoner's dilemma. As Trump tried to stuff hugely unfavorable deals down the throats of each bondholder group, asking them to accept way less money than they were due, each bondholder group had to play ball with Trump lest they become the odd man out, hungrily left out in the cold while the pie was split without them. This saga dragged on for years before Trump's casinos declared bankruptcy at long last—but not before Trump had successfully offloaded at least $1 billion of his own liabilities into the hands of those unlucky enough to trust him with their money.

Trump might have passed some of the buck on to others, but there's no denying the battering his finances took from his '90s ordeal. Even the grandmaster of divide and conquer could not find a way to shimmy off the hook entirely as the bills came due. The enduring scars were very real, with Trump losing virtually the entirety of his equity stakes in the Plaza Hotel in New York, as well as the Trump Taj Mahal, Trump Plaza, and Trump Castle in Atlantic City, while liquidating Trump Shuttle, *Trump Princess*, and other "non-core" holdings to pay back creditors encompassing many of Trump's most cherished playthings and personal pet projects. That didn't even begin to account for the countless other more petty humiliations, like losing his corporate jet or being placed on a spending plan by his bankers like an exorbitant child put on an allowance by concerned parents.[25]

The financial scars never fully healed, and Trump's fortunes did not meaningfully recover for many years—not truly until quite recently, with his return to the White House. But let's not jump ahead in the story—more on that later.

Trump remained so strapped for cash through the '90s and into the first few years of the 2000s (before *The Apprentice* catapulted him from "has been" to superstardom) that Fred Trump had to repeatedly help prop him up with massive gifts disguised as business contracting "fees" for years, prior to Fred's death in 1999.[26] And after the death of the patriarch, Trump liquidated, nearly immediately, the empire his father had spent his entire life building at what in hindsight appear to be bargain-basement, fire-sale prices, apparently desperate to scrounge up another much-needed $1 billion.[27] A subsequent analysis found that if Trump had held on to his father's company instead of selling it at a low point, it would now be worth twenty times more. How Fred must be rolling in his grave.

In addition to rather ineptly liquidating his father's business legacy, Trump also squandered his father's considerable wealth during the '80s and '90s as he was bleeding cash. Per our analysis, if he'd merely taken the $200 million that Fred Trump started him out with in 1976 and put it in a generic stock index, such as the S&P 500, which has returned an average 10 percent annually since then, Trump's net worth would be at least four or five times what it is today.

That first $200 million, mind you, doesn't even begin to factor in the hundreds of millions more that Fred Trump transferred to Donald over the rest of his life; nor does it include his inheritance when Fred passed, which would be worth tens of billions more today. The greatest irony here is not only that Trump was handed a golden spoon, as many of his critics have pointed out, but that he, despite his braggadocio, largely squandered that golden spoon, which few appreciate.

Interestingly, the hundreds of millions Fred gave to his son would surely have been less—a lot less—if Fred hadn't come up with particularly creative ways to evade reporting income and gifts to the IRS. Recent investigations of the Trump family's shady tax practices found that Fred spared no scintilla of energy and creativity in tax avoidance and tax minimization schemes, including setting up shell companies, hiring his children as "contractors," and even letting them skim from subsidiary accounts. In one particularly audacious scheme, Fred set up a shell procurement company, which apparently functioned solely to mark-up items it purchased and resold to the Trump Organization, effectively shuffling money (and taxable income) off its books and into an opaque network of LLCs, where that money became difficult if not impossible to track.[28]

Trump may not have always heeded his father's financial advice, but he was an apt student on matters of tax avoidance, making it normal business practice to find creative ways to get around owing taxes to the IRS, believing that to simply be smart business. Not only did he take maximum advantage of net operating losses (NOLs) but his opaque network of hundreds, if not thousands, of interconnected LLCs shuffling money between themselves in shadowy related-party transactions made his business activities substantively impossible for tax authorities to understand, much less scrutinize.

Trump takes special joy in getting away with paying as little taxes as possible, routinely bragging that it reflects his smartness as a business person. One former Trump advisor remembers sitting in Trump's office when a tax refund check for $10 million arrived in the mail. "Can you believe how f*cking stupid the IRS is?" Trump squealed with delight. "Who would give me a refund of ten f*cking million dollars? They are so stupid!"[29]

Another fallout of Trump's financial travails was that the self-proclaimed master builder would never again develop a project of the same scale as his early deals from start to scratch after the early 2000s. Despite playing a real estate builder and tycoon on television, the reality was that he was merely sitting around, bored, collecting rents from a collection of properties he had managed to hang on to through his travails, not building new skyscrapers in city after city as he liked to portray himself as doing. The extent of Trump's real estate wheeling and dealing became confined to buy-low deals he would strike for distressed assets, such as the Trump Winery deal from desperate bankrupt divorcée Patricia Kluge or the acquisition of the Doral golf course in 2011 in the depth of the Great Recession. Trump never again built the type of skyscrapers from start to finish on which he had built his brand. That part of the story rarely seemed to penetrate the public consciousness, thanks in part to Trump constantly feeding positive stories and spin to the press touting his vaunted real estate developer image, including masquerading as "John Barron," his own fictitious PR spokesperson, in calls to the press, when in reality that spokesperson was Trump himself.

Just as Trump was sitting around bored, looking for second acts, a thunderbolt of luck struck him in the form of *The Apprentice* in 2004. When NBC cast him in the role he always pretended to occupy but hadn't really for many years—that of the high-flying billionaire real estate developer and tycoon with money to toss around—Trump found the sudden fame, fortune, and cultural relevance that had eluded him since his heyday in the 1980s. He rose to instantaneous superstardom as his name became a brand more valuable than any of his properties. From that point on, Trump the real estate investor morphed into Trump the media personality, for whom a majority of income derived from lucrative, if somewhat dubious, brand licensing deals. Trump would endorse basically anything as long as he received a cut and didn't have to put up any money, a classic, Trumpian "heads I win, tails you lose" setup.[30]

Just take a look at the comically long list of products Trump has endorsed over the years, many of which carry a whiff of the used car salesman, so to speak: Trump Steaks, Trump Vodka, Trump Ice Natural Spring Water, Trump Signature Collection Menswear, Trump Watches,

Trump fragrances and perfumes, Trump cologne, Trump home furnishings, Trump chocolates, *Trump* magazine, Trump board game, Trump video game, Trump trading cards, Trump Mortgage, Trump Model Management, Trump Productions, Trump sneakers, Trump coins, Trump guitars, Trump meme coins, Trump tokens, Trump NFTs, and, of course, the infamous Trump University, of which I was once offered the presidency.[31]

If you think being president might make Trump even a tad more reluctant to endorse dubious products, think again. Months after settling in to his second term, a little known, obscure company made waves debuting a splashy new wireless phone service called Trump Mobile, promising to offer made in America cell phones for less than $500. It rapidly emerged that this made in America phone was little more than a made in China phone with a layer of gold paint applied to it in the US.[32] There seem to be no bounds to what Trump is willing to endorse, even offering up signed Trump Bibles during his time in the White House.[33]

But the monetization of Trump's name, as ludicrous as some of those instances may be, is one of the more tame, mild, and entertaining ways in which he has profited since his rise in politics. Critics have noted that his profiteering often takes on a far more ruthless sheen, giving the appearance of blatantly, directly, and shamelessly monetizing the highest office in the land regardless of what the actual facts may be.

Perhaps those who expected that Trump would adhere to any of the long-held ethical guidelines and norms of conventionally acceptable business behavior for elected officials were misguided; to obediently comply with bureaucratic procedures and rules would have been the most un-Trumpian move ever. But even his most ardent critics have been surprised by the degree to which they believe Trump has seemingly mixed his personal business interests with genuine US commercial and national security priorities. For his entire life, in

As Barack Obama memorably quipped, "He's got constant attempts to sell you stuff. Selling you gold sneakers and $100,000 watches and most recently, a Trump Bible. You know, he wants you to buy the word of God, Donald Trump edition. Got his name right there, next to Matthew and Luke. You could not make this stuff up. If you saw it on Saturday Night Live, *you'd say, 'Now, that's going too far.'"*

every deal, in every negotiation, Trump is always looking out for his wallet, as that remains the consummate way he keeps track of score, in cold, hard cash. It's his yardstick for measuring success and benchmarking himself against peers.

Trump's first term featured several prominent examples where critics accused him of mixing personal profit with national security. For example, US tech companies were bewildered when he reversed course in sanctioning China's ZTE despite massive, well-documented export violations, helping Iran's march to the nuclear bomb. Trump's explanation that his reversal was due to concern that it would cost fifty thousand jobs in China, brought to his attention by China's Xi Jinping, raised eyebrows when it emerged that the Chinese state-controlled Bank of China had been considering issuing a $500

Trump repeatedly called me to Trump Tower to offer advice, and I often brought along a diverse set of voices whose insights I thought might benefit him.

When I brought a group of top Chinese business leaders from my Yale Program to visit Trump at Trump Tower, not only did Trump exhibit genuine interest and spend over an hour with them, he called Ivanka and Don Jr. down to his office and then brought some friends from the New York branch of ICBC in as well to create a classic impromptu Trump confab. Even when the party moved to the ICBC offices, Trump came along, charming the entire group with his stories and personal warmth.

President Trump and members of his family have regularly joined our Yale CEO Summits, in off-the-record discussions with the CEOs of our nation's largest companies.

Trump exemplifies the hub-and-spokes model of leadership with no conventional hierarchical chain of command. He has centralized power in himself with all his deputies reporting directly into him. Trump is the sun around which everything else must revolve.

Loyalty can be a one-way street in Trump world, as countless disgruntled staffers have found out the hard way.

With Trump, there is a lot of "will no one rid me of this meddlesome priest," with suggestive musings almost akin to a mafia don.

Conjuring up the ghost of Hugh Hefner?

Trump's negotiating style is distinctly not based on building mutual trust. He starts most negotiations by striking the first blow and staking out the maximalist stance, creating maximum leverage for himself.

Trump is a master of lawfare—using the legal system to wear down opponents.

Trump is a master at using divide and conquer to ensure his adversaries cannot unite against him.

To Trump, his resistance to unified action by perceived adversaries is essentially equivalent to Gulliver resisting the efforts of the tiny Lilliputians to bind and blind him in the famous 1726 book Gulliver's Travels.

Trump has endorsed an almost comically long list of branded products over the years.

Trump's first big major transaction, the Commodore Hotel, embodied the prototypical Trump deal of offloading much of the downside while retaining the upside.

As Barack Obama memorably quipped, "He's got constant attempts to sell you stuff. Selling you gold sneakers and $100,000 watches and most recently, a Trump Bible. You know, he wants you to buy the word of God, Donald Trump edition. Got his name right there, next to Matthew and Luke. You could not make this stuff up. If you saw it on Saturday Night Live, *you'd say, 'Now, that's going too far.'"*

Many of Trump's business ventures, such as the ill-fated Trump Shuttle commercial airline, failed to get off the ground, figuratively and literally.

The Trump Perpetual Noise Machine is an ever-spinning engine of new headlines, intentionally outrageous statements, and sudden moves designed to overwhelm, scatter, and redirect public attention—especially when he's intent on driving attention away from bad news.

To Trump, it's a world of winners and losers—though his definition of winning and losing is unique.

Trump's verbal attacks tend to be calculated, calibrated, and above all, effective for what he is trying to achieve.

Behind closed doors, Trump can display a surprisingly wry sense of humor and even a willingness to poke fun at himself— traits seldom seen in his public persona. One exception came in a commercial for a now-defunct computer company, which mocked his reputation for pursuing attractive women.

For Trump, building is a physical manifestation and expression of his heroic drive, of the image he wishes to present to the world—a point underscored when he personally directed the demolition of the White House's East Wing to make way for a new Grand Ballroom.

In Trump's universe, every trophy requires another; every superlative must be topped. The Kennedy Center Honors were not enough; he needed to chair the Kennedy Center, and rename the Kennedy Center after himself.

Trump implicitly understands that chutzpah is necessary to transcend ordinary constraints and achieve heroic, even mythic stature. He is constantly inventing and perpetuating his own heroic myth.

Critics argue that Trump's grandiosity is shattering norms, weakening institutions, and rupturing alliances.

million loan to finance a theme park near Trump-affiliated projects and Trump-affiliated business partners in Indonesia around the same time. Surely a coincidence! The prospective loan was ultimately dropped after public outcry.[34]

Similar public outcry arose after what some media outlets reported was the diversion of US military personnel to the Trump-owned Turnberry Resort in Scotland for stays during refueling stops on trips to the Mideast—despite the fact Turnberry was not particularly on the flight path to the Mideast or any US bases.[35] From the outside at least, it appeared to be another Trump gimmick to fatten his own accounts at the expense of the government, similar to charging rent to Secret Service staff and others who have no choice but to stay at his properties. That doesn't even begin to factor in the desperate attempts of foreign officials to steer cash to the Trump family, coming up with creative schemes such as booking out entire blocks of rooms at the Trump National Hotel in DC, paying sticker price for rooms they never used and didn't need.[36]

Trump's shenanigans during his first term, however, amount to child's play compared with what critics see as the blatant, wholesale monetization of power seen in his second term. It was almost as if he restrained himself from indulging his worst impulses during his first term and now feels released from any such inhibition. As Don Jr. quipped offhandedly in Qatar, "In the first term, we actually said we're not going to do any foreign deals. The reality is, it didn't stop the media from constantly saying, 'You're profiteering anyway.' We're like, 'We stopped entirely, even the deals that were totally legit, it didn't stop the insanity.' So this time around, we said, 'Hey, we're going to play by the rules, but we're not going to go so far as to stymie our business forever, lock ourselves in a proverbial padded room, because it almost doesn't matter—they're going to hit you no matter what.'" Virtually declaring to the entire world that he was open for business and willing to indulge the highest bidder, Trump Jr. seemed to capture the ethos that pervaded the Trump family's wide-ranging moneymaking efforts, essentially that everything was fair game with little, if anything, off the table.[37]

The gloves started coming off even prior to his second term, during the interregnum. While Trump has always resented underlings cashing in at his expense—such as when he unceremoniously dumped campaign manager Brad Parscale for allegedly skimming off the top of campaign accounts and diverting campaign funds to his own businesses, and similarly blew up at subsequent campaign advisor Chris LaCivita when he got wind of how much money LaCivita was allegedly making—he doesn't seem to mind schemes by underlings to monetize his name as long as they kick some to the big guy. Plenty of cronies and clingers-on found ways to do so after Trump was booted from office in 2021. One underling, Sergio Gor, set up a lucrative publishing enterprise that catapulted to success by publishing picture books of Trump. It may be no coincidence that Gor would go on to become director of personnel in Trump's second term. Similarly, a pair of failed serial entrepreneurs partnered with Trump to take his no-income shell of a social media company, Truth Social, public through an SPAC offering so dubious that it remained bogged down in SEC investigations for two years prior to finally being nudged through, despite continuing concerns from many quarters. Trump benefited immensely, immediately earning around $4 billion thanks to highly unusual, generous provisions in the SPAC awarding him warrants for additional stock based on certain stock price benchmarks. Of course, the stock price of Truth Social has always been absurd. The company's valuation hovers in the billions, depending on the day, despite revenues of less than $30 million and annual losses of nearly $500 million. That valuation of over 2,000x revenues makes even the most bubbly, overvalued AI start-ups look pretty cheap in comparison. One wonders who is buying all those Truth Social shares.[38]

But even Truth Social pales in comparison to some of Trump's business schemes since returning to office, which have only grown more brazen and unprecedented in the eyes of many critics. The Trump family's launch of a crypto venture with the Witkoff family—including Steve Witkoff, who doubles as Trump's special envoy for virtually everything—has steered billions of foreign money directly into the pockets of the Trump family. Critics argue that foreigners seeking to influence Trump are buying literally billions of dollars' worth of Trump meme coins that lack any fundamental intrinsic value, not to mention billions of dollars' worth of Trump stablecoins. Not only does Trump not hide from these activities; he actively embraces crypto, even hosting a party for top buyers of his crypto coins at his Virginia golf club, flying in from the White House to visit this group over dinner. This was not a political fundraiser but a direct, for-profit event benefiting his family's crypto empire. Predictably, a who's who of shadowy figures with turbulent reputations bought oodles of Trump meme coins for this once-in-a-lifetime access, such as notorious Chinese crypto tycoon Justin Sun buying tens of millions of dollars of meme coins explicitly for the occasion—money that flowed directly into the president's pockets. Similarly, disgraced Binance founder Changpeng Zhao boosted the crypto ventures of the Trump family prior to supposedly coincidentally receiving a presidential pardon.[39]

Even beyond Truth Social and Trump's crypto pursuits—which account for a vast majority of his newfound wealth, contributing over $6 billion total to his net worth by many estimates, a value literally double that of his real estate holdings[40]—it seems Trump has found other creative ways to cash in on his power, and no amount is too small. As we noted previously, he has cleverly used litigation as another way to line his own pockets, most blatantly by suing media companies he doesn't like. He's already made quite a bit of money this way. Elon Musk and X settled with Trump for $10 million, ABC/

Disney settled with Trump for $15 million, and Paramount/CBS is settling with Trump for $16 million after prolonged negotiations; plus, Trump has demanded $230 million from his own Department of Justice. These are not payments due to Trump's campaign but to Trump's foundation and library, almost akin to Trump personally.

Unsurprisingly, other Trump family members have quickly joined in on the act. Even Melania seems to have embraced this free-for-all, rushing to publish what critics panned as a rather superficial and unrevealing memoir before the election, almost as if she were expecting her husband to lose and possibly go to jail and it might be her last chance to cash out. She then took things even further when the election turned out favorably by auctioning off the rights to her life to Amazon for a cool $40 million, far more than comparable documentaries, and launching her own cryptocurrency token, $MELANIA.[41]

Trump's sons have made Melania's activities look tame by comparison, however, with what critics see as unvarnished money grabbing of their own. As the widely respected journalist Bethany McLean

Critics argue that Trump's brazen ways of cashing in on his power are unprecedented.

documented in *Business Insider*, despite Trump and his family's vocal attacks on Hunter Biden cashing in on his father's name, Trump and members of his family set up an unprecedented number of what appear to be pay-to-play arrangements. These include a private, exclusive Executive Branch Club in Washington, DC, that advertises its proximity to top MAGA leaders, charging membership fees of up to $500,000 each. Criticized for what appear to be blatant pay-to-play practices, Don Jr. reacted with rage to McLean's factual reporting, accusing *Business Insider* and its owner, Axel Springer, of foreign election interference without actually addressing the facts.[42]

The family has also found creative ways to profit beyond Don Jr.'s chicanery, with several Trump skyscrapers in development around the world, from the Middle East to Asia to Central Europe. While those appear to be genuine businesses, critics argue some of the foreign deals have started to resemble outright shakedowns, such as when Trump cajoled the emir of Qatar into surrendering an exorbitant 747 jet as a "donation" for the new Air Force One. As an extra kicker, the plane wouldn't stay Air Force One forever but would leave office with Trump, with ownership reverting to Trump's "presidential library," which could be nothing more than a front for Trump's indefinite personal ownership.[43]

For many, this gift from the emir of Qatar epitomized the conflict of receiving lavish gifts from foreign officials while in office. As the conservative American Enterprise Institute reported, "The issue of Trump's receipts of gifts and money from foreign government sources goes well beyond the airplane deal. Trump has expressly organized his business interests in his second term to facilitate the receipt of foreign gifts. These arrangements probably violate the Foreign Emoluments Clause of the Constitution."[44]

Critics of Trump's business activities point out that the section of the US Constitution titled "Foreign Emoluments Clause" in Article I, Section 9 provides that "no Person holding any Office of Profit or

Trust under [the United States], shall, without the Consent of the Congress, accept of any present, Emolument, Office, or Title, of any kind whatever, from any King, Prince, or foreign State." The intention of the Constitution's framers was to prevent foreign government corruption of the presidency through a form of bribery or the appearance of extortion. The Council on Foreign Relations reported last year that "the oldest form of foreign influence remains one of the most widespread: using money or other material benefits to win elite favor."

Of course, Democrats in Congress erupted in outrage over such self-enriching deals by President Trump in office, but even Republicans shared many concerns about the president accepting foreign gifts. "I'm not flying on a Qatari plane. They support Hamas," Sen. Rick Scott (R-Fla.) said. "I don't know how you make it safe." Similar criticism of these deals has been voiced by some of the most prominent MAGA true believers and Trump loyalists, such as Laura Loomer, Ben Shapiro, Mark Levin, Senate Majority Leader John Thune, Rand Paul, Ted Cruz, and other Republicans in Congress. *Politico* labeled the outrage "a rare bipartisan moment in Washington."[45]

It's not just overseas where the Trump family is flexing its muscle. In a particularly provocative case close to home, the Trumps steamrolled local opposition in Doral, Florida, where many citizens opposed their attempts to build thousands of condos on the Doral golf course, by threatening local politicians and injecting presidential endorsements into obscure city council races, all but muscling through the condominium project and barreling through opposition.[46]

It's not the art of the deal, it's the art of stealing the deal—where Trump retains as much of the upside for himself as possible while offloading as much of the risk and potential downside to others as possible.

CHAPTER 5

Trump Behind Closed Doors One-on-One

The Fluidity of Friends, Foils, and Foes

The oft-cited book *On War* by the nineteenth-century Prussian general and military theorist Carl von Clausewitz is still taught around the world in sixteen languages. Clausewitz did not object to friendship and alliances, but advised that they should be based on mutual, strategic interests rather than open-ended emotional bonds or shared values. The later, related term, "Realpolitik," describes this transactional approach based on practical and material factors rather than ideology, norms, values, or enduring friendships. While practicing power politics rather than friendship politics is often criticized derisively as being amoral, coercive, or Machiavellian, such pragmatic perspectives on relationships have been advanced by such far-ranging leaders as Otto von Bismarck, Charles de Gaulle, Deng Xiaoping, Lee Kuan Yew, George H. W. Bush, George Kennan, Henry Kissinger, Zbigniew Brzezinski, and yes, Donald Trump. There is no better reflection of Trump's transactional approach to relationships than his personal relationships—and the remarkable fluidity of friends, foils, and foes in Trump's universe.

The public act of Trump the showman is quite different from what Trump can be like in one-on-one settings behind closed doors, in surprising and often disarming ways. Don't get me wrong, the exaggerated caricature of himself that Trump knowingly and intentionally cultivates as his public persona—all the chaos, vulgarity, and frenzy—is genuinely Trump. But very few see the other Trump, the private side, and even those inclined to hate the man acknowledge that he can be charming and flattering, if not mesmerizing, on a personal level. And funny too. He gets to the edge of self-effacing humor. He can poke fun at "Trump this" or "Trump that" knowingly in ways that surprise. (And yes, he does refer to himself in the third person.) If all that fails, he can usually find someone or something you can laugh at together.

One-on-one, Trump is even willing to listen when you disagree with him in ways that he never would or could publicly. Of course, you have to be thoughtful in how you go about it. He chafes at being scolded; he finds it demeaning, insulting, and disrespectful. Even worse is to be humiliated in public. One infamous example of the latter was when he attended the White House Correspondents Dinner in 2011 as the guest of Lally Weymouth, daughter of *Washington Post* owner Katharine Graham. During his humorous speech, President Barack Obama made several jokes at Trump's expense, poking fun at Trump's reality TV show, his gaudy taste, and his advocacy of the "birtherism" conspiracy theory about Obama's country of birth. The emcee that evening, late night comedian Seth Meyers, poured fuel on the fire with repeated mockery of Trump throughout his remarks. No matter how adamantly Trump denies it, there may be some degree of truth to the assertion that being so humiliated on the world's largest stage provoked Trump to treat his presidential aspirations far more seriously.[1]

This sensitivity to how he is addressed is the lesson that President Zelenskyy of Ukraine, however heroic he may be, never understood

The public Trump is nothing like the Trump you get behind closed doors. One-on-one, Trump can be thoughtful, charming, solicitous, flattering, and even self-effacing and funny.

when he went to the Oval Office thinking he could fight it out with Trump. You can't lecture him or moralize at him—as Zelenskyy found out the hard way, thanks in part to the poor advice of his incompetent underlings. That's not how it works with Trump, ever. It inevitably backfires.

However, just when you think you're Trump's friend by treating him deferentially and being warmed up by his buddy act—think again, because for Trump, unlike virtually anybody else, the dividing lines between friends, foils, and foes can be blurry, possibly even nonexistent. There's not the slightest hint of contradiction in Trump's mind as he rotates people in his orbit through those three categories, because ultimately, that's the transactional way he sees the world. Very few things are really personal with him. People think he holds personal grudges, and he certainly can be vindictive, but his grudges aren't what people think they are. He'll just as often try to drown the squeaky wheel in oil rather than replace it or throw it out completely. When he does hold a grudge, it's strategic. Simply put, he picks only the fights that he thinks he can win and that play to his favor to fight it out. Winning or gaining an edge motivates him much more than genuine personal animus or hatred.

That's how I first got to know Trump myself. As I detailed previously, Trump converted me from critic to friend after first attacking me publicly, then laying on the charm. And so it was with many similar tales of Trump foes turned friends turned foes then turned friends again before turning who knows what? It could be called the art of Trump's flip, for he really can let bygones be bygones when he's dealing with people outside his immediate family and staff, much more so than his "vindictive" reputation would suggest. Of course, his staff and family are a whole other story (see chapter 1), and he is fiercely possessing and unforgiving of any minor hint of disloyalty or slight. But when it comes to the wider world outside his staff and family, it's entirely different, with foes, friends, and foils constantly in flux as people move seamlessly between categorizations. It can be almost disorienting and head-spinning to watch, unless you understand the fluidity with which Trump treats relationships.

Consider all the folks in politics who have crossed Trump and not only lived to tell the tale but turned into Trump favorites and stalwart Trump loyalists. Lindsey Graham started out calling voting for Trump in the 2016 election "a choice between getting shot or taking poison," yet he's turned into one of Trump's fiercest defenders. "Lil Marco" Rubio, as Trump derogatorily nicknamed him, went from questioning Trump's manhood to compliantly putting out Trump's fires on the foreign policy front as the Henry Kissinger of the second Trump administration. "Lyin' Ted" Cruz went from being the victim of JFK assassination smears by Trump to becoming one of Trump's most trusted Senate allies.

Another vivid example of how quickly Trump can flip foes into friends is how he and New York Mayor Zohran Mamdani attacked each other viciously on the campaign trail, only to buddy up in a White House presser merely days after the mayoral campaign was over. Observers from both sides were startled by how quickly Trump and Mamdani warmed to each other—one *New York Times* headline screamed, "The Surprise Ending to the Trump-Mamdani Buddy Movie Has Heads Spinning"—but they should have seen it coming. Trump has no ideological grounding whatsoever, and the fact that he attacked Mamdani as a radical leftist "communist" on the trail means far less than the transactional benefits he perceives from being able to work productively with Mamdani. If anything, as he admitted in the joint presser, he was genuinely impressed by Mamdani's campaign, his relentless focus on economic populism and affordability, and how many of Mamdani's supporters had also voted for Trump. After all, as he admitted to me in 2015, before he was taken seriously as a presidential candidate, he had mused about going to the left of Bernie Sanders before realizing that tapping into populist anger on the right might be the more realistic path. Another similar flip was how Trump's vice president, JD Vance, once called Trump a Nazi and "America's Hitler," amid other vicious remarks, and made a career out of his Trump criticism, which Trump dramatically forgave.

In fact, if anything, JD Vance's history of vitriolic statements may have helped him in Trump's eyes, counterintuitively. There's nothing that gives Trump more pleasure than to convert erstwhile critics into loyal cronies, for it represents a pure, undeniable show of brute force. Nothing makes Trump look stronger than having his loudest critics beg for forgiveness. Trump's not just sitting around waiting for his critics to flip; he's proactive, even indefatigable, in making it happen, no matter what it takes.

Far-right Trump critic Tim Burchett is another critic-turned-ally who received the "Sonnenfeld treatment" from Trump. After Burchett, a true-believer Tea Party fiscal hawk in the mold of the unyielding Thomas Massie, came out swinging against Trump's Big, Beautiful Bill on the basis of insufficient spending cuts and debt concerns, Trump hosted Burchett at the White House, pouring the charm on so thick that Burchett, on cloud nine, forgot all about his policy complaints, flipped completely, and couldn't stop singing Trump's praises after the meeting, raving on social media and television appearances, "The president told me he likes seeing me on TV, which is kind of cool." Trump didn't even have to offer Burchett any material inducements or use any bludgeons—laying on the personal charm thick worked its magic, no carrots or sticks needed. Trump, one-on-one, is mesmerizing enough to be able to pull it off sincerely.[2]

Similarly, Trump was able to convert even strident, longtime critic Bill Maher, who had mercilessly mocked him on television for years, through nothing more than his personal charm. After a mutual friend set them up for dinner, Maher emerged a seemingly different man, recounting how Trump was "gracious and measured," and heaped praise on Trump's "enormous successes."[3]

Trump's charm works because it's authentic—as much as Trump can be authentic and empathetic. He gets to know people personally, wants to know their fears, dreams, desires, and secrets, and is a tireless, even fun gossip for whom no topic—sex, money, you name it—is taboo for conversation. He asks about your family members and remembers what you tell him about them. Even though he's been divorced twice himself with as messy a personal life as they come, there's a genuine grounding in family in him, a family-first orientation, which is instantaneously visible and draws people in. And few realize that Trump is a connector of people; he's always trying to connect very different people in his wide-reaching orbit with others they wouldn't otherwise encounter, taking genuine delight in creating collisions of very different worlds. When I brought a group of top Chinese CEOs of the largest state-owned enterprises from my Yale program to visit Trump at Trump Tower, he not only exhibited genuine interest and spent over an hour with them but proudly called Ivanka and Don Jr. down to his office to have them dutifully parade through, even though they didn't seem to know what their father wanted from them. He merely wanted to show off his attractive kids and to graciously deepen a personal bond

When I brought a group of top Chinese business leaders from my Yale program to visit Trump at Trump Tower, he not only exhibited genuine interest and spent over an hour with them, he called Ivanka and Don Jr. down to his office and then brought some friends from the New York branch of ICBC in as well to create a classic impromptu Trump confab. Even when the party moved to the ICBC offices, Trump came along, charming the entire group with his stories and personal warmth.

with his guests. Then he took us to visit his tenants from the New York branch of ICBC in Trump Tower—playfully referring to it as "some little Chinese bank," to the humor of the Chinese guests, who thought he was teasing them, and who were unsure whether Trump realized it was the largest bank in the world at the time. Still, Trump charmed the entire group with his stories and personal warmth.

Trump can pull this off with authenticity because he doesn't have to fake it. There is a genuinely disarming, subversive side to Trump that defies expectations and gives him an innate connection with the underdog—no matter how much of a contradiction that might sound like to his detractors. Just as Trump's never been the kind of high-minded, civic-spirited statesman immortalized in Jon Meacham or Michael Beschloss's glowing presidential portraits, he's never been a generic, run-of-the-mill, stuffy tycoon either. While most of his billionaire peers would be more comfortable hiding away in an Aspen chalet, skiing down a mountain, sipping on thousand-dollar champagne, Trump would rather be on the WWE floor, smacking down Vince McMahon in front of thousands of cheering fans. His everyman habits are genuine, and not just for show—as evidenced by his well-documented fondness for McDonald's despite being able to afford any gourmet cuisine he wants.

Trump has always connected more deeply with the guy in the street or the construction worker sweating in the heat than with an Ivy-trained banker or lawyer. Even before his political turn, those were always his people—his undying, unwavering everyman fans, his truest loyalists and core constituency. It's class for the masses: Trump may have been repulsive to fellow moguls, but he remains irresistible to the many millions who aspire to be like him, to be him, but who aren't there yet and who will never get there.

Trump's subversiveness throws people off-balance because even though it often doesn't make any rational sense, it's truly authentic. Take his choice of music at campaign rallies—and if you think this is trivial, you don't know Trump, and the many hours he spends personally curating his music playlists. In fact, it's a safe bet that for any given rally, Trump devotes much more time to obsessing about the music to be played than he does about the speech itself or any other preparation for it, every single time. Whereas he could just stick with the classic patriotic songs—and yes, there's some of that, with Lee Greenwood getting hauled in to perform "God Bless the USA" live over and over again—Trump also picks subversive music, which confuses people. The crossover songs often don't seem to make sense, from the infamous gay anthem "YMCA" to "You Can't Always Get What You Want," when politicians are supposed to be promising to give you exactly what you want. He's staged live operatic performances at rallies where 99 percent of the attendees don't even know what opera is, and blasted Andrea Boccelli tunes at the White House to staffers who have never heard of the Italian tenor, all while keeping some foreign head of state waiting in the anteroom. It throws people for a loop but it's authentic, it's disarming, and it makes Trump impossible to typecast in ways that endear him to many.

Trump's subversiveness also works because he relishes inverting social hierarchies and violating protocol rules in ways that nobody else in his position ever would. He brings world leaders to eat cake and drink Cokes with him on the patio at Mar-a-Lago, where strangers who are members of the club walking through can run into the world's most powerful people just sitting there munching away on junk food. He'll crash random weddings of strangers, uninvited, on a whim, and spend time taking pictures and getting to know the bride and groom. That accessibility and informality make him genuinely engaging to many. Though his door is always open for other top leaders to deal with him directly, he's just as likely to call up a CEO as he is to pull in a random landscaper off the street, quite literally, and quiz him for his views on world affairs—which happened to a group of landscapers working on the White House grounds who were suddenly called in to act as Trump's kitchen cabinet on weighty tariff discussions in the aftermath of Liberation Day. Trump will meet with virtually anyone, often impromptu, such as when he ushered a group of thirty HBCU presidents who were on a tour of the White House into the Oval Office spur of the moment in a way no other president ever would. As MSNBC anchor and ardent critic Stephanie Ruhle quipped about Trump, "I called DJT on his cell phone and he picked up first ring, and I said, 'Yo, can I get an interview?' And he told me to go f*ck myself, but I still was able to connect with him just like that." In contrast, Ruhle lamented, "If I were to want to connect with Kamala Harris or Joe Biden, there are fifty people between me and them. I could write a note that maybe could get to somebody to get somebody that (through) Pony Express and a pigeon, something might end up in a mailbox near them."[4]

Trump's charm also comes across as authentic, because he can be genuinely funny in unexpected ways, capable at times of knowingly self-effacing, even self-deprecating humor that gently mocks his own outsized public persona. Although that private wit seldom surfaces in public, one rare example appeared two decades ago in a timeless advertisement he recorded for a now defunct computer company.

The concept of the commercial was deliberately absurd: Hiring the wrong technicians to fix your computer was like asking Donald Trump to make pottery. What made the ad memorable was not simply the sight gag of Trump bungling his way around a potter's wheel, shattering molds, dropping clay pots, and wreaking havoc in the studio, but how willingly he leaned into parodying himself. He exaggerated his own caricatured public persona: trying to solve his pottery failures by throwing money at the problem, attempting to buy replacement pots from passersby after destroying his own, nickeling and diming them in price negotiations. The commercial closes with Trump hitting on a pretty young female pottery artist, who dispatches his advances by witheringly rolling her eyes in unmistakable disgust while he ogles at her chest.

What shone through was the kind of humor that is common in private interactions with Trump but rarely seen in his public

Behind closed doors, Trump can display a surprisingly wry sense of humor and even a willingness to poke fun at himself—traits seldom seen in his public persona. One exception came in a commercial for a now-defunct computer company, which mocked his reputation for pursuing attractive women.

performances: his own ability to lampoon the bluster and bravado of the Donald Trump persona he has created and cultivated, revealing a sliver of self-awareness and a willingness to laugh at himself.

THE FLUIDITY OF TRUMP'S PERSONAL RELATIONSHIPS

Despite the genuine personal warmth and charm, you should not be fooled into thinking you are his pal. For Trump, the dividing lines between friends, foils, and foes can be blurry if not nonexistent.

The fluidity of Trump's friends, foes, and foils is on full display in his complex relationship with the media. Critics of Trump who lampoon his "the media is the enemy" commentary often don't fully comprehend the complexity of his interactions with the press as simultaneous, interchangeable foils, messengers, sounding boards, and even quasi-therapists. He truly likes meeting people on a personal level, and his genuine cultivation of the press alongside his genuine malicious attacks are paradoxical and disorienting, but pure Trump.

Make no mistake, Trump understands the value of the press because he never stops cultivating them and makes spinning stories for them a top priority. It's no coincidence that he watches hours of cable TV every day and obsesses about print newspaper coverage about him, because he is a more canny manipulator of the media and a shaper of his own public image than anyone else, and has been for decades. He'll bring favored journalists into his universe, give them exclusive access and juicy stories, and then call them the enemy of the people when they publish the exact stories he wanted published. He'll invite the press in for briefings in the Oval Office, as he does nearly daily nowadays, and then lambast the journalists he hand-selected on live television for asking the exact questions he knew they would. He will invite press to fly with him on Air Force One, then attack journalists as "piggies" as he is speaking with them. It's all a part of the show, attacks and all.

The hot-and-cold nature of many of Trump's dealings with the press is perhaps most vividly captured by Trump's hate-love-hate-love-hate-love saga with former Fox anchor Megyn Kelly, she of the "blood coming out of her ears, blood coming out of her whatever" infamy. After Trump attacked her so viciously in 2016, Kelly reportedly basically refused to show up for work, forcing Roger Ailes to beg Trump to tone down his onslaught, which, of course, prompted Trump to double down with relish and glee, sensing he had the upper hand. Kelly tried to reinvent herself as an anti-Trump, soft-news women's advocate during her ill-fated run at NBC, but after she quickly flamed out, she ran back to Trump, carving out a lane for herself as a pro-MAGA provocateur with a culture-wars focused podcast that quickly soared in popularity.

Even as Trump was publicly shaming and humiliating her, posting on Truth Social that Kelly was "making a career by pretending she likes me," he was simultaneously fueling her ascent, providing her with an exclusive sit-down interview at a time when she desperately needed it. As soon as he did the interview, he attacked Kelly as "nasty," which only drew more attention to their interview.[5] Of course, for someone who is always obsessing over people's appearances and whether they are straight out of "central casting," it never hurts when someone looks attractive in Trump's eyes. Still, the 3D chess is enough to leave anyone confused—especially after Trump invited Megyn Kelly to speak onstage at a campaign rally shortly after she attacked him for having a bush-league comic make derogatory jokes about Puerto Rico. But all these head-spinning turns are just classic Trump. He needs the press; they need him, and the more they fight, the more both win—at least sometimes.

It doesn't always work out so happily. At times, it all blows up on him, and badly. He repeatedly brought in Bob Woodward and Michael Wolff for exclusive tell-alls, and then after they spilled the beans, threatened to sue and attacked them furiously, which, of course, only draws more attention to whatever it is Trump didn't like and sells more books. Then, when it all settles down and everyone's happy again, Trump will invite them in for round two, followed by the same attacks and Kabuki theater, and so forth. Trump will treat Maggie Haberman of *The Times* as his de facto therapist and confessor, only to spin around and attack her on Truth Social as "nasty," then call her up again with more juicy stories. There are times, however, when he succeeds in co-opting hostile media, such as when he hired away staunch Never-Trumper Mary Kissel of *The Wall Street Journal*'s editorial board as a senior advisor in his State Department or former Carly Fiorina campaign manager and media commentator Sarah Isgur as a senior Justice Department official. He demonstrated considerable magnanimity in both these cases. A prominent critic who regularly scorched Trump prior to his 2016 win, Kissel scolded me once at Larry Kudlow's house for taking Trump's

The hot-and-cold nature of many of Trump's dealings with the press is perhaps most vividly captured by Trump's hate-love-hate-love-hate-love saga with former Fox anchor Megyn Kelly.

candidacy seriously in August of 2015. Similarly, Isgur launched repeated barbs at Trump during the campaign and even attacked me in vicious personal terms, to which Trump thoughtfully personally called me to see if I was okay and reassured me that I had gotten the upper hand in the exchange, with the truth shared.[6]

That Trump forgave and forgot with both these critics he once tangled with demonstrates his complexity as well as his deftness in drowning the squeaky wheel in oil. Other times, the more some media commentators vacillate and waver, such as on-again, off-again Trump critic and on-again, off-again Trump fan Ann Coulter, the more attention they draw for themselves.

The head-spinning volatility of Trump's relationships serves a purpose: He needs foils, all the time, constantly, because without them, his shtick can't work. In Trump's worldview, there always needs to be someone to blame for the problems of the world: illegal immigrants, other countries ripping us off, crazy leftists taking over the country, "Sleepy Joe" Biden, Haitian immigrants eating their neighbors' pets, you name it. For Trump to be Trump, he has to have a convenient target he can rile his supporters up to train their fury and ire on—even if, in many cases, there's nothing personal driving the rage he voices toward the unfortunate victims he targets. The turns from foil to friend can be dizzying, such as when he went from calling Mexican immigrants rapists and drug dealers to cutting Spanish-speaking campaign ads while dancing the salsa when he realized he needed Hispanic votes to win in crucial swing states.

Sometimes there really is some extra oomph, some real animus, behind Trump's attacks on his foils. Many critics have pointed out a certain strain of apparent misogyny in how he disproportionately targets women as "nasty," from Rosie O'Donnell to Nancy Pelosi to Hillary Clinton, with "nasty woman" becoming a rallying cry for many opponents. When he feels betrayed by his own staffers, especially staffers who he thinks he "made," he'll go after them with a vengeance: calling for Mark Milley's execution for treason, prosecuting James Comey, sending Michael Cohen to solitary confinement, issuing an executive order targeting Chris Krebs, raiding John Bolton's house, completely exiling Mike Pompeo and Jeff Sessions and Mike Pence and Marjorie Taylor Greene as sacrificial lambs for their disobedience, however minor. These attacks are often more intentional and selective than he lets on, for he reads people—and their vulnerabilities—unfailingly, with an instinct for the jugular and an outsider's unerring talent for shunting adversaries from disadvantage to disadvantage. He is capable of genuinely inimitable, perceptive insights into the critical vulnerabilities of his opponents. Indeed, many of Trump's nicknames for his opponents—"Low-Energy Jeb," "Lil Marco," "Lyin' Ted," "Crooked Hillary," "Sleepy Joe"—caught fire instantly because they captured something deeply resonant about his opponents' perceived weaknesses, puncturing their softest underbelly. There's no vulnerability too low for Trump to exploit, no matter how underhanded, wrong, and morally offensive it may be, such as when he shamelessly promoted the birtherism nonsense about President Obama even though it was complete bunk.

For all Trump's fluidity, he can't always avoid getting boxed in when his schemes backfire, as they sometimes do. In other words, he sometimes gets foiled by the foils he sets up. Trump trapped himself badly by fanning the flames of conspiracy theories that Democrats were hiding information about Jeffrey Epstein, only to end up cornered himself when details emerged that Trump's own friendship with Epstein was deeper than anyone imagined, including pictures of naked women and poems Trump wrote to Epstein that *The Wall Street Journal* reported on and that Trump promptly sued over. His foils sometimes don't need to fight back, they just need to sit back and watch Trump twist himself into knots in his desperation to find ever-shifting targets to go after. But Trump will soon find a new foil, forget about the last one, and maybe even try to drown the squeaky wheel in oil later on. It's all a part of his fluidity with the art of the flip, where foes, friends, and foils are interchangeable and often indistinguishable from one another. Friends one day are foils the next, and vice versa.

CHAPTER 6

The Wall of Sound

Trump's Perpetual Noise Machine of Constant, Overwhelming Distractions

What appears to many outside observers to be the constant chaos surrounding Trump is, in fact, sometimes anything but chaos.

Actually, it *is* chaos, but often it is manageable chaos of Trump's own creation, the difference between a wildfire and a controlled burn. Rather than accidental or undisciplined, the constant commotion and turbulence surrounding him is a deliberate, calibrated churn of calculated distractions, manufactured controversies, and intentional provocations.

It's Trump's own "Wall of Sound," borrowing from Phil Spector's iconic music production technique, which is characterized by a large, overpowering ensemble of musicians playing multiple instruments and doubling parts, their sheer frenetic energy combining to fill the entire sonic spectrum and drowning everything else out.[1]

In Trump's case, the Trump Perpetual Noise Machine is an ever-spinning engine of new headlines, intentionally outrageous statements, and sudden moves designed to overwhelm, scatter, and redirect public attention—especially when he's intent on driving attention away from bad news. Through sheer force of will and frenetic activity, Trump is able to bend the news cycle to his will and reshape the public narrative, disorienting and exhausting opponents while preventing any story from dominating the narrative long enough to inflict lasting political harm.

President Trump's skill at changing the entire media narrative and public discourse in a sweeping manner is well demonstrated by his efficient US military raid on Venezuela to seize President Nicolás Maduro for alleged drug trafficking and to secure opportunity for massive investments by US oil companies. Instantly, the entire US media wiped clean their 24/7 coverage of faltering domestic issues

The Trump Perpetual Noise Machine is an ever-spinning engine of new headlines, intentionally outrageous statements, and sudden moves designed to overwhelm, scatter, and redirect public attention—especially when he's intent on driving attention away from bad news.

where Trump's polling was plummeting to instead debate the legality of this action. Oil executives told me that they resented being used as foil as they had no advance knowledge of this military action and that the current oil glut has depressed prices discouraging them from Venezuela's expensive antiquated oil infrastructure.

For someone who says as many reckless, politically incorrect things as Trump does, seemingly stream of consciousness, it is ironic how completely intentional many of his most controversial statements and actions have been. Indeed, when a damaging headline looms, Trump has often, fully intentionally and knowingly, introduced a new, even more sensational headline of his own making, a distraction that scrambles the media's focus and divides his critics' energy.

The Trump Perpetual Noise Machine reaction when Michael Cohen testified before Congress in February 2019 is a great example. Cohen accused Trump of being a con man, a liar, and a cheat, revealing information that had never before been revealed, including the hush money payments to Stormy Daniels that would ultimately get Trump convicted as a felon in New York. It seems a bit more than sheer coincidence that as Trump got wind of Cohen's testimony being scheduled, it just happened to be that at the same time he scheduled a high-profile summit with Kim Jong Un, the mercurial "Little Rocket Man" dictator of North Korea.[2]

That news helped divert some attention away from Cohen's otherwise headline-dominating testimony, but to Trump's credit, he understood that both good and bad news have power. Many experts and even some of his own aides, such as John Bolton, feared that Trump would be so eager to divert attention away from Cohen's testimony that he might trade major concessions for empty promises in order to have a success to feed the press. But when Little Rocket Man proved so intractable, Trump did the entirely unexpected: He walked away, all but admitting that his weeks of buildup, flattery, and reality TV–style showmanship and courtship of the little tyrant had ended with a flop. "Sometimes you have to walk, and this was just one of those times," a deflated Trump admitted during a hastily scheduled press conference. That was a spectacle no TV channel could refuse, with live coverage flipping back and forth between Cohen's testimony and Trump's press conference—whereas on any other day, Cohen's testimony would have aired nonstop on every major channel.

Of course, in turn, Trump then cast around for a way to divert attention from that disappointment of his own making, desperately seeking to recast the narrative away from Cohen's bombshell congressional testimony and the unsuccessful effort at diplomacy with North Korea. Hours after the summit broke down, Trump was already at it, announcing on Twitter his grandiose plans for a "Salute to America" military-style July Fourth celebration, something nobody had ever asked for and that had never existed other than as a figment of Trump's imagination. That kind of ostentatious spectacle, replete with military displays, fireworks extravaganzas, and himself speaking from the Lincoln Memorial's steps in the shadows of Lincoln and Martin Luther King Jr., was exactly the kind of distraction Trump knew could divert his followers.

Of course, such pomp and spectacle did not hold the public's attention for long. The bad news cycle catalyzed by Trump's domestic and foreign policy failures in 2019 provided Trump little relief as he was hit over and over again with reminders of his own missteps every time he turned on the TV for months. It took another major scandal of Trump's own creation to shift the narrative, and once again, he was seemingly pouring fuel on his own fire.

That scandal, of course, was Trump's call with then-newly elected Ukrainian President Volodymyr Zelenskyy, with Trump seemingly extorting Zelenskyy on the call to investigate Joe Biden, threatening to withhold hundreds of millions in congressionally appropriated and approved assistance for Ukraine.

It took the bravery of a courageous whistleblower—Col. Alexander Vindman on the National Security staff—to break this "drug deal" into public knowledge, but once it was out, Trump did something counterintuitive: He poured more fuel on this fire by voluntarily releasing the verbatim transcript of the call, revealing his apparent extortion in flagrante delicto for the whole wide world to see.[3]

This is the part that critics of Trump often misunderstand. Many journalists rushed to portray the release of the transcript as a delusional screw-up by an out-of-touch tyrant cosseted into his own cocoon and detached from reality, buying into the nominal cover story that Trump thought the memo would be "exculpatory." But it's more likely that Trump knew full well the transcript wasn't and would never be exculpatory. If anything, he would have likely known exactly how explosive the memo would be—and that might explain why he released it.

He'd never admit to it, but the Trumpian way of looking at this situation would posit that Trump knew exactly what he was getting into by releasing the read-out. The transcript was so blatantly transgressive and shocking that Democrats on Capitol Hill, already looking for any excuse to launch impeachment proceedings, would surely run with it, which was exactly what Trump would have wanted. He handed Democrats ammunition for his own impeachment, on a cause where he knew his own base would rally behind him, knowing full well that nothing would divert attention from all the bad news in 2019 more effectively than impeachment proceedings launched by "them," the evil Democrats, against "us," all the MAGA true believers. For, of course, it wouldn't be seen as an impeachment of Trump but as yet another attack against MAGA, against all his people. Even if this was a bunch of bunk, Trump repeated it so frequently that many of his followers truly believed it. Plus, Trump would have remembered how much of the general public, including not only Democrats demoralized by the protracted Monica Lewinsky scandal but also some GOP voices, rallied around

Bill Clinton during Clinton's own impeachment, when the Inspector Javert–style Kenneth Starr inquisition moved from the empty Whitewater real estate investigation to impeachment proceedings based on his sexual indiscretions. Thus, Trump would have figured that his own impeachment might engender some political capital for him in addition to rallying the base.

Confused? This is exactly what makes Trump, Trump, and why so many of his critics can never understand his approach to manufacturing scandals and controversies of his own creation—even when it appears to involve shooting himself in the foot.

Trump is far more self-aware than most would expect. He once told me in Trump Tower, in a rare moment of genuine self-reflection and accurate self-perception, about a time when he was entering a Manhattan party and saw a confused older man turned away by security. Trump went over and asked if he could help. The man smiled and said, "Donald, how are you? How is your father, Fred?" The older man turned out to be renowned mega homebuilder and real estate titan William Levitt. Now in his eighties, Levitt had taken on big bets to revive his career long after selling his business and had lost all his wealth. Trump's lesson? "You must always know your limits. Despite my flamboyant public fights, I always know where the line is for me—even if that is not where you would draw it. You have to know where to draw your lines, and don't cross those lines. My lines aren't where you or anyone else would draw them, but I know where my lines are."[4]

Trump himself captured it more incisively than anyone else ever has when it comes to his inimitable approach to courting controversy intentionally. Trump will knowingly pick fights that nobody else would ever choose to get into, and even sometimes fights where he incurs genuine damage. Yet, for Trump, who always looks at every situation as one to be exploited and manipulated, there is nothing quite like fighting an enemy he chose to provoke, even when he has to shoot himself in the foot to rally his base and create the urgent "us vs. them" mentality crucial to his ability to lead.

It's that quality of his—being deliberately, intentionally provocative—that many of his critics miss. By reacting exactly the way he expects them to react to his rage-bait—with unadulterated rage—he is able to harness that reaction to exploit the situation for his own advantage, flipping conventional rules of behavior on their head. He turns ostensibly catastrophic missteps into his superpower, a grand puppeteer always in control of the situation even when the house is seemingly burning down around him.

At least that's Trump's playbook *sometimes*. A lot of the time it's not quite so thought-out. Trump flies by the seat of his pants, taking each day as it comes, and it's abundantly obvious to those who've worked with him when he is in pure, frantic, desperate improvisation mode. When he has no idea how to divert attention away from the crisis du jour, he will throw anything and everything against the wall to see what sticks.

Consider his response to the renewed media and public interest in his ties to Jeffrey Epstein as a classic example of the Trump "I have no plan, let me try anything and everything" playbook. After Pam Bondi's DOJ released a memo claiming there was never any "client list" of Epstein's and affirmed Epstein's death as a suicide, Trump suddenly, unexpectedly faced a revolt from his true believers, with longtime loyalist FBI Deputy Director Dan Bongino apparently ready to resign in frustration over how Bondi handled the Epstein case. The coals were stoked when Elon Musk posted on X that Trump appeared in the Epstein files.[5]

This crisis was most certainly not intentionally created by Trump. He seemed caught entirely off guard by the fervent blowback from his true believers, even musing on social media that his "friends"—quotation marks his—were out to get him.

Trump initially tried to dispose of the unexpected crisis in his tried-and-true way, dismissing it as an "us vs. them" thing, claiming the renewed interest in Epstein was a politically motivated "Democratic hoax" and claiming "nobody cared" about Epstein anymore, noting dismissively that Epstein had been dead for years.

This time, the fuel added to that fire most certainly did not come from Trump, who genuinely wished the Epstein story would go away forever. Merely days after the DOJ declarations over the Epstein case set Trump's world ablaze, *The Wall Street Journal* published a bombshell explosive scoop, reporting that Epstein's fiftieth birthday celebration book in 2003 included a letter from Trump, which contained a hand-drawn figure of a voluptuous woman.[6]

Trump's desperation to make this unwelcome news cycle go away became abundantly obvious in the scattershot way he threw out everything and anything to try to divert attention. First, it was the classic "deny, deny, deny" response, with Trump promptly suing Rupert Murdoch and *The Wall Street Journal* for $10 billion in damages for what he claimed was false reporting, after personally warning Murdoch not to publish the story and even removing Murdoch-linked media from the press pool for his Scotland trip.

From there, Trump doubled down on his classic "us vs. them" instinct, working feverishly to rally his base around a rotating cast of old foils. First, out of the blue and without a scintilla of new evidence, Trump accused former President Barack Obama of "treason" and nudged his DOJ and FBI to investigate Obama, seemingly as a diversion to get malcontents at the FBI and DOJ occupied with red meat, anything other than Epstein. Similarly, on Truth Social, he floated stripping the citizenship of his timeless foil, Rosie O'Donnell. Even Melania got in on the act, issuing a $1 billion cease-and-desist threat to Hunter Biden for merely mentioning the possibility she was introduced to Trump by Epstein and ran in similar social circles in an apparent bid to paint the Biden family as part of some criminal cabal pulling the strings of Epstein-gate behind the scenes.

Meanwhile, Trump simultaneously tried to smother the greasy wheel with oil by trying to control as much of the Epstein fallout as he could, even as the situation spiraled beyond his clutches. Most prominently, he tried to co-opt the lone surviving witness who could make or break him, Epstein's longtime accomplice, Ghislaine Maxwell. His personal lawyer turned deputy attorney general, Todd Blanche, made a personal pilgrimage to visit and interview Maxwell in jail. Of course, for the deputy attorney general to visit a low-level prison to interview an inmate, in lieu of a nonpolitical line prosecutor, was a massive and unprecedented breach of protocol, but who cares about standard procedure in Trump's world? This was a situation that needed fixing, and nobody better for this sensitive job than his former personal lawyer, who helpfully happened to now hold sway over the pardon process—not that Maxwell should ever read too much into that (cough, wink, nudge).[7]

Similarly, Trump defaulted to his classic "invert, invert, invert" logic by making it seem as if he was on the side of the Epstein truthers all along, portraying himself as a lonely crusader for transparency against the evil forces that be by throwing a canard into the works, seeking to release Maxwell's grand jury transcripts, which nobody had ever asked to see and which not even the hardest-core Epstein truthers really cared about. The diversion was so transparent that a judge bluntly dismissed the motion, stating the transcripts would add no new evidence.

As all that was playing out, Trump reportedly furiously called aides trying to find "a big thing" to divert attention definitively away from Epstein.[8] Announcing Coca-Cola's return to real cane sugar didn't quite have the splash Trump was hoping for, generating more derision for why this was a top priority for the leader of the free world. Upping the ante by calling for the ouster of the CEO of Intel and provocatively suggesting the CEO of Goldman Sachs, David Solomon, return to deejaying also didn't quite land, provoking cries of

Maoism and Marxism from aggrieved prominent voices in the business community, while failing to register with the broader public. And Trump's architectural overhauls of the White House grounds, paving over the Rose Garden—the same Rose Garden that his wife, Melania, had spent millions and over a year carefully redesigning during his first term, only for all that to fall victim to a few hours of concrete-pouring—also fell flat amid lamentations that Trump's plans to replace the First Lady's office with a grand ballroom were "ugly." Even more substantive diversions, such as taking over the Washington, DC, police and deploying the National Guard to several cities such as Los Angeles, Memphis, and Portland, as well as plotting major geopolitical pivots with a Putin summit in Alaska, failed to put out the Epstein fire.

It was only after it appeared that the dam would break over Epstein—with even MAGA loyalists in Congress such as Marjorie Taylor Greene, Nancy Mace, and Lauren Boebert threatening to join the perennially intransigent Thomas Massie and all House Dems in voting to release the Epstein files, despite Trump's best efforts to forestall such a vote—that Trump finally bowed to the inevitable in a classic Trumpian move: He tried to outflank himself, claiming that he had always been for the release of the Epstein files and arguing that it was Democrats like Larry Summers and Bill Clinton who came off far worse. As Trump anticipated, public attention quickly shifted away from him and toward figures like Summers, whose exposure in the released Epstein messages proved devastating. Amid withering fire from liberal critics such as Elizabeth Warren, Summers was forced to withdraw from public life, resigning from all his boards and paid media contributor positions. Trump reveled in watching his adversaries tear themselves apart, exactly the outcome he had engineered.

Trump's response to the Epstein allegations reflects his tried-and-true diversion tactic, where he quickly diverts attention away from unfavorable news by flipping it on his adversaries and going on the offensive. He similarly diverted attention away from the Billy Bush "grab 'em by the p*ssy" leaked tapes during his 2016 campaign, an episode that would have proven fatal to virtually any other mortal politician. Trump's deflection when confronted with that crisis captures his go-to diversion strategy, which is to downplay his own guilt, portraying himself as the victim of a witch hunt while pointing a finger at his enemies for being more guilty of what he himself did but refuses to admit.

With prominent Republicans calling for his withdrawal from the race after the release of the *Access Hollywood* tapes, including his own soon-to-be chief of staff and then-head of the RNC, Reince Priebus, Trump was not only defiant but redirected fire by holding a surprise press event featuring four women—Paula Jones, Juanita Broaddrick, Kathleen Willey, and Kathy Shelton—who accused the Democratic nominee, Hillary Clinton, of complicity, if not enablement, of her husband's sexual forays. Broaddrick memorably quipped, "Trump may have said bad words, but Bill Clinton raped me and Hillary Clinton threatened me."[9] The optics were unmistakable, as Trump turned a moment of vulnerability—his own offensive remarks—into a counterattack, frame-shifting from his rhetoric to Bill Clinton's alleged actions. Trump succeeded in so sufficiently muddying the waters that a cut-and-dried scandal of moral outrage became diluted into a spectacle of partisan sexual allegations, with his die-hard followers once again rallying around his banner when confronted with an "us vs. them" moment.

Trump transformed what could have been a candidacy-ending scandal into a spectacle of circular allegations and apparent moral equivalence, and attention shifted elsewhere as the potency of the *Access Hollywood* tapes faded. Unsurprisingly, Trump more or less dropped the four women soon thereafter, never really delivering on his promises to win them justice. It seemed to be always about just surviving the moment. As soon as his own purposes were met, these

What happened to Trump ideas as varied as the annexation of Greenland and taking over Canada as the fifty-first state?

women, like everyone else in his orbit, became essentially replaceable, akin to widgets that had outlived their usefulness.

It's not only people who get dropped by Trump. When ideas that he floats aren't greeted with a rapturous reception or the news cycle moves on, he often forgets them as quickly as he tossed them out. Remember the annexation of Greenland? Or Canada as the fifty-first state?

With Trump's "Wall of Sound" approach, accountability is dropped just as quickly as ideas and people. His own missteps are quickly forgotten amid the constant maelstrom of his own creation. When DOGE fizzled out despite the initial hype surrounding Trump and Elon Musk's promised cost-cutting rampage—with the promised $2 trillion in cuts dwindling into merely $100 million in cuts, if that, Trump more or less washed his hands of responsibility, blaming Musk and moving on.

All that noise disguises the lack of a comprehensive plan for much of anything. Trump can opportunistically take whichever ideas resonate and run with them, quickly covering up mistakes and disappointments by throwing even more against the wall to see what sticks. It allows Trump to play to his strengths. By operating horizontally, across many different planes, he doesn't ever have to go deep on anything and can effectively paper over his lack of knowledge and boredom with specialized expertise, not to mention his comically short attention span. It allows him to drive and dictate the news cycle, steering away from bad news and toward things he wants to talk about. All it takes is a tweet for Trump to singlehandedly divert the news cycle. One analysis found that Trump tweeted over twenty-five thousand times during his first term alone, with many of those tweets driving news cycles for days afterward.

It didn't matter that some of his tweets were completely incoherent: In fact, that may have been exactly the point. Case in point: the infamous "covfefe" tweet from May 2017—where Trump posted "Despite the constant negative press covfefe" at midnight and left it up for hours. Was "covfefe" a typo? A coded message? A medical episode? The speculation consumed news cycles for days. Late-night comedians made it into a running joke. #Covfefe became a trending hashtag. The White House was asked about it repeatedly.

Here's what got lost in all the breathless coverage of "covfefe": That same month, Trump had fired FBI Director James Comey, triggering the appointment of Special Counsel Robert Mueller, unleashing a bad news cycle that threatened to engulf his nascent presidency. Yet with a single enigmatic tweet, Trump managed to divert attention and create a worthy distraction at exactly the moment when sustained scrutiny of the Comey dismissal might have proved most damaging. In that light, "covfefe" functioned as a perfectly timed reprieve, shifting the conversation from an external crisis he could not control toward the manageable, controllable chaos of Trump's own creation. Intentional or not, "covfefe" demonstrated a key principle of Trump's "Wall of Sound": Sometimes the most effective distraction is the most inexplicable one. When people are trying to decipher something inexplicable, they're not focusing on anything else.

The aggregate effect of Trump's Perpetual Noise Machine is disorienting for his opponents, who find it impossible to respond effectively to an overwhelming fusillade of provocations or to effectively shine a spotlight on Trump's missteps. Moreover, with Trump staying in constant attack mode, it seems futile to try to fight him on any one issue, because he is everywhere, all the time, across all issues, and the overall effect makes him appear an even larger force than he is because of the ricochet effects.

This is why the rational response for any of the many groups attacked by Trump, from universities to law firms to companies, should be to ally together—at least on paper. In practice, that is impossible because they get too distracted trying to protect their own flanks against Trump's constant pokes and jabs, and Trump works to ensure that their separate interests are constantly broken down, so that they remain embroiled in internecine squabbles with one another rather than ganging up against him. Meanwhile, Trump fills the void with an exhausting, flood-the-zone maelstrom of activity such that the sheer volume and ricochet effects overwhelm opponents and create a manufactured sense of inevitability.

Trump might not be the type to appreciate Phil Spector's iconic, aforementioned "Wall of Sound" music production technique characterized by layering instruments and reverb to create such a dense, immersive sound experience that it drowns out distractions, but in his own approach to leadership, he certainly intuits enough of Spector to make every day Trump's own "Wall of Sound," as the Trump Perpetual Noise Machine drowns out everything and anyone else and ensures he remains fully in control in driving the narrative day in and day out.

CHAPTER 7

Trump's World of Winners and Losers

Class for the Masses, Avoiding Losers like the Plague, and Selective Retribution

It's not surprising to anyone who hasn't been living under a rock that Trump tends to see the world as winners versus losers. Trump relies on this binary lens to size up just about anyone and everyone instantaneously. It is not just a rhetorical tic or branding instinct; it is the fundamental framework of his basic worldview, how he measures people's worth, and how he keeps score.

Trump's definition of a winner is unique and doesn't match how most others define it. For Trump, a winner is not necessarily the most honest, the most capable, or the most deserving individual, or even a respectable person who you'd want to associate with. It's nothing about the person themselves—it's all about how the world sees that person and their standing. A winner is someone who projects success, glamour, toughness, and, above all, relevance. A winner has a following, an audience, a crowd that affirms their status—even more simply put, as Trump would say, "a star." Conversely, a loser is not defined by crime, immorality, or even failure in the traditional sense. Being a loser has more to do with status than any innate reflection of self-worth—someone who has lost their constituency, someone without glamour, someone who threatens to taint and tarnish Trump's brand with their own failure. Yet, paradoxically, the more interesting nuance that few appreciate is that Trump doesn't always fully abandon losers, contrary to public perception. Often he'll even keep stone-cold losers hanging around the hoop in cases where most would be running for cover. If they retain a constituency, if they remain sympathetic victims in the eyes of certain groups, or if their plight can be repackaged as proof of Trump's own persecution, these losers become useful to him. This calculus, brutal in its simplicity, explains both his loyalty and his ruthlessness. He will defend

To Trump, it's a world of winners and losers—though his definition of winning and losing is unique.

a convicted felon without hesitation, if that felon still commands a constituency and can be reframed as a martyr. He will abandon a once-trusted advisor if they slip into irrelevance, no matter their years of service. He gravitates to glamour and power the way a moth seeks a flame, while avoiding failure as if it were a contagious disease.

At its heart, it's all about power. Consider how Trump ruthlessly discarded erstwhile allies for rather trivial foot faults, when they had lost their independent standing and all utility to him. The saga of Rudy Giuliani is particularly tragic but representative of Trump's approach. The hero of September 11, once celebrated across the land as "America's Mayor," Giuliani's descent into caricature—replete with leaking hair dye, rambling speeches, and financial ruin—made him toxic, never mind the fact that critics noted his demise was in part catalyzed by carrying out the dirty hatchet jobs Trump seemingly put him up for, such as shaking down Ukrainian President Zelenskyy and undermining the 2020 election. Trump, who once leaned on Giuliani as his legal warrior and celebrated his news hits, promptly dropped him like a hot potato, going so far as to allegedly refuse to pay his legal bills for a time, while freezing him out.[1]

Trump's penchant for dropping even his most loyal consiglieres, even if their reputations are sullied due to taking risks on behalf of the boss, is striking—as Michael Cohen found out when he carried out the Stormy Daniels hush money affair, allegedly at Trump's behest.[2] The list of Trump's associates who faced reputational fallout is long and continues to grow, as everyone seems to somehow think it will be different when it's their turn up. Mike Lindell, who not only trumpeted Trump's election denial claims in 2020 but spent a significant chunk of his personal fortune bankrolling and amplifying them, is now substantively bankrupt, with his fortune depleted and defamation lawsuits still pending. Naturally, Trump has done little to help the man who was his staunchest ally in fanning the flames of his 2020 stolen election claims.[3] Likewise with

Trump, who once leaned on Giuliani as his legal warrior and celebrated his news hits, promptly dropped him, going so far as to allegedly refuse to pay his legal bills for a time, while freezing him out.

Sidney Powell, the lawyer Trump once turned to as the linchpin of his stolen election lawsuits.[4]

Lindell, Powell, and Giuliani may be extreme cases where their excessive zeal and questionable judgment gave perhaps even Trump cause for concern, but Trump has the same callous, ruthless pattern of dropping allies cold when it comes to political allies who've done little wrong other than seeing their stars fade. Sarah Palin, the Tea Party favorite whose blunt, outspoken candor helped pave the way for Trump's candidacy in 2016, was initially a strong ally of Trump's when few other GOP establishment figures rallied behind him. As Palin's star faded, however, Trump iced her out as if she wasn't worth his time, despite Palin having done nothing to cross him. She was left to complain to anyone who would listen, "I didn't even get credentials to attend the GOP convention, if you can believe it. I mean, wow, they're tight," she said. "And I'm the only living Republican nominee who had run for VP or president who supported Trump. And even I couldn't get in."⁵ Palin did nothing to cross Trump personally, mind you, but sinking into irrelevance apparently counts as a crime far worse in Trump's eyes. Their crowds have vanished. Their spectacle has soured. Their glow has faded. Their energy has sapped. They threaten to contaminate his own image. That, in Trump's world, is what is truly intolerable.

Contrast Palin's treatment with how Trump rehabilitates erstwhile political opponents and critics if they have some usefulness, constituency, public standing, or reputation. Many critics have committed far worse sins and said far worse about Trump than the still-loyal Palin, but Trump has a pragmatic instinct for welcoming former rivals into the fold if they can prove useful, reach important constituencies, or bend the knee.

Sarah Palin, the Tea Party favorite whose blunt, outspoken candor helped pave the way for Trump's own candidacy in 2016, was a strong ally of Trump's before her star fizzled. Trump subsequently iced her out, despite her having done nothing to cross or offend him in any way.

Consider how Trump was willing to overlook JD Vance's previous virulent anti-Trumpism, even going so far as to overlook Vance dubbing Trump "America's Hitler" and his depictions of Trump as "noxious" and "heroin." But when Vance reinvented himself as a MAGA populist, Trump happily endorsed him for Senate, recognizing the symbolic power of having one of his loudest, most prominent conservative critics bend the knee. If anything, Vance's previous track record of impassioned Trump criticism was an asset, not a liability: Nothing spoke to Trump's complete and utter domination quite like having the superstar author of *Hillbilly Elegy*, with all his cultural cachet, become converted to a loyal, dependent acolyte.[6]

Vance's brother-in-arms in Trump's cabinet, Marco Rubio, went through a similar rehabilitation. Despite "Lil Marco" questioning the size of Trump's manhood—a special no-no in Trump's world where size is always paramount—Trump recognized Rubio's unique star power and his potential as a young GOP banner carrier commanding the loyalty of important constituencies within the party. Thus, he was willing to let bygones be bygones, even supporting Rubio when he changed his mind and sought reelection to his Senate seat after dropping out of the presidential race, at a moment when Trump could have easily twisted the knife and left him for dead. Although Rubio continued expressing doubts about Trump both publicly and privately, Trump was willing to overlook that disloyalty in selecting Rubio as secretary of state and subsequently empowering him with broad control over the foreign policy portfolio as both secretary of state and national security advisor.

Obviously, that stands in stark contrast to the way Trump discarded a rotating cast of individuals from his first administration whom he perceived to be stone-cold losers, ex-loyalists mercilessly shunted aside and forgotten like Jeff Sessions, Sean Spicer, and Reince Priebus—staffers without real independent constituencies of their own—who were unhesitatingly tossed aside for far lesser "sins." Similarly, external allies such as Marjorie Taylor Greene or Elise Stefanik were similarly tossed aside when their usefulness waned. This contrast underscores certain peculiar truths about the way Trump sees the world: If rivals retain a platform, constituency, or glamour and are contrite, they can be rehabilitated. If they lose these underpinnings of independent stature, they are discarded as losers irrespective of what they may or may not have done to offend Trump. Staffers without real constituencies of their own, who are entirely dependent on Trump for their refracted glory and standing, are prone to being treated as interchangeable and immediately disposable should their usefulness wane.

Of course, what it really comes down to is power. Trump will feel more emboldened to toss aside people who he feels he "invented" or "discovered," and who owe their entire position to him, whereas those with independent constituencies and independent underpinnings of power outside of their relationship with Trump will get more leeway. Take, for example, Trump's ginger handling of frenemy Elon Musk. Too powerful to be tossed aside, yet too independent to be embraced as an unquestioningly loyal follower anymore, Trump struggles to handle him, sometimes mocking him but sometimes courting him and reaching out with olive branches. Even after Musk called for Trump's impeachment and surfaced Trump's appearances in the Epstein files, the two embraced gingerly in the aftermath of the Charlie Kirk murder, with Musk invited back in the fold for certain events, such as a presidential state dinner with Saudi leader Mohammed bin Salman. In this way, Trump treats Musk like a rival warlord—dancing awkwardly around him, sometimes gingerly extending olive branches, waiting for the power dynamic to shift and/or an opportunity to pounce, as if Musk is the American Prigozhin, a threat to his own power who cannot be trusted and who has already crossed the Rubicon, and thus needs to be neutralized at the right time, but not immediately.[7] In a less dramatic example but similar vein, Trump clearly respects Bobby Kennedy's independent constituency and has given RFK much more room to run and freedom to maneuver than his other cabinet secretaries, whom he tends to keep on a much tighter leash. Trump has stood by Kennedy despite strong criticism from historically GOP constituencies, ranging from GOP senators to pharmaceutical companies to rare disease experts. Contrast that to Trump's treatment of the other former Democrat in his cabinet, Tulsi Gabbard, whom Trump has kept a close watch over amid rising frustrations. Trump himself aptly summarized the difference: According to *The New York Times*, Trump quipped, "Bobby's a star. Tulsi? Tulsi wants to be a star."

Simply put, Trump handles those with independent constituencies, power bases, and forms of legitimacy that he respects or fears differently than those without them. Even when he insults them, he calibrates the attack differently than he would with true "losers" who are dispensable. Trump never dismisses Barack Obama as an outright loser. Instead, he traffics in conspiracy theories like birtherism and accusations of deep-state plotting and muses about prosecuting Obama for treason, but he treats Obama as a cunning, powerful rival. He knows Obama is still adored by millions, so he recasts Obama as an illegitimate winner and a traitor, a dangerous manipulator who represents what Trump's base despises, but never a down-and-out, stone-cold loser.

This is Groucho Marx logic applied politically: Any club that would have him, Trump doesn't want to join. If the only people still loyal to you are nobodies, you are radioactive. Trump is always grasping to move up, always with an eye on folding into his own tent those he respects, with independent constituencies of their own and for whom Trump sees some use. Trump collects people the way others might collect baseball cards or stamps, and is always striving to upgrade his collection.

That explains why Trump has sometimes defended even ostensibly left-in-the-dust losers, those whom few others would dare associate with, much less defend. These are the sympathetic losers—or at least losers whom Trump tries hard to paint as sympathetic. These are very different from the losers without a following, whom Trump is so quick to drop. If anything, with these losers who have a constituency, Trump opportunistically wants to "buy low"—his brain spinning a thousand miles an hour about how to capitalize on their misfortune, this person who might be down-and-out at the moment but still has a following, and what Trump can get out of the fact that they now need Trump's help.

Once again, the decisive factor with these cases is constituency above all else. Trump does not ask whether someone has repented or proven their worthiness in a moral sense. He asks whether they still command an audience that could benefit him and what advantage that may give him—especially when it appeals to society's sense of sympathy or injustice—with a victim who is perceived in some circles to have been wronged.

That's why Trump has defended such fallen stars as Martha Stewart, who remains glamorous and beloved and whose indictment aligns perfectly with Trump's sense of grievance over unfair treatment by prosecutors; Former New York City Mayor Eric Adams, who may be embroiled in tawdry scandals repulsive to Park Avenue but who retains strong support within his working-class base in the NYC outer boroughs; his longtime friend Mike Tyson, who retains his die-hard fandom even though allegations of abuse have sullied his name in the decades since his rise; and even the Tate brothers, whose sex crimes shock polite society but who retain cult status on the extreme far-right and within bro circles, not dissimilar to Trump's commutation of the con man George Santos. Trump's benevolence toward these disgraced, even criminal, yet still magnetic figures are not mistakes or coincidences, nor are they borne out of altruistic kindness.

These cases contribute to why people who don't know any better often think Trump is a loyal person. Those who know better would argue he has no loyalty but to himself. But to those who don't understand how his mind works, this seemingly irrational loyalty to fallen stars that members of polite society would normally shun becomes misconstrued as fervent, undying personal loyalty, when it could be little more than naked opportunism. After all, whether it's with financial assets or people, Trump always seeks to buy low.

The losers Trump redeems are those who still have something to give him: a constituency, a symbol, a victimhood narrative. These figures, disgraced though they may be, retain constituencies, networks, or symbolic power. They remain glamorous, sympathetic to some, even when untouchable in others' eyes. To disparage them is to risk alienating their followers; to defend them costs little other than some polite scorn and strengthens Trump's image as magnanimous.

Trump's hesitance to drop losers with independent power bases and constituencies is heightened when those individuals may have leverage of their own. For example, for years before the Jeffrey Epstein files exploded back out into the open, Trump assiduously refused to disparage Epstein's longtime girlfriend Ghislaine Maxwell, repeatedly "wishing her well" and making her out to be a sympathetic figure. There may be ample self-interest there, with skeptics noting Trump could be possibly fearful of what dirt Maxwell may have on him. Maxwell plays perfectly into the idea that Trump finds it more appealing to play ball with certain losers than to drop them.

That same logic applies to Trump's consistent defense of certain disgraced political allies, an odd bunch of offbeat, quirky characters whom more conventional politicos would wash their hands of in a heartbeat. Instead, he reframes them as political martyrs and turns their plights into useful value for himself through their ability to foment public resentment toward Trump's enemies. As the adage goes, "I'd rather have them in the tent pissing out than outside the tent pissing in."

Consider the number of oddball political allies whom Trump has remained loyal to over the years. This group of eclectic characters includes Roger Stone, whom Trump has painted as a loyalist unfairly targeted by Mueller and whose sentence he commuted; Paul Manafort, whom Trump rebranded from a for-hire felon who has done dirty deals with some of the world's shadiest characters into a victim of the deep state "witch hunt"; and Michael Flynn and Steve Bannon, both of whom Trump treats as persecuted victims of his enemies.

Their value lies in how they symbolize Trump's central claim: that the establishment is out to destroy him and his allies. In defending them, Trump defends himself.

These men are losers by conventional political standards. But because Trump can spin their plights as symbols of a larger narrative of persecution and because he would rather have them with him than against him, they are redeemed; whereas more conventionally palatable political allies such as Jeff Sessions and Bill Barr are dropped for their lack of utility to Trump and their lack of leverage. This is also why Trump's choice of losers can sometimes appear so jarring, because his definition is so different from anyone else's. General John Kelly and other top generals from his first administration claimed that Trump often derided fallen soldiers as losers, believing that real winners were only wounded, not killed, and routinely skipped the transfers of the remains of dead service members at Joint Base Andrews as well as national cemetery visits.

Constituency is everything for Trump in how he deals with those he perceives to be losers, and that manifests in the targets he selects for revenge and retribution. Contrary to public perception, Trump's vindictive streak is hardly indiscriminate; he pursues revenge only when he is confident he has the upper hand, with great selectivity and intentionality. He has a knack for picking targets he perceives to be unsympathetic, whom he believes are unlikely to be able to mobilize much support for themselves. In cases where he does not believe he can strike a knockout blow, he will just as frequently try to drown the squeaky wheel in oil than try to replace it altogether.

It is hardly a coincidence that some of the targets he has selected for retribution in his second term tend to be former Republicans turned independents who are, for all intents and purposes, politically homeless and without party—maverick voices such as John Bolton, James Comey, and Chris Krebs, all of whom have never held elected office, only appointed positions. Although Trump will, on occasion, target elected Democratic officials for retribution—such as New York Attorney General Letitia James—he also understands that such cases tend to mobilize support for his targets and that oftentimes he ends up helping them more than he can hurt them. Thus, those cases are far less frequent than his targeting of mavericks such as Bolton, Comey, and Krebs. Trump apparently perceives them to be far more vulnerable with their lack of independent constituencies, having become isolated from their erstwhile political parties and allies, with little reservoir of goodwill remaining on either side of the aisle and having never run for office or built any public support apparatus outside of insular DC policy and government circles to begin with.

Indeed, when the news was announced that John Bolton was being indicted, Bolton was seen by many Dems as so unsympathetic a character that they were not only loath to defend him, but some prominent Democratic voices seemed almost rather pleased, joining Trump in criticizing Bolton. Former Florida congresswoman Val Demings, who had served on the impeachment committee, posted, "John Bolton had an opportunity to testify during the first impeachment trial of Donald Trump and do his duty to get an unprincipled man out of power. He chose to write a book instead. Chickens coming home to roost."[8]

Indeed, Trump's tendency for picking targets he perceives to be unsympathetic extends far beyond just revenge and vindictiveness. He is always casting about for the soft underbelly of his adversaries, through which he can accomplish his goals and exert his power, in all situations. For example, although Trump has been feuding with Federal Reserve Chair Jay Powell for years, in a dispute over the direction of interest rates that has become highly personal, it is interesting how Trump chose to carry out his campaign to undermine Powell's authority. While Trump initially targeted Powell personally—claiming that the Fed chair's gross mismanagement resulted in the Fed squandering billions of taxpayer dollars on construction projects—he quickly pivoted course when prominent GOP senators rushed to Powell's defense, unconvinced by Trump's accusations. Instead of going after Powell directly, Trump seized on allegations of mortgage fraud by Fed Governor Lisa Cook, after housing agency head Bill Pulte surfaced documents allegedly showing that Cook had taken out multiple mortgages for different properties while claiming each of them as her primary residence. Although Cook is innocent until proven guilty, with her case winding through the legal system, even her supporters admitted that the facts looked rather damning in her case, making it hard for her supporters to substantively defend her amid Trump's assaults. The saga is an illuminating example of how Trump picks his targets and how he discriminates between vulnerability and strength in different adversaries, seeking to strike only when and where he senses weakness.[9]

Of course, Trump has never shied away from using the specter of retaliation as a preemptive tool to achieve what he wants. Take an illustrative instance from his early career, around the opening of the Trump Taj Mahal in 1988 in Atlantic City. As the casino was gearing up for its grand opening, a Wall Street research analyst at the securities firm Janney Montgomery, Marvin Roffman, published research suggesting, rather presciently, that the casino would be unable to generate enough money to cover its debts.[10]

In response, Trump faxed a letter to the chairman of Janney Montgomery directly, demanding that the head of the firm dismiss Roffman and issue a public apology, warning that he would bring a lawsuit against the firm. Trump correctly perceived Roffman's weak position inside his company—as a low-level research analyst employed by a securities firm that sought to do business with Trump, and with the potential business Trump represented dwarfing whatever financial revenues Roffman brought in. Trump hit his mark as the firm promptly folded and terminated Roffman. Even though Trump succeeded in his goal of taking out Roffman, ironically, the fired analyst had the last laugh: After Roffman's prediction proved correct with the eventual bankruptcy of the Trump Taj Mahal, he won a multimillion-dollar settlement in a wrongful termination case. Nevertheless, Trump accomplished what he set out to do.

The transactional, cold way through which Trump calculates and carefully selects his targets for revenge and retaliation reflects his little-appreciated intentionality. Though widely seen as thin-skinned and hot-tempered, he only picks targets he thinks he can win against. Furthermore, when he pursues vendettas, it tends to be for strategic reasons, whether muzzling a thorn in his side, establishing a strong deterrent effect to intimidate would-be others, or trying to see how far he can push in extending his own power and domination.

That is the essence of how Trump picks his targets, which many observers and even some who have worked with Trump still fail to understand. For example, according to Jonathan Karl in his book *Retribution*, Trump's first-term vice president, Mike Pence, was genuinely startled and caught off guard by how quickly Trump turned against him when Pence decided not to block incoming President Joe Biden's certification by the Electoral College on January 6, 2021. Pence had remained steadfastly loyal to Trump across the entire four years of his term, after all, and Pence had deluded himself into thinking that he had a strong relationship with Trump, which he figured had to count for something.[11]

How wrong that was. Not only did Trump berate Pence personally, he turned a blind eye to the January 6 rioters chanting "Hang Mike Pence," leaving Pence to fend for himself. But what made no sense to Pence made nothing but sense to Trump. Forget the fact that Pence had stayed loyal to him and had been a willing and loyal #2 to him for four years. For Trump, after four years as president, he knew that he no longer needed the mainstream conservative and evangelical Christian imprimatur Pence originally brought to his ticket. From that angle, Pence was yet another interchangeable, constituency-less official who could easily be tossed aside and replaced. In how Trump chooses his targets and how he handles "losers," there is a cold, hard logic to it all.

In pursuing selective retribution, Trump typically probes the limits of what is permissible—pressing forward incrementally, testing resistance, and retreating once he encounters barriers that cannot be overcome. This pattern reflects not a do-at-all-cost obstinacy, but an opportunistic and strategic instinct. He advances only as far as the system allows, calibrating his actions to societal tolerance rather than defying it outright. Power, in this view, is something to be stretched, not shattered.

That dynamic is evident in the deliberate elevation of longtime loyalists to some of the most sensitive prosecutorial posts in the country—Alina Habba as US Attorney in New Jersey and Lindsey Halligan in the Eastern District of Virginia—only to pull back when faced with insurmountable obstacles. Habba's interim appointment functioned as a calculated test of institutional elasticity, but it collided with statutory limits, judicial refusal to extend her tenure, and ultimately a unanimous appellate ruling stripping her of lawful authority, leaving no viable path forward. In Virginia, Halligan's high-profile cases against perceived adversaries likewise unraveled not because of public controversy, but because of procedural failure: a judge found her appointment unlawful, a grand jury declined to indict, and key evidence was barred. Faced with these obstacles, Trump ultimately largely let his efforts to pursue legal retaliation lapse, abandoning his appointments of loyalists as US attorneys and reverting back to the traditional blue-slip–Senate confirmation process for US Attorneys. In short, Trump pushed retribution until the system pushed back—and then he stepped back.

The flip side of the coin is who Trump chooses to surround himself with. Calling them "friends" is a bit of a stretch. Trump doesn't really have many friends, at least not in the conventional sense of the word, though he obviously has too many cronies and loyalists to count. He has been a lone wolf his entire life, even before politics, though not a conventional loner either. There's a good reason that you've never heard of Trump having a wolfpack of childhood friends he keeps up with or of college buds he goes to reunions with. It's because they're virtually nonexistent.

And for all his supposed playboy image, there's a good reason you've never heard of Trump having girlfriends or exes outside of the women he married and one-night stands and casual dalliances with porn stars—because they're virtually nonexistent too. The man is, at his heart, a lone wolf who views his relationships with anyone and everyone else as fundamentally transactional. Paradoxically, he genuinely enjoys the company of those he can control when he sits at the center of a social network of his own creation—but he trusts none of them wholly. Put most simply: Trump has few friends, only followers.

That is even more the case now, after he transitioned into politics and as he enters into his eighth decade. He's outlived many of his true contemporaries, including the sibling with whom he was closest, his younger brother Robert Trump, as well as the only person left he truly feared, his sister, Judge Maryanne Trump Barry. Almost all of Trump's current advisors and staff are Johnny-come-latelies who haven't known him very long.

If anything, that's been an advantage. Unlike other politicians who are caught off guard by some longtime loyalist violating their trust or stabbing them in the back, Trump trusts nobody in politics to begin with, because he spent his entire adult life until age seventy outside of politics, and thus barely really knew anyone in politics outside of New York until he dove in. He didn't rise up the ranks with anyone, which is how so many friendships are formed, in the salad days of youth, and thus lacks a reservoir of early career friendships or personal goodwill to draw on. His staffing has been almost entirely opportunistic and transactional, with Trump treating his staff as the professionals for hire that they are rather than as trusted intimates or genuine friends. He is under no delusions and believes, in classic Trumpian "see the worst in everyone" form, that those who come to work with him are opportunists whose first loyalty is to themselves, not him.

But even though calling them friends is a stretch, who Trump does choose to surround himself with, his hand-picked cronies, is revealing and insightful. As Don Quixote memorably quipped, "Tell me your company and I'll tell you your manners." In Trump's case, there is an almost caricatured gravitation, so extreme as to be almost laughable, toward ostentatious glitz, exaggerated grandeur, gold-covered everything, beautiful women, and tough guys.

This unique package captures Trump's real appeal for so many of his followers, which is that he offers class for the masses. Rather than calibrating his tastes toward how fellow billionaire peers would act and behave, with low-key expressions of luxury, Trump caters to the everyman with outsized dreams of grandiose glamour. One might say that his ostentatious luxe life pursuits are how a construction worker or a police officer would live if they were suddenly given many billions of dollars.

Let's admit it, it can make for a great show. This is why he lauds Sylvester Stallone at the Kennedy Center, praises the bombast of KISS, or courts celebrity endorsements with theatrical gusto. High culture bores him; Nantucket cultural capital means little to him. Trump delivers mass entertainment, not high entertainment. What matters is spectacle that translates across the television screen. Crass glitz becomes a form of democratic glamour—accessible and appealing to the average voter who, like Trump, associates it with winning.

This instinct helps explain his survival in politics even as he defies all the conventional rules. As rivals preach policy or morality, Trump curates the Trump show, and it's always a stage of one, the stage of Trump. He knows that voters, like audiences, are swayed not only by arguments but by the spectacle of who is standing beside you.

When he assembles a staged event, it is not by accident. At his Republican National Conventions, the roll call of celebrity endorsers looks more like the lineup for a Las Vegas pay-per-view than a traditional political event: Hulk Hogan, Dana White of the UFC, Kid Rock, Ted Nugent. These names are chosen because they project toughness, spectacle, and mass-market recognizability across broad swaths of the population who don't follow politics or haute couture and who've never watched a fashion show or tasted crudités. To Trump, these are the kinds of stars, with loyal independent followings of their own, who can help him.

When it comes to Trump's favorite sport of golf—and boy does Trump love golf, playing roughly sixty-two days a year by some counts, or more than once every five days—his regular playing buddies tend to be similarly strategic, symbolically important figures such as Tiger Woods, Rory McIlroy, Jack Nicklaus, and other such celebrities, professional athletes, and powerful influencers with independent constituencies and followings of their own. On occasion, he will also use golf to cultivate strategic political alliances, often playing with senators such as Lindsey Graham or top advisors such as Steve Witkoff. By contrast, the golf buddies of other presidents who enjoyed the game, such as George H. W. Bush, Bill Clinton, and Dwight Eisenhower, tended more toward genuine, long-term friends without explicit strategic agendas or ornamental status value.

In short, Trump's social collection is a curated stage of the eclectic associations that make him so unique among his peer set: boxers, rock stars, strongmen, sympathetic victims. He discards those who threaten his brand and clings to those who he believes enhance it. The logic is not moral but performative.

At root, this explains Trump's endurance. By defining losers on his own terms, he defines himself as a winner by contrast. Every loser discarded, every martyr defended, every glamorous ally paraded—all serve to reinforce his central claim: that Trump himself is the ultimate winner, surrounded by spectacle, untouchable and untainted by failure.

It is a coherent, if brutal, philosophy of association: Avoid losers like the plague, cling to glamour and toughness, redeem those with constituencies, and drop those without. In this cold, but effective, logic lies the key to understanding the fluidity of Trump's politics, his alliances, and his enemies.

CHAPTER 8

Rewriting History Through the Sleeper Effect
When Relentless Repetition Becomes Truth

Knowingly or not, Trump has fully internalized the concept that "history is written by the winners," fully presuming that victors can influence historical narratives regardless of what the facts may be, through cold, hard power. Winston Churchill's adaptation of this ancient proverb was revealed in a speech before the House of Commons in 1948: "For my part, I consider that it will be found much better by all parties to leave the past to history, especially as I propose to write that history myself."

More darkly, a year later, in George Orwell's dystopian novel *1984*, a core theme was the rewriting of history, driven by the totalitarian Party, through the government's Ministry of Truth. Written fully seventy-three years before the release of ChatGPT, this agency continuously altered all records, from birth notices and obituaries to news articles and photographs, to fortify political narratives presenting the governing party as infallible. The Party's slogan was "Who controls the past controls the future," targeting the complete elimination of any facts that did not support the Party's dogmatic view of history.

A few years later, in 1961, Yale psychologists Carl Hovland and Walter Weiss, in their mass communications research, suggested a process where such facts can be rewritten in the public consciousness.[1] They found that people often remember a message long after they've forgotten its source—and more troubling still, that unreliable sources become more persuasive and compelling over time, with enough repetition. They further revealed that more sophisticated audiences need to hear some version of both sides of a story to form their own opinion; but for mass audiences, they are content with a strong message repeated unrelentingly as a single forceful explanation, which they accept unquestioningly. That brings a comforting and ostensibly comprehensive but in fact inaccurate understanding, lacking nuance. They called this phenomenon the "sleeper effect," a powerful tool in the arsenal of those who seek to reshape reality through repetition.

Trump surely has never heard of Hovland or Weiss and might not be familiar with their sleeper effect theory, yet he has intuited the sleeper effect with remarkable consistency throughout his career. His approach represents a master class in exploiting cognitive vulnerabilities in shaping perception and understanding. If one repeats an assertion relentlessly and with absolute certainty, regardless of whether it's factual, even skeptics begin to doubt their own judgment. Over time, those untruths become conventionally accepted "fact." Or, at a minimum, the waters are sufficiently mucked up for there to be genuine confusion over the facts. As I once heard quipped at Trump Tower, there is the recognition that one can tell, as he would put it, "stupid" people one side of the story without allowing for another perspective, persuading them by brute force rather than letting them reach their own conclusions. This was intuitive, closely mirroring the pioneering research of renowned Harvard and Yale psychologist Chris Argyris, a disapproving student of Carl Hovland who confided in despair to me that this work could help leaders "intentionally manipulate the masses. You tell sophisticated people both sides of the story, and they think you've been fair. For unsophisticated people, you just hammer them with one side of the story, as they do not want the nuances."

The genius of this approach lies not just in repetition but also the absolute certainty with which these claims are made. When someone states falsehoods with unwavering confidence, people begin to think, *Maybe there's something I've missed.* This is precisely how the sleeper effect works: The messenger's confidence becomes more memorable than the message's accuracy.

The sleeper effect is one of Trump's most potent tools. He repeats assertions so many times that even the most dubious, those initially dismissed as ludicrous, gradually become conventionally accepted facts. *The Washington Post* previously documented 30,573 false or misleading claims by Trump during his first term, but the sheer volume and consistency with which Trump repeated these messages has ended up

Trump surely has never heard of Hovland or Weiss and might not be familiar with their sleeper effect theory, yet he has intuited the sleeper effect with remarkable consistency throughout his career.

shaping public belief regardless of their factual veracity.[2] In July 2025, my team and I tested the veracity of twenty of President Trump's most often-repeated economic, social, and diplomatic pronouncements by running them through leading AI large language models, including OpenAI's ChatGPT, Anthropic's Claude, Perplexity, Google Gemini, and xAI's Grok. As we revealed in our *Washington Post* publication, those different AI models unanimously found most of Trump's statements to be untrue—yet Trump has continued repeating those same lines to great effect, with many people truly believing what he says.[3]

Consider how Trump's sheer repetition of untruths can shape the public narrative. In a viral *Fortune* publication during the 2024 presidential campaign, I pointed out how many of Trump's most-repeated campaign talking points included dubious assertions that strained credulity, across every core pillar of his 2024 campaign platform. Yet through sheer repetition they eventually seeped into mainstream media narratives, before eventually becoming accepted as conventional wisdom with time.[4]

Immigration was one of the most blatant manifestations. In the June debate against Biden, Trump said, "We had the safest border in history." Trump then doubled down on his border record at the Republican National Convention, saying, "Under my presidency, we had the most secure border and best economy in the history of our country," while hammering Biden for being weak on illegal immigration.

While the Biden administration showed clear weakness on illegal immigration until it was too late, Trump substantially overstated his own record. Looking at the numbers revealed that Trump did not have the safest or most secure border in recent or not-so-recent history. Annual encounters at the US-Mexico border under President Trump averaged 488,164. Under his predecessor, President Barack Obama, annual encounters averaged 408,493, more than 16 percent lower. Even in the final couple of months of Trump's presidency, Obama had lower numbers, with 43,251 in December 2016 and 31,576 in

January 2017, compared to 73,994 and 78,414 for Trump. In fact, during the time of Trump's speeches, the Biden administration also had lower numbers, 56,408 in July 2024, and steadily declining after the Biden administration took executive action to secure the border at long last. Yet, through sheer repetition, Trump was so effective in popularizing the narrative that he was tough on immigration whereas Biden was soft that it became accepted as conventional wisdom by both sides throughout the campaign. Popular opinion polls showed a vast majority of Americans from both the left and the right believed Trump's claims that Biden was weak on immigration whereas Trump was stronger. Whatever corrective steps the Biden administration pursued, they came too late to dislodge the entrenched narrative of weakness on stopping illegal immigration—one relentlessly amplified by Trump at every turn.

During the 2024 campaign, Trump's assertions about the economy, inflation, and wage growth were similarly repeated so frequently that the narrative that Biden had let inflation get out of control and the economy tank also became widely accepted, even as inflation had already slowed by the time of the election.

At an August rally, Trump criticized the Biden and Harris administration's "radical liberal policies . . . [that] have caused horrific inflation," blaming Bidenomics for the rapid rise in prices since 2020. Such claims oversimplify the sources of inflation—but that was entirely the point. Economists generally argue that inflation can be attributed to many sources beyond pure fiscal policy and government policy, and that at least some recent inflation was attributed to COVID-19 and idiosyncratic supply shocks, factors that no president could control.

Under Biden, inflation did spike to 9.1 percent coming out of the pandemic, but it had fallen to 2.9 percent by the time of the presidential campaign in summer 2024, near historic averages. However, by virtue of Trump's effective sleeper effect-esque assertions that Biden had wrecked the economy and was responsible for runaway inflation, popular opinion polls consistently showed that voters preferred Trump on economic issues. Amazingly, though inflation remains near those levels today with fears of resurgent inflation among economists and market strategists, inflation just about completely vanished as a political football after Trump's election, a remarkable testament to how effectively Trump controls the narrative through relentless repetition of certain assertions, singlehandedly driving narratives into the news cycle. The actual facts and figures related to inflation were lost in the cacophony as Trump replayed the message that "Biden killed the economy" over and over until it became accepted as conventional fact.

Trump similarly attacked the Biden and Harris government for overspending, a charge that proved incredibly effective for the Trump campaign and lethal to his adversaries. The irony is that even as Trump was bashing Biden for overspending, it was Trump who had passed the original pandemic relief programs that injected $3.6 trillion into the economy and who has repeatedly blown through budgetary ceilings and flouted traditional GOP concerns about balancing the budget. If anything, some of the worst cases of COVID spending excesses, such as the widely panned, fraud-ridden PPP programs, were implemented under Trump, not Biden, despite Trump's effective attacks of wasteful Biden government spending. But Democrats were so cowed by the efficacy of Trump's messaging that they more or less completely surrendered the point, with nary any counterattacks.

Likewise for Trump's attacks on the federal debt. Trump claimed in the June 2024 debate, "The country was growing like never before, and we were ready to start paying down debt." Again, in the June debate, Trump said, "But [Biden's] got the largest deficit in the history of our country." This is ironic, because on an equivalent basis, as debt accumulated per year in office, Trump saddled America with more debt than any president in US history during his first term. Controlling for the effects from COVID-19, the Biden administration added less debt than the first Trump administration did during their respective presidencies, all things considered. It was Trump who oversaw the largest spending deficit in any year since World War II. Full-term net spending increases under Trump 1 were also greater than those under the Biden administration, with or without pandemic relief. Yet thanks to Trump's powerful messaging, it became widely accepted as fact that Biden had overspent coming out of the pandemic, with even liberal economists like Jason Furman and Larry Summers lending credence to Trump's arguments that Biden was guilty of reckless federal spending while largely absolving Trump of any blame.

Another manifestation of the efficacy of Trump's inaccurate economic assertions, repeated until they became accepted as conventional wisdom, is infrastructure spending. "Dollars that are not yet spent, we will redirect that money for important projects like roads, bridges, dams," Trump stated at the 2024 Republican National Convention. Trump made similar promises to invest in infrastructure during his 2016 primary campaign against Hillary Clinton, promising to spend more than $500 billion. He never delivered. Infrastructure weeks were touted in the media, but there was no substance behind the glitz. In contrast, the bipartisan Infrastructure Law and Inflation Reduction Act passed after Trump left office dedicated more than $700 billion to strengthen and modernize US infrastructure, and Biden announced nearly $454 billion in funding for more than 56,000 projects and awards across the country. Projects included more than 165,000 miles of roads, 9,400 bridges, 450 ports and waterways, and 300 airport terminals, among others. Yet public polling repeatedly revealed that voters gave little credit to Biden and the Democrats for achievements related to infrastructure, and that voters were just as likely to give infrastructure credit to Trump as Biden despite Trump's failure to pass major infrastructure legislation.

The story is similar when it comes to Trump's claims about employment. An August Trump post on Truth Social claimed, "Most new jobs under Biden went to illegal Immigrants. Additionally, he got what is known as Covid Bounce-back jobs. . . . He did terribly on jobs." Trump repeated variations of the same claim for the rest of the campaign. Controlling for COVID-19 complexities, the Biden administration still saw more employment gains than Trump 1 by a wide margin, with jobs going to both native-born and foreign-born workers. Federal Reserve data shows that over half of all changes in employment levels went to native-born workers under Biden. Yet, once again, public polling showed that voters were frustrated with employment gains under Biden, and a large segment of the population believed that most new jobs under Biden went to illegal immigrants, as Trump had asserted.

The facts are even more stark when it comes to manufacturing employment, despite Trump's oft-repeated assertions. In a *Meet the Press* interview, JD Vance claimed Trump brought manufacturing jobs back to America, when in reality, the Trump presidency saw manufacturing jobs decline, largely due to COVID-19. Trump even went so far as to claim credit for AI, innovation, and technology, a brazen assertion that he repeated time and time again. After his Silicon Valley campaign fundraiser, Trump bragged, "One of the primary reasons for the endorsement was the four years that we had in office, which was the best four years ever for high tech . . . especially as it relates to AI and all of the other new and brilliant technologies coming right at this moment." However, during the first Trump administration, little was done to incentivize domestic chip production, contributing to the major chip shortages during the pandemic, while the Biden administration passed the CHIPS Act to reshore semiconductor production. Biden also acted to restrict the transfer of sensitive technologies to competitors such as China without unduly impeding global free trade through the "small yard, high fence" philosophy.

But all these facts fell by the wayside, with even prominent Democratic officials starting to believe Trump's pronouncements, no matter the facts, giving Trump the opportunity to dominate the narrative unchallenged across all fronts.

In fact, during the 2024 campaign, I was told directly by top economic advisors to Joe Biden and subsequently Kamala Harris, including but not limited to Ron Klain and Jared Bernstein, that they were reluctant to celebrate the Biden-Harris administration's economic triumphs because the public genuinely believed Trump's claims that the economy was faltering, and because Trump was so effective in hammering home this message. Secretary of the Treasury Janet Yellen, Secretary of Commerce Gina Raimondo, and others were dispatched for what amounted to misguided apology tours, while other Biden-Harris officials wrongly attacked CEOs and companies for price gouging. Ironically, we found business leaders, even Republican-leaning CEOs, to be more appreciative of the genuine Biden/Harris economic accomplishments than those Biden/Harris administration officials themselves, who were so cowed by Trump's messaging efficiency that they all but surrendered the point. With Democrats chronically unable and unwilling to trumpet their own accomplishments, Trump capitalized on his opportunity to dominate the narrative, no matter any inconvenient facts.

Trump began honing his skills at leveraging the sleeper effect well before the 2024 election. That it's long been a classic, go-to tool is evident from his decades-long campaign to establish a Trump origin story through constant, incessant repetition of stories that strain credulity. As discussed in chapter 4 ("How Trump Makes Money"), the reality is well-documented: Trump received the equivalent of nearly half a billion dollars from his father's real estate empire, much of it through questionable tax schemes that helped the family evade hundreds of millions in tax obligations. Yet, through constant repetition of an alternative narrative, Trump successfully implanted a "rags to riches" myth in the public consciousness. That tale has been roundly debunked by biographers, reporters, and even former friends and colleagues, but Trump has successfully drowned out all efforts to correct the record by continuing to loudly and passionately repeat his version of the story, overshadowing any actual facts regardless of what they are.

As we detailed in chapter 4, Trump stops at nothing in his full-scale communications war to defend his rags-to-riches origin story. That includes litigation against many media outlets who truthfully reported the facts. Trump sued *The New York Times* for $5 billion when Tim O'Brien reported that Trump had dramatically exaggerated his wealth, pegging his actual net worth at closer to $250 million rather than the billions Trump contended. The courts ultimately dismissed Trump's claims, but only after three years of expensive litigation and O'Brien's exit from *The New York Times*.[5]

This rewriting of history extends to every aspect of his biography that might suggest weakness or failure. A minor but revealing example is the lengths Trump goes to in order to control the flow of any records, ensuring nothing surfaces that might undermine the story he wants told.

For example, when Trump started championing the "birtherism" movement, falsely claiming he had evidence to prove his bogus assertions that Barack Obama was not born in America, he simultaneously attacked Obama as a beneficiary of affirmative action, even though Obama had been first Black president of the *Harvard Law Review* and a best-selling author and public intellectual in his twenties. He called Obama a "terrible student" and demanded that he release his transcripts. Naturally, detractors responded by demanding to see Trump's own academic record. A Trump staffer had to resort to intimidation, even brazenly threatening educational officials at Trump's alma mater, to keep Trump's academic records sealed, ensuring that Trump's actual school grades would never see the light of day. Controlling the flow of information in this way allowed Trump to define the public narrative regardless of the actual underlying facts.

Trump's devotion to constructing alternate realities extends beyond his personal history and reflects his fundamental understanding of how the world works. His admiration for strongmen, from Putin to Andrew Jackson, extends beyond what historian Thomas Carlyle called the "great man" theory of history. In Trump's worldview, history—and what drives events in the world—is a series of contests and conquests, won by superior strength and will rather than collective action, humanitarian progress, or any bottom-up grassroots movements driving the progression of society.

In this worldview, complex historical events become simple stories of winners and losers, strong leaders and weak ones. Nuance disappears in favor of dramatic narratives that are easier to remember and more emotionally satisfying. When Trump compares himself to Lincoln or claims to be greater than Washington, he's doing something more sophisticated than making grandiose statements. He's planting seeds with the capacity to grow, which he then feeds with statements that may initially seem ludicrous but with time and repetition become more credible and sometimes even evolve into conventional wisdom. For example, early in his first term, most laughed it off when Trump repeatedly suggested he ought to be on Mt. Rushmore or that he ought to receive a Nobel Prize, but now, die-hard Trump proponents are actually hard at work trying to nominate him for a Nobel Prize and trying to etch his face on Mt. Rushmore in the pantheon of Lincoln, Jefferson, Washington, and Roosevelt—exactly the company in which Trump wants people to believe he belongs. When Trump was passed over for the Nobel Peace Prize in 2025, which instead went to the Venezuelan democracy activist María Corina Machado, there was genuine disappointment among his supporters, many of whom had come to believe he would really receive it, a testament to how far his once-implausible aspiration had grown.

That view of history is why Trump is always seeking to rewrite his own political history. His continued claims about the 2020 election being "stolen," and that he won "three" times, represent perhaps the most comprehensive application of the sleeper effect in American political history. Despite losing more than sixty court cases and finding no evidence of significant fraud, the determined repetition of election denial claims has convinced millions of Americans that the election was stolen, with polls finding that over 60 percent of GOP voters doubted the veracity of the 2020 election outcome.[6]

This campaign succeeded because it followed the sleeper effect playbook: Make the claims with absolute certainty, repeat them endlessly, and dismiss all contradictory evidence. The specific allegations—voting machines, ballot harvesting, dead voters—may have been thoroughly debunked, but no matter; the overall impression of illegitimacy took root in the public consciousness. Even now, after his remarkable comeback, Trump still insists that he won the 2020 election when he no longer has any reason to do so. With Trump, however, acknowledging shades of gray is never an option. There is always only a single version of the truth—his version—which he'll stick to with un-Trumpian discipline and remarkable consistency, reiterating them at every opportunity until repetition results in the perception of some degree of validity, and sometimes even acceptance as fact.

That may also explain why Trump has long shown a willingness to accept revisionist history from others, such as Vladimir Putin's account of who started the Ukrainian conflict.[7] By echoing Putin's false narrative, whether knowingly or not, he legitimizes it through repetition. Each time the claim is made, it becomes slightly more plausible to those hearing it, regardless of the mountain of evidence contradicting it.

It's the same phenomenon with Trump's continued insistence that he witnessed Muslims celebrating in New Jersey after 9/11—a claim for which no evidence exists[8]—which exemplifies his understanding that vivid, emotionally charged narratives can become "true" through repetition alone and plays into his overall worldview, to which his supporters ascribe. The specific details may be questioned, but the emotional impression lingers: that there was celebration, that something suspicious happened, that the official narrative might be incomplete, feeding suspicion and distrust of authority with Trump as the alternative savior, the only one courageous enough to surface the real truth.

Trump's tendency to deploy the sleeper effect across everything he sees or doesn't like manifests clearly in his relationship with polling data. His approach is remarkably consistent: Every losing poll is fake, every winning poll represents perfect science. He has never acknowledged a negative poll as accurate publicly or dismissed a positive one as flawed. This isn't random. It's a systematic construction of an alternative reality, in the universe of Trump-land, where his support is always strong and growing. That is a narrative that he is always feeding, and he refuses to ever concede any shades of gray or setbacks.

By repeatedly dismissing unfavorable data while amplifying favorable results, dismissing all nuance, Trump creates a parallel information ecosystem—"alternative facts," as his first-term staffer Kellyanne Conway inelegantly labeled them.[9] Trump is too clever to ever reveal his hand so tactlessly, and never would have used that term himself, yet it does perfectly capture his approach. His supporters, incessantly bombarded with his selective interpretation of the facts, gradually absorb the underlying message: Trump is more popular than mainstream sources suggest. The specific polls fade from memory, but the impression of hidden popularity remains—just as Trump intended.

By systematically applying the sleeper effect across multiple domains—personal history, current events, economic data, electoral outcomes—Trump has created nothing less than an alternative reality, "Trump's World," if you will. This practice is leagues beyond ordinary political spin. Traditional politicians might shade the truth or emphasize favorable facts, but they generally operate within a shared framework of what constitutes evidence and reality. Trump's approach challenges that framework, suggesting that reality is whatever can be

Trump is too clever to actually call his approach "alternative facts," but he has effectively created a parallel reality through his repeated, consistent use of the sleeper effect approach.

made to seem true through sufficient repetition and forcefulness, no matter how seemingly outlandish or baseless at first glance. Even basic believability falls by the wayside.

The sleeper effect's power lies in its durability. Long after specific claims have been debunked, the impressions created through the sheer volume of repetition linger in public consciousness. At that point, even factual corrections may have limited effectiveness—as underlying beliefs have already taken root and been reinforced. That's how Trump has succeeded in creating his own version of reality, dragging millions of Americans along with him into a realm where his word is paramount.

Of course, Trump is hardly the first politician to traffic in factually dubious claims and promises. While Yale's Carl Hovland was inspired to research the sleeper effect based on the success of German Third Reich propagandist Joseph Goebbels, throughout American history, demagogues on the political left and right have successfully promoted false narratives to electrify the American electorate. Columbia and Harvard historian Alan Brinkley's Pulitzer Prize–winning book, *Voices of Protest: Huey Long, Father Coughlin & The Great Depression*, unraveled the dangerous political rhetoric and popular appeal of Huey Long and Father Charles Coughlin during the Great Depression. Brinkley uncovered many specific examples where Long's personal declarations about his background were false or exaggerated, all while Long was spinning up populist charm in a colorful, anti-intellectual style.[10]

Just as Huey Long's populist charm built on factually dubious foundations worked for him, until his assassination at least, Trump's populist language has demonstrated great effectiveness no matter the factual foundation. When, in 2015, one US automaker CEO asked me to try to get Trump to stop promoting the false message that they were shifting work from the US to Mexico—noting that in reality, they had closed an engine plant in Hungary without taking any jobs from the US—I passed on the message to Trump, who basically told me that he couldn't care less, because the public loved his message and it was working for him.

Trump's messaging savvy means that he can get messages amplified even when he isn't the one stating them. In 2015, when Trump failed to correct a supporter at a New Hampshire town hall who made blatantly false anti-Islamic assertions, I unwisely counseled Trump that I thought he missed a chance for his McCain moment—referring to the famous incident when John McCain corrected a bigoted supporter in 2008. Trump replied to me and to his then-communications lieutenant Hope Hicks breezily with an effort at plausible deniability, "Hey, it wasn't me who said it." Trump is so effective in brilliantly crafting his messages, executing his delivery with flair in ways that draw attention, and then relentlessly staying on message with uncharacteristic discipline that it is unlikely most of the country will ever awaken to realize his mastery of the pernicious sleeper effect.

As the old quip goes, "A lie can travel halfway around the world while the truth is still putting on its shoes." Ironically, the veracity of even this quip is disputed, with some attributing it to Mark Twain and others believing Jonathan Swift might be the original inspiration, and several others are also credited. That just goes to show that when it comes to separating truth from fiction, things can be very difficult indeed.

CHAPTER 9

Sultan of Insult

Reducing Complexity to Simplicity

Trump is often mischaracterized as reckless, impulsive, and undisciplined with his words. Observers fall into the trap of believing his constant fusillade of stream-of-consciousness insults, attacks, and musings reflect an ostensibly unfiltered candor. Similarly, many misguided observers assume his penchant for nicknames, mockery, and cutting one-liners are the product of a short fuse and impulsive temper. There may be some degree of truth to that, but to reduce Trump's rhetorical arsenal to a lack of impulse control or a hair-trigger temper is to miss the deeper truth of his intentionality and the underlying logic behind it all.

Trump's insults are not always random or impulsive. While he may have thin skin, his verbal attacks tend to be calculated, calibrated, and, above all, effective for what he is trying to achieve. He has mastered the art of insult as both weapon and theater.

Trump's inspiration here draws not from other politicians, historical or current, which is what makes him unique in the political realm. He absorbed much more from cultural and entertainment

Trump's verbal attacks tend to be calculated, calibrated, and, above all, effective for what he is trying to achieve.

predecessors than he did from any political predecessors. Those shock jock entertainers tap into something in the collective psyche that yearns for that kind of subversive behavior, which academics have been trying to explain for decades.[1]

Decades of research suggest that offensive humor, which violates expectations and norms, can pierce the dense fog of messaging. A 2016 study in the *Journal of Social Neuroscience* found that "insults are no laughing matter."[2] These researchers found that insults can be devastatingly effective for bullies and equally devastating for their victims. Their research found that messages tend to be more memorable when they contain insults, and when the audience laughs along, that laughter is often a nervous release of stress or an instinctive reaction of shock by the audience. Unsurprisingly, insults have a far more emotionally detrimental impact on their targets, especially if the victims are laughed at by a crowd rather than insulted in private. Furthermore, the emotional intensity of insults towers over the impact of praise, compliments, and honors.

Thus, such bullying can pierce the attention fog to reach mass audiences effectively, regardless of the emotional damage done to the target. Nobel Prize–winning economist Herbert Simon of Carnegie Mellon warned of information overload when, in the late 1960s, he coined the term "attention economy," stating, "A wealth of information creates a poverty of attention and a need to allocate that attention efficiently among the overabundance of information sources that might consume it." My former Harvard colleagues Thomas Davenport and John Beck's 2001 book *The Attention Economy: Understanding the New Currency of Business* explained that the supply of information has grown exponentially, while the amount of human attention is fixed, creating a fundamental economic problem.[3] And that was written a quarter century ago, before the quantum leaps of information from social media, streaming, and AI exacerbated that phenomenon even further.

Social psychologist Howard Garfinkel's 1967 book, *Studies in Ethnomethodology*, which created an entire subdiscipline, focused on how people's attention can be seized by transgressively breaking social norms.[4] The humor of the often startling *Seinfeld* show, "shock jocks" like Howard Stern, and comedians such as Don Rickles, Joan Rivers, Andrew Dice Clay, Jackie Mason, and Robert Smigel's puppet "Triumph the Insult Dog"—all of whom built their careers around violating social expectations with shocking, socially inappropriate pronouncements—reflect the efficiency of that approach.[5]

This prior generation of comedians and entertainers pioneered insult as art form, hurling crude barbs that audiences devoured, with an irrepressible mix of subversiveness, shock value, and a willingness, if not eagerness, to push conventional boundaries. Trump clearly internalized or perhaps intuited the key lesson from these insult comedians: Insults silence hecklers, disarm critics, and, most importantly, draw a crowd and keep them entertained.

Other business moguls have similarly used insult as spectacle. Ted Turner, the brash media tycoon, had such a penchant for controversial statements that his nicknames included "Captain Outrageous," "Terrible Ted," and "The Mouth of the South," reflecting his splashy stunts and his willingness to shock. Likewise, shock jocks like Howard Stern proved that salacious, taboo-breaking commentary attracted massive audiences and found ways to monetize that attention with commercial success. Trump appeared as a guest on Stern's shows and other similar formats (recall his "grab 'em by the p*ssy" shock comments on the Billy Bush tapes), and he also evidently intuited the format, the laughter, the ratings.

While Trump did not invent insult as spectacle, perhaps his genuinely original, novel insight was to fuse entertainment and politics. He understood intuitively what few others in politics previously grasped: Conversation is cluttered, attention is scarce, and repetition of the same dull clichés leaves audiences numb. The people were tired of conventional politicians speaking in politically correct ways.

To break through, one must not merely talk differently but talk memorably. Trump discovered long before entering politics that insults—vivid, personal, plainspoken, and preferably funny—stand out in a world of the information overload, and he transposed that same business model into American politics. His insults jolt, entertain, and linger. They turn stump speeches into spectacles, debates into theater, and a single leader into a cultural phenomenon. In this sense, Trump has mastered the art of becoming a shock entertainer with the largest stage of any performer in the world.

That's why Trump discards the conventional playbook of political rhetoric and oratory altogether. In politics, candidates typically echo poll-tested phrases: "working families," "invest in the future," "fight for you." These lines are safe but forgettable. More original candidates, such as JFK or Barack Obama, rally support with hopeful, uplifting, soaring oratory that inspires but can often leave followers disenchanted over time by the inevitable gap between promise and reality. Trump does none of this. When others say "my distinguished opponent," Trump says "Crooked Hillary." When others debate marginal tax rates, Trump says his rivals are "low energy," "little," or "lightweights." He rarely offers policy proposals or promises; he focuses on delivering the most entertaining version of the Trump show. His followers attend his rallies not to hear about tariffs or taxes but to be entertained and participate in his cultural glow. His insults, rather than his policy proposals, are the highlight reel across every media show. A Trump rally without nicknames and insults would be like a boxing match without punches.

The attraction is not unlike watching a car crash in real time to see how it will end up: shocking, unpredictable, impossible to look away, akin to a reality television show with the highest possible stakes. Audiences are transfixed, and even critics cannot look away. Insult ensures no sameness, no monotony, and absolutely, positively no boredom. Every event carries the promise of a new target, a new phrase, a new moment to be replayed on cable news and social media. The constant ostensible spontaneity makes every new moment freshly exciting and unpredictable. He is not just campaigning; he is performing.

This dual role—politician and entertainer—explains Trump's durability. Other politicians fade when the campaign ends or the policy promises fizzle into disappointment. The Trump Show, conversely, never stops, with a steady stream of new material created and spewed out to his followers on a daily, if not hourly, basis.

A METHOD TO THE MADNESS: THE ART OF TRUMP'S INSULT

When it comes to the art of Trump's insult, paradoxically, Trump doesn't have many arrows in his quiver. He relies on recycling the same tried-and-true gimmicks over and over, honing the timing, cadence, and targets of his insults to maximum effect.

Among his favorite and most effective are the mocking, derisive nicknames he bestows on his targets, which even his most fervent critics acknowledge are unerringly effective and catchy. Many of his nicknames—"Crooked Hillary," "Sleepy Joe," "Lil Marco," "Lyin' Ted," "Low-Energy Jeb," "Crazy Bernie," "Pocahontas Warren"—enter the cultural lexicon. The tactic of diminishing adversaries by reducing them to a label has proven devastatingly effective, especially as they invariably capture some shred of perceived truth about his targets' weaknesses, however unfair or exaggerated. Once affixed, these brands stick and take on lives of their own. Potent nicknames reduce opponents from complex, complicated human beings into caricatures, defined by and remembered for their most devastating, irredeemable weakness. This allows Trump to fully control the frame of reference, keeping his adversaries off-balance and on the defensive.

By repeating these nicknames relentlessly, Trump ensures that they overshadow his opponents' messaging and self-defenses. They reshape perception entirely. Hillary Clinton's policy proposals became irrelevant once "Crooked Hillary" dominated coverage; millions of Americans might not be able to say what Hillary planned to do on health care or trade, but they could sure remember how "Crooked" Hillary was. Jeb Bush's résumé mattered less than the image created by labeling him "low energy." This is branding and marketing 101, applied to politics. Trump, a real estate developer who stamped his name on every building he built, learned that repetition and branding cements identity. He branded his rivals as effectively as he branded his hotels.

Interestingly, despite Trump's prowess with nicknames, there are some adversaries for whom he has struggled to come up with an adequate nickname, those struggles apparent in plain sight. Consider how difficult it was for him to come up with an appropriate nickname for Kamala Harris, experimenting with a series of experimental monikers that fell flat, including "Laffin' Kamala" and "Comrade Kamala." Similarly, Trump has never quite come up with the right nickname to tar his predecessor, Barack Obama, with "Cheatin' Obama" failing to capture the hearts and minds of even his most diehard supporters. That fumble is a reminder that Trump's go-to tools do not always work, with some adversaries escaping being placed into a box so easily by lacking such distinguishably caricaturable weaknesses or vulnerabilities.

Another of Trump's favorite tricks is the disproportionate counterpunch. He has said, "If someone hits me, I hit back harder." This mantra nicely encapsulates his approach to insults and attacks. He rarely responds in kind. If a rival lands a glancing blow, his response is to bring out the sledgehammer. When a pundit questions his poll numbers, he does not merely rebut with data; he attacks their character, stamina, or appearance in viciously personal terms. The disproportionate escalation raises the stakes. The cost of criticizing him, or even correcting him, becomes too high, and rivals think twice before striking. It acts as a form of deterrence. Just as military strategists preach overwhelming retaliation to prevent future attacks, Trump applies overwhelming verbal force in the form of humiliating insults.

Consider, for example, when Senator Rand Paul took a jab at Trump's poll numbers in a 2015 debate, not without some basis in truth. Trump replied not by defending the poll numbers or by questioning Paul's own underwhelming polling but by viciously mocking Paul's looks in devastatingly personal terms, sneering that he should not even be on stage.[6] The message was clear: Criticism, no matter how minor or factual or legitimate, will be met with personal humiliation and massive escalation. There is no line between factual and personal disagreement; they become one and the same.

Another go-to tool in Trump's insult toolbox is humor as deflection. Many insults contain a strain of mean humor that his most rabid fans appreciate, which can either blunt the blow of cruelty or emphasize it. When audiences laugh, they give permission for the attack. That kind of humor, no matter how cruel, transforms hostility into entertainment.

Trump's treatment of Rosie O'Donnell illustrates this style of comic insult, no matter how mean. Years before his entry into politics, Trump clashed publicly with O'Donnell, calling her names, mocking her weight, and ridiculing her television career. The attacks were purposeful, because Trump knew not only that the feud would make for perfect tabloid fodder but also that O'Donnell was the perfect foil for Trump, and vice versa, given her public persona and all that she represents. In the 2015 presidential primary debate, Trump pulled out this card again to turn a serious political vulnerability into a flashpoint of Trumpian humor. When Megyn Kelly asked about his track record of disparagement of women, Trump glibly replied,

"Only Rosie O'Donnell," to uproarious audience laughter. This kind of humor works only when the audience laughs along, giving permission for transgressive humor, and laugh they did. The line landed with the GOP primary electorate, with Trump deflecting what Kelly perceived to be his misogynistic comments into a laugh line targeted at his most rabid supporters.[7]

Rather than deny or soften, he amplified. It shocked viewers, but in an unexpected and humorous way, if also cruel and unwarranted. In that moment, Trump turned what could have been a liability into an asset. By appearing candid and even funny to his base, he defied the conventions of apology politics and turned traditional rules on their head.

Of course, it should surprise nobody that Trump's sense of humor is unlike almost anyone else's. Though he can be funny, he is not "fun" by conventional standards, not the type to grab a beer after work, cracking casual jokes with colleagues. However, he does excel in finding opportunities to get audiences laughing along with him instead of at him, by finding foils and targets that unify disparate constituencies. Trump's humor is almost always laced with cruelty because there is, necessarily with this type of humor, always a butt of his jokes, some poor target being diminished or ridiculed. Without a foil, without a target, Trump has little humor and little ability to provoke or generate laughter.

The Rosie O'Donnell episode also illustrates Trump's ownership of, rather than apologetic approach to, humor. Where other politicians might deny or express regret, Trump repeats and doubles down. Rather than retreat from his misogynistic attacks on women, he owned the insult and doubled down by targeting Rosie O'Donnell. That moment crystallized the Trump playbook: Denial is weak. Retreat is boring, but repeating the insult, preferably louder and sharper, is powerful. Where others retreat, he doubles down and escalates. He violates norms and, in doing so, signals strength.

The adage "There's no such thing as bad publicity" is often attributed to the nineteenth-century Bridgeport, Connecticut, showman P. T. Barnum, who believed that any attention, even negative, was better than being ignored, because it enhanced name recognition and provided differentiation. Trump's flamboyant insults are rarely random expressions. Rather, he tends to be strategic and intentional with his timing, tone, and targeting, with surprising flexibility and ability to shape-shift. Consider, for example, how he dialed down his heated rhetoric about "Mexican rapists," which helped him rally the base in his 2016 candidacy, once Hispanic votes became crucial for his pathway to win the Electoral College in 2020 and 2024. In fact, during his 2024 campaign, he even released Hispanic language ads showing him dancing to salsa music—a head-spinning reversal of the Trump of 2016.[8] But that's Trump: where even insults can shift on a dime. At the end of the day, he views boredom and irrelevance as the most lethal threats of all.

By refusing sameness, Trump distinguishes himself from virtually every other politician. Politics is often monotonous, with candidates droning through similar talking points on similar issues. With Trump, insults guarantee unpredictability. No one knows what he will say next, which ensures constant attention in a media circus flywheel. This unpredictability fuels media coverage. Journalists, like audiences, cannot look away. Outrage is newsworthy. Shock ensures airtime. Trump's insults generate more coverage than policy, and more coverage means more dominance. Networks air his rallies live, knowing that put-downs will come and ratings will spike. He delivers spectacle. Politics becomes reality television.

To acknowledge the method behind Trump's ostensible madness does not mean ignoring the costs. Often his insults are mean-spirited, bigoted, and damaging, frequently directed at vulnerable groups, the weak, the underprivileged. They are usually unprovoked, cruelly damaging those least able to defend themselves. And critics point out that the collective impact has been to degrade societal discourse, corrode civility, and pull people apart.

Despite these costs, the method to the madness is worth understanding because of how effective this method can be. Most politicians would suffer career-ending backlash for comments deemed offensive. Trump, by contrast, often gains support. Many interpret his refusal to apologize as strength. For his base, it signals defiance of political correctness, an authenticity missing from conventional politics. His different style of speaking gives his followers the impression that he also *thinks* differently than other politicians, that his shocking words reflect unconventional thinking, his insults transcending rhetorical flourishes to become invitations to reconsider, jarring the listener into rethinking long-held precepts. That is a powerful impression—if often illusory. For every rejected cliché that forces reconsideration of outdated paradigms, there are many more times when it is all simply a branding exercise.

Trump's status as a "Sultan of Insult," for better or worse, is secure. He has uniquely weaponized mockery into a political art form, transforming weakness into perceived strength, criticism into cruel laughter, credible rivals into punchlines and caricatures. His insults are not random or impulsive but diabolically strategic, shocking, entertaining, and branding along the way.

In short, Trump weaponizes insults with intention. It is not theory derived from books but instinct derived from watching people, listening to reactions, and constantly iterating.

Trump drew from Ted Turner's outrageousness, Howard Stern's shock, Don Rickles's humor, and Joan Rivers's bite and transformed them into political ammunition. He discovered that insult, wielded disproportionately, deters rivals. Humor, injected into cruelty, entertains crowds. Ownership, not apology, signals authenticity.

Trump showed that politics could be theater, that insults could be strategy, that entertainment could be dominance. For his supporters, this was ineffable entertainment. For his critics, it was corrosive. But for all, it was unforgettable—and effective. Like a comedian gauging laughs, Trump adjusted in real time. He saw what drew attention, what stuck, what entertained. He has built a political movement on principles drawn from the world of entertainment. In doing so, he rewrote the rules of political communication.

CHAPTER 10

Donald the Great

The Role of Grandeur, Image, and Heroic Aura

In a curious twist of history, the thirtieth episode of the largely forgotten 1950s television show *Trackdown* featured a con man named Walter Trump, who claims he alone can save the masses from impending doom—by building a wall. The episode, which aired May 9, 1958, was titled "The End of the World." His shakedown scam worked on the villagers in a small Texas town until a Texas Ranger exposed the hoax and arrested him for fraud and larceny.[1] The Trump of that TV series was a villainous scammer, a huckster exploiting and manipulating people's fear. While he would resent that exaggerated and overwrought characterization, the real Trump, with his brash confidence and "I alone can fix things" self-confidence, might perhaps recognize certain uncanny parallels in his TV predecessor of the same name. In fact, *Washington Post* journalist Bob Woodward's 2018 book on the Trump administration, *Fear: Trump in the White House*, cited some of the many ways Trump manufactures or inflames public anxiety to then present himself as a savior.[2]

Presidents traditionally couch their appeals in collectivity—we the people, together, united we stand, and so on—but Trump's rhetoric is a blatant inversion of that. He habitually presents himself in the singular: "I alone can fix it," he memorably declared in his convention speech. He routinely casts himself as not a mere candidate or even a mere mortal but a savior, presenting himself in almost messianic terms.

There are many such parallels to anthropologist Joseph Campbell's classic research on the monomyth of the hero across continents, cultures, centuries, and civilizations, where the hero's journey seeks to prove their greatness and valor in Odyssean adventures, through necessary trials of resilience from failure and near-death crises.[3] In my own book *The Hero's Farewell*, I differentiate two heroic drives with different psychological motives and different societal purposes. One, *heroic mission*, is driven by a quest for immortality through lasting contributions. The other, *heroic identity*, is driven by a quest for stature and an image of elevated, even unique, power.[4]

Trump's presentation of himself in almost messianic terms is not merely campaign rhetoric but rather a worldview. In Trump's universe, it's all about Trump. Cabinet secretaries are diminished, generals are sidelined, and institutions are ignored. Trump believes in Trump first and foremost, comparing himself without a shred of exaggeration or doubt in his own mind to Lincoln, to Washington, and to even larger mythic figures. His claims to singular greatness have become central to his self-perpetuated mythic story.

Many were surprised when in December 2025 President Trump announced the creation of a new fleet of guided-missile warships to be called Trump-class battleships. That same month, ticket sales plummeted and artists performances were cancelled at the John F. Kennedy Center for the Performing Arts when Trump put his own name on this cultural institution. Such historically unparalleled, grandiose moves should not have been a shock to the public.

Trump is not the first president to appeal to such grandiosity. Prior US presidents such as FDR, Teddy Roosevelt, and Ronald

Reagan also knowingly cultivated such auras of heroic stature with exciting fanfare through sweeping, inspiring ceremonies exhibiting pomp and grandeur. Perhaps a bit of grandiosity is a requisite for the position. Jimmy Carter's humble, low-key persona—even carrying his own bags and doing his own chores—worked against him. I became personally friendly with Carter and found that while he had an ego, it manifested in the self-righteousness of his positions and his judgment of others rather than through public displays of grandiosity.[5]

It is ironic, however, that Trump so often uses George Washington and Abraham Lincoln as his benchmarks or "gold standards," as they were renowned for their personal humility and lack of self-declared grandeur yet still enjoyed enormous acclaim as colossal leaders—even though, or perhaps in part because, they did not rely on cheap devices of self-aggrandizement but were victorious due to their bold visions and humble, skillful execution. Biographer Ron Chernow in *Washington: A Life* detailed Washington's consistent reluctance to assume power.[6] When he was given command of the Continental Army in 1775, he expressed reluctance that he was not up to the enormity of the role. He was cautious about serving as president and about curtailing his own exercise of power, as he did not want to be seen as establishing a tradition of reassembled military dictatorships. Biographer Joseph J. Ellis documented the "truly exceptional character" of Washington's voluntary surrender of power, both as commander-in-chief and president, in works such as *His Excellency*, stating that Washington was afraid that creating a model of leaders who die in office would undermine the foundations of the new republic.[7] Yet another renowned Washington biographer, Garry Wills, in *Cincinnatus: George Washington and the Enlightenment* likened our first president to the classical parallel of the Roman general Cincinnatus, who returned to his farm after saving the republic, representing a strong symbol of civic virtue and the peaceful transfer of power.

Thus, few who studied Washington would ever conflate his leadership contributions and style with Trump's. The same is true of Abraham Lincoln's lack of grandiosity. His humble origins in a log cabin were iconic to his image as a "self-made man" who understood the struggles of ordinary people. He was renowned for his humility and was not someone trumpeting or touting his own sense of destiny. His distinguished biographers, including Carl Sandburg, David Herbert Donald, and Doris Kearns Goodwin, all described his preternatural self-awareness, his unpretentious lifestyle, and his authentic self-effacing voice, even regarding his physical appearance. During one debate, Stephen Douglas accused Lincoln of being "two-faced." Lincoln, drawing on his great wit, supposedly replied, "If I had another face, do you think I'd wear this one?"[8] That kind of self-deprecating humor is hardly characteristic of Trump.

Of course, the humility that defined the leadership of Washington and Lincoln is exceedingly rare. Across American history, presidents have flirted with the trappings of grandeur. Long before Trump, presidential politics had already drifted into the territory that Arthur Schlesinger Jr. famously labeled *The Imperial Presidency*—an office swollen beyond constitutional design, buoyed by ceremony, image, and a public appetite for executive mythmaking. The presidency, Schlesinger warned, had accumulated the symbols and prerogatives of an "imperial court," complete with its own rituals, courtiers, and carefully choreographed displays of executive majesty, undermining the other coequal branches of government through increasing executive prerogative and far exceeding what the framers of the Constitution had in mind.

Franklin D. Roosevelt understood this dynamic long before the term "imperial presidency" entered the lexicon. His 1940 bid for a third term stands as a master class in presidential stagecraft—the kind of political theater that Theodore H. White, in his later *Making of the President* chronicles, would treat as foundational to the modern performative nature of the presidency. Publicly, Roosevelt maintained the posture of a reluctant statesman, telling reporters in the spring of 1940, "I have no wish to run for a third term; I do not choose to run—unless circumstances should require me to continue."

Behind the scenes, however, Roosevelt had already resolved to stay in the race. The Democratic National Convention in Chicago became the stage for what was billed as a "spontaneous" draft Roosevelt movement—but was, in truth, a meticulously choreographed pageant. The Chicago Stadium, stifling under July heat and thick with cigar smoke, pulsed with orchestrated anticipation. Delegates, as well as busloads of municipal workers brought in just for the occasion, had been primed to erupt at prearranged moments. When the pre-agreed signal words were spoken—"No man has the right to turn his back on destiny"—on cue, the hall exploded in chants of "We Want Roosevelt!" a tidal roar so overwhelming that veteran political reporters later admitted they were momentarily deafened. What they didn't know was that loudspeakers had been placed strategically across the venue to amplify the chants—a sign of just how choreographed the entire "spontaneous" episode really was.

Roosevelt himself, listening by telephone from the White House, received breathless updates on the unfolding drama. The dimming of the lights, the sudden illumination of his portrait, the scripted pleas for continuity in a world on the brink of war—all of it echoed Schlesinger's "imperial presidency." FDR's mastery of political theater transformed the convention ritual into a coronation, blurring the lines between democratic acclamation and imperial inevitability. In Chicago that summer, the presidency was no longer simply an office; it was becoming a stage on which power itself could be performed.

Even if Trump has never heard of the 1940 "Draft Roosevelt" campaign, he has intuited the performative nature of power and of politics, and the necessity of building an image of inevitability through grandeur. The use of heroic stature as a device can feed the ego of a strong leader, but it also can provide reassuring confidence to a leader's constituents that he or she has a greater, almost regal authority and is worthy of following. It implies that they may know far more than the rest of us and possess powers to save us from shared peril.

Trump implicitly understands that chutzpah is necessary to transcend ordinary constraints and achieve heroic, even mythic stature. He is constantly inventing and perpetuating his own heroic myth.

DONALD THE GREAT: THE ROLE OF ILLUSION AND HEROIC AURA

Nobody ever called Alexander III of Macedonia Alexander the Great until he invented the title, claiming a false lineage to Odysseus and Achilles. Trump implicitly understands that type of chutzpah is necessary to transcend ordinary constraints and achieve heroic, even mythic stature. He is constantly inventing and perpetuating his own heroic myth, acting as his own best salesman.[9]

Carefully cultivating that heroic stature and that image is what has allowed Trump to become "Teflon Don," transcending the quicksand of wonkish policy traps, failed promises, risqué personal scandals and shortcomings, and even felony criminal convictions that would have sunk any lesser politico eons ago. To Trump's followers, there is a mythic, almost messianic quality to the man, as if he were

Where else would Trump take a group of visiting EU leaders but to the MAGA gift store in the White House for a display of MAGA merchandise?

a savior. In times of great economic uncertainty and global security risk, people search for strong, confident leaders who purport to know and see more than the rest of us.

Trump has mastered the paradox of a political base with deep-seated populist resentment of snobby cultural elites and exclusive institutions but that also celebrates recipes for success and shows of wealth. Throughout history, Americans actually identify with success and do not resent it as long as it is obtained fairly, across athletic, artistic, entrepreneurial, technological, and financial success—which is why the self-help literature in magazines, books, and websites has always sold so well. Popular examples through the ages include Benjamin Franklin's proverbs in *Poor Richard's Almanack* of 1732, Dale

Carnegie's 1936 *How to Win Friends and Influence People*, Norman Vincent Peale's 1952 *The Power of Positive Thinking*, and Stephen Covey's 1989 guide *The 7 Habits of Highly Effective People*.

Trump delivers to the masses a notion, justified or not, that success can be achieved via understandable, transparent formulas, befitting the Alger tradition—even though, ironically, the Horatio Alger "rags to riches" myth is a media creation. The real Horatio Alger was a pedophiliac minister from Brewster, Massachusetts, who fled to New York to write formulaic short stories for newspapers. He died penniless in 1899. However, decades later, a New York author created a fictionalized biography fusing Alger's name with the image of self-made business success to sell to a nation eager for a hero. While lacking veracity, the Alger myth speaks to the wellsprings of American motivation into which Trump taps, the inherent attraction of an ostensible self-made success story.[10]

As Thorstein Veblen's *Theory of the Leisure Class* predicted in 1899, rather than resent success as Marx anticipated, Americans would seek to emulate the successful. Trump plays to that desire for success and the belief in a fluid American class structure.[11] With Trump, there is the added dimension that, like a reality television show playing out live in front of your eyes, the fate of his high-wire act depends on you, his audience. That is an irresistible setup, even for his critics. As Michael Wolff alluded, it's "all or nothing": Either you elect me or I go to jail and lose my fortune. You, the audience, hold my fate in your hands. Nobody can turn away from such a spectacular setup, with critics and supporters alike eager to find out whether Trump wins—or loses, in which case jail and bankruptcy likely await.[12]

It's unlikely that Trump has heard of Leo Braudy's concept in *The Frenzy of Renown*, but he seems to have intuited the key points. Braudy argues that fame breeds more fame; renown is insatiable, demanding constant renewal. Once on the stage, one cannot step off without vanishing. Trump embodies this principle perfectly.[13]

Every trophy requires another. Every superlative must be topped. The Kennedy Center Honors were not enough; he needed to chair the Kennedy Center, and rename the Kennedy Center after himself. Hosting *Saturday Night Live* was fun only while he was adored; once lampooned, he declared the show unwatchable. *Time* magazine's "Person of the Year" thrilled him until *Time* came out with an unflattering cover. Then it became "rigged."

Braudy's framework explains Trump's constant pursuit of validation. Grandeur for him is never static; it is a treadmill. In his perpetual quest to build and sustain that grandeur, one might say Trump has ended up living much of his life as what the Platters once sang about in their 1956 Billboard #1 hit, "The Great Pretender." The song's lyrics—about putting on a show of gladness while masking the truth—were meant as balladry, but for Trump they could almost serve as a biography.

Everything in Trump's orbit is the biggest, the greatest, the largest, the grandest. Numbers are inflated, floors invented, crowds expanded. His first inauguration crowd had to be the biggest ever, even if he had to draw up dubious photos and order his spokesman to stretch the truth to make it so. It's why if you've ever been in the elevator bank of any Trump skyscraper, you'll notice that there are more floor buttons than actual floors, a classic Trump trick to make you think there are more levels than there actually are, with a bunch of decoy buttons supporting the illusion. Even his language obeys the rule of the superlative. He is never content with "large." It must be "the largest ever." He cannot leave "good" unembellished; it must be "the greatest in history." Stretched numbers, like fake floors in Trump Tower, are not slips—they are the design. As Susie Wiles, his chief of staff, told Chris Whipple of *Vanity Fair*, Trump has "an alcoholic's personality." He "operates [with] a view that there's nothing he can't do. Nothing, zero, nothing."[14]

Trump memorably quipped, "I don't like to analyze myself because I might not like what I see," all but acknowledging that he is a Freudian psychoanalyst's dream. An analyst might well attribute his grandiose behavior to a manifestation of a unique combination of insecurities and idiosyncrasies deriving from his past.[14]

Of course, nobody can understand how Donald Trump became Donald Trump without first looking at the influence of his domineering, harsh, dismissive father, Fred Trump. From the Freudian view, it is hard not to see the endless boasting of the adult Trump as an unending quest to prove and validate himself to a father who never believed anything he did was ever enough, one who constantly made a younger Donald feel unworthy, humiliated, and beaten down.

That unending Oedipal battle, equal parts rebellion against authority and desperate quest to please, is combined with the classic outer-borough chip-on-his-shoulder edge where grandiosity compensates for insecurity of origin and pedigree. Born in Queens, in a modest brick home in middle-class Jamaica Hills, Trump longed to prove himself to Manhattan—that he belonged among the power and

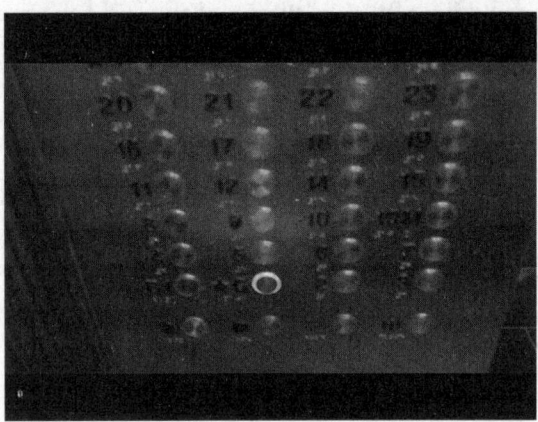

If you've ever been in the elevator bank of any Trump skyscraper, you'll notice that there are more floor buttons than actual floors, a classic Trump trick to make you think there are more levels than there actually are, with a bunch of decoy buttons that don't work supporting the illusion.

Nobody can understand how Donald Trump became Donald Trump without first looking at the influence of his domineering, harsh, dismissive father, Fred Trump.

moneyed elite, and in more respectable company. To cross the East River from Queens to Manhattan was more than just transcending geography or origin; it was transcending class and status. That's why Trump has never bothered playing in the Queens real estate businesses where his father made the family's fortune; it's always been about building in Manhattan from the very start. It was Manhattan or bust for far more than economic reasons.

That grandiosity may also stem from a third factor, far less understood. This third factor has seemingly eluded even many critics of Trump, which is that Trump has built his image of business tycoon on somewhat precarious foundations. Despite presenting himself as a real estate titan, unlike CEOs of multinational corporations who climbed corporate ladders and answered to independent boards, Trump never truly helmed a large, public company. His company, even at its peak, has always been organized as a rather haphazard family business and has never been close to entering the Fortune 500, in stark contrast to genuine business titans who have founded and run some of the world's largest, most well-known corporations. The scale of his Trump Organization real estate activities, while not insignificant, was dwarfed by those whom Trump liked to consider his peers, real estate tycoons such as Sam Zell and Steve Schwarzman.

Together, these insecurities fused into a relentless, never-enough, always-striving drive to project success and surround himself with grandeur that serves as armor. Other very wealthy politicians radiated noblesse oblige across the political spectrum, such as Ned Lamont in Connecticut—grandson of Thomas Lamont, handpicked protégé of J. P. Morgan—or the Rockefellers before him. They were men who exhibited a quiet assurance that came with inherited stature, whereas Trump substituted noise, spectacle, and self-promotion. He was not of Manhattan's old aristocracy, so he became its loudest, greatest pretender.

GRANDIOSITY TRUMP STYLE: CLASS FOR THE MASSES

That contrast between patrician, wealthy noblesse oblige politicians and Trump's distinctly opposite style carries into far more than just political approach and self-presentation. It extends into every aspect of his being, including his tastes and his style.

For patrician types, grandeur is usually understated. The Rockefellers' townhouses and the patrician clubs of Manhattan radiate restraint, marked by understated but priceless works of art rather than gawk-inspiring shows of brazen, brash wealth. True wealth, the argument goes, does not need to shout. That, of course, has never been Trump's design playbook.

By gilding his buildings, plastering his name everywhere in giant letters, and putting gold leaf where others would put wood or stone, Trump created a visual vocabulary of success that people could easily and immediately understand. The shimmer did not require insider knowledge of pedigree or lineage or understanding of the subtler signs of wealth. You didn't need to know who his grandfather was or which private school he attended. You only needed to look at the gold. That's why Trump has gold everywhere. He is obsessed with gold, because gold screams money to the masses.

Just think of how infatuated Trump is with gold.[15] He places brazen, over-the-top displays of it everywhere and anywhere possible. Trump Tower on Fifth Avenue set the template. Completed in 1983, the skyscraper's lobby features a six-story atrium clad in pink marble with eighty-foot waterfalls. But the element that dominated every review, every tourist photo, every promotional brochure was all the glittering gold. Escalators were flanked by polished brass railings that gleamed like treasure. Doors were trimmed in gold. Fixtures were gilded. Even the air seemed to shimmer.

Trump made gold not just an accent but also a brand identity. His personal apartment at the top of the tower was covered in gilded molding, gold-leaf ceilings, and gold-plated fixtures. When journalists were given tours, they invariably wrote about the gold.

This obsession carried into his casinos in Atlantic City. The Trump Taj Mahal, opened in 1990, was marketed as "the eighth wonder of the world." Its chandeliers sparkled with crystal. Its signage was edged with gold. Even the slot machines were designed to glitter.

Trump is now trying to import that same golden style to the White House, not just metaphysically by calling his presidency a new "golden age" but literally, physically. Trump redecorated the Executive Mansion in a more gilded style, with gold ornament and trim across the once-sedate Oval Office, and bulldozed the East Wing of the White House to construct a new, gold-laced grand ballroom. He even redesigned the Oval Office curtains in gold tones. Plus, of course, abundant gold trim is a hallmark of his new Air Force One plane, "donated" by the Qataris.

With Trump, it's over-the-top gold, all the time.

That captures Trump's entire shtick: class for the masses. He democratizes the performance of luxury, almost in a comically over-the-top, exaggeratedly accessible and understandable way. He offered middle-class tourists the chance to walk through Trump Tower's golden atrium, ride its escalators, bask in a glow that felt like royalty. His casinos and hotels did the same. His gold was accessible luxury, not behind velvet ropes but displayed in lobbies and atriums for all to experience. It was a performance anyone could consume. It's the kind of ostentatious shows of wealth that make people who've never enjoyed wealth think, *That's how I would live if I made $1 billion overnight.*

Gawking at all that gold is the whole point. Trump wants people to gawk, he wants to throw so much gold around that it is understood as brazenly over-the-top, because it is the whole point of class for the masses. It's why he has a private jet that was nicknamed "Trump Force One," even before he became president. It's why he purchased what was then the world's largest yacht from the Saudi royal family, which he promptly renamed the *Trump Princess*. It's why his name is stamped on all his buildings so prominently. It's why Trump shows off a silent, smiling Melania, expecting her to perform as the perfect trophy wife. All of this is not so much business or even utility as much as one great big performance, to show that he is living the great dream and that "this is how you would live if you had my money." What it all amounts to is one giant, continuous billboard of Trumpian grandeur, giving his followers the opportunity to see in all that gold-plated bravado a reflection of their own most brazen, Id-esque aspirations.

That's also why building physical spaces is so essential to the Trump image. Trump is always obsessing over the smallest details in his construction projects, because he knows that for his followers, his

There are echoes of the ancient Roman phrase "bread and circuses" in Trump's playbook of delivering class to the masses.

buildings are a reflection of how they see him. For Trump, a building is a physical manifestation and expression of his heroic drive, of the image he wishes to present to the world.

It was hardly an accident that even though as president he was weighing consequential global diplomatic and economic issues, one of his personal pet projects became the demolition of the East Wing of the White House and the building of a new, grand ballroom. Trump admitted that this was a project that mattered very much to him personally, and indeed, he had expressed fascination with the idea of building a White House ballroom even before he became president, cold-ringing advisors to President Barack Obama to try to sell them on the concept.[16]

For Trump, the ballroom is so much more than an event space serving a practical need: to host grand affairs at the White House without having to set up tents on the lawn, even if that might be the official rationale and not untrue. But it runs far deeper than that. The ballroom is Trump leaving his physical imprint on the most iconic of American sites, the White House, for generations to come, creating a physical legacy through tangible monuments and physical spaces. That is the same motivation driving the proposed "Arc de Trump," with Trump hoping to construct a new monument in DC with echoes of the Arc de Triomphe in Paris. For him, all these physical monuments he constructs, whether skyscrapers or ballrooms or arches, are physical reflections of his heroic aura and the grandiose image he wishes to present to his followers at all times.

That grandiosity is manifest in the distinctly unnatural, idiosyncratic way Trump refers to himself in the third person when telling stories, almost always addressing himself as "Sir." If there aren't enough voices of supplicants to feed him what he wants to hear, he'll even masquerade as someone else to feed the chorus. Take the now famous story of him inventing the John Barron persona in the 1980s, supposedly his spokesman. When reporters called the Trump Organization for comment, Barron would answer the phone, affect a slightly altered voice, and praise Donald Trump in the third person. "Mr. Trump is a great success," Barron would say, "very rich, very powerful."[17] The charade was transparent, with Trump only slightly adjusting his real voice, but it captures the fact that if no one else would flatter him sufficiently, he would invent and impersonate someone who did. This self-conjured spokesman demonstrates the core of Trump's leadership style: He manufactures grandeur when reality withholds it and envelops himself in the false persona he created.

The danger of this heroic self-image comes when all the grandiosity melds into megalomania and demagoguery. Charisma can spark group spirit and lead to great collective accomplishment, but it can also lead to a series of pathologies when it spirals out of control, sans any guardrails.

Unconstrained grandiosity can be almost diametrically at odds with how a society based on norms, shared values, and respect for systems was designed to operate. Consider how the institutions of democratic society thrive on humility, on the recognition that no single leader embodies the greater whole. Grandiose leaders see institutions as obstacles to personal glory. Frequent attacks on the judiciary, the intelligence community, his own Department of Justice, and so many more entities reflect this impulse to dismiss institutional constraints as unfair or "deep state" conspiracies. If courts are dismissed as biased, if elections are claimed to be rigged, if independent agencies are painted as enemies, then citizens lose trust in the very systems that sustain democracy. Delusions of grandeur personalize power in a way that hollows out institutional expertise. Such excess sidelines experts, distrusts process, and leads to critical decisions being made on impulse, confident that instincts are superior to analysis.

The weakening of alliances is the flip side of the same coin. Grandeur thrives on bilateral theater—two leaders on a stage, two flags, two handshakes. Multilateralism, by contrast, dilutes the spotlight.

Trump shows consistent disdain for NATO, the G7, and other international institutions and multilateral fora, which dilute the Trump show with what he perceives to be clingers-on and flunkies from "sh*thole countries" stealing his spotlight. Unsurprisingly, Trump much prefers one-on-one summits where he can dominate.

This approach often leaves natural allies uncertain of their place and adversaries emboldened. When grandeur dictates policy, loyalty is measured not in shared values but in personal deference, as personal relations become the only currency of the realm. Leaders who flatter Trump are embraced; those who criticize him are scorned. Such a framework undermines collective alliances and partnerships, replacing them with volatile relationships centered on ego and obsequiousness toward Trump and Trump alone. Leaders abroad learned that flattering Trump—praising him personally, hosting him with pomp, awarding him symbolic trophies—could win concessions. Whether it was a military parade in Paris or a royal welcome in Riyadh, spectacle often outweighed substance. Critics argue that such excesses fracture democratic norms, turning politics into little more than one big, continuous cult of personality where supplicants perpetually try to outdo one another in their ostentatious displays of complete, subservient fealty.

Perhaps it's little surprise that a president who is constantly promoting a grandiose view of himself as the greatest in history is unlikely to lose much sleep over the constitutional limits of his office. Trump frequently described Article II of the Constitution as giving him "the right to do whatever I want." This was not a slip of the tongue or mere braggadocio, but a fundamental worldview rooted in that same grandiosity: that he, as president, was above checks and balances. Trump even went so far as to echo Napoleon's declaration that "he who saves his Country does not violate any law."

Critics such as distinguished political scientists Tim Snyder, Anne Applebaum, and Jason Stanley or renowned legal scholars such as Laurence Tribe and Judge Michael Luttig argue these delusions of grandeur create fertile ground for creeping authoritarianism, sounding the drumbeats of alarm practically every day on TV shows such as CNN's *Erin Burnett OutFront*, MSNBC's *Last Word with Lawrence O'Donnell*, and MSNBC's *Morning Joe*.

To them, it was only a matter of time before a leader who sees himself as uniquely indispensable would chafe against electoral limits, which is why many of those who knew Trump best were already warning that he would try to subvert the 2020 election long before he claimed the election was stolen from him. Likewise, it comes as no surprise to those same voices now that Trump is musing about serving more than two terms, praising leaders who held power for life, and continuing to cast doubt on the legitimacy of elections that do not favor him while doing everything he can to subvert the rules of fair play in the electoral process, whether through brazen mid-decade gerrymanders or flippant interference with state and local electoral officials.

Critics argue that Trump's grandiosity is shattering norms, weakening institutions, and rupturing alliances.

Of course, the other side of Trump's obsession with grandiosity and delusions of grandeur is an inevitable fragility beneath all the glitz and glam. Gold plating, after all, is only a thin veneer. Inflated numbers—inflated crowds, inflated vote counts, made-up numbers—are easily punctured by reality. Yet because grandeur depends on constant reinforcement, every contradiction becomes a threat.

This fragility helps explain Trump's hostility to satire (think *Jimmy Kimmel*), to criticism (the press), to oversight (Congress). His first instinct is to attack anything that tarnishes the gold-plated image of himself that he is constantly creating. A leader who sees cracks as existential cannot tolerate dissent. The result is that preserving that fragile illusion of greatness, no matter at what cost, becomes the only real, overarching leadership priority.

When such a quest for heroic stature and grandiose identity overtakes the quest for heroic mission, the coveted frenzy of renown is short-lived. The ephemeral nature of fame is made concrete in the Kinks' wistful 1972 hit song "Celluloid Heroes" with these lyrics:

> Everybody's a dreamer
> And everybody's a star
> And everybody's in movies
> It doesn't matter who you are
> There are stars in every city
> In every house and on every street
> And if you walk down Hollywood Boulevard
> Their names are written in concrete. . . .
>
> You can see all the stars as you walk down Hollywood Boulevard
> Some that you recognize, some that you've hardly even heard of
> People who worked and suffered and struggled for fame
> Some who succeeded and some who suffered in vain

The futility of leaders arrogantly seeking fame for fame's sake alone is warned about even more starkly in the 1818 sonnet "Ozymandias" by English Romantic poet Percy Bysshe Shelley, invoking the Greek name for Egyptian pharaoh Ramesses II:

> I met a traveller from an antique land
> Who said: Two vast and trunkless legs of stone
> Stand in the desert. Near them, on the sand,
> Half sunk, a shattered visage lies, whose frown,
> And wrinkled lip, and sneer of cold command,
> Tell that its sculptor well those passions read
> Which yet survive, stamped on these lifeless things,
> The hand that mocked them and the heart that fed:
> And on the pedestal these words appear:
> "My name is Ozymandias, King of Kings:
> Look on my works, ye Mighty, and despair!"
> No thing beside remains. Round the decay
> Of that colossal wreck, boundless and bare
> The lone and level sands stretch far away.

For all his sneering arrogance and trappings of conceit, this once-almighty but long-forgotten pharaoh was unprotected by the ravages of the sands of time. The cold indifference of history buried this grandiose tyrant in the oblivion of the desert sands—a haunting reminder that even the greatest of leaders are but fleeting shadows in the long arc of history. Not that Trump loses any sleep over such lessons, for he exists entirely in the present: For him, the only power that matters is the power he can wield in the here and now.

CONCLUSION

In this book, I have put forward an explanation for how Donald Trump leads, his strategic road map, and how he thinks, based on my quarter century of personal history as an advisor, friend, critic, adversary, and everything in between, and based on my five-decade anchoring as a scholar of leadership. I have tried to analyze his leadership strategies as factually and objectively as I can, regardless of what you, the reader, might think or feel about Trump personally. As noted earlier, his son-in-law Jared Kushner has repeatedly told my Yale CEO forums, "Before you judge Donald Trump, you have to understand him. He thinks differently than you do."

This background allows me to explain Trump's leadership style not as an anomaly or as mere impulsiveness but rather as a strategic model that contains its own logic. For his actions have shown time and time again: Trump lives by his own Ten Commandments. He may not be a religious person, but he has strategic guidelines that he follows. They are not Moses's laws from Sinai governing ethical conduct; they are his own rules for gaining, wielding, and keeping power, politically incorrect and often uninformed by societal norms, conventional wisdom, or prevailing groupthink, yet startlingly effective and street-savvy. Many of them are, surely to his surprise, anchored in decades of supportive scholarship.

Where popular leadership doctrines and trendy "how-to" manuals promote emotional intelligence, servant leadership, empowerment, and consensus decision-making—all of which preach empathy, contrition, and humility—Trump practices much the opposite: domination and rigid self-assurance, never admitting an error. His commandments explain how he came to seize control, neuter, and manipulate power centers long thought impregnable to a single domineering individual, whether that be political parties, government agencies, international coalitions, or the media.

Unlike predecessors who avoided third rails and sacred pillars—religion, veterans, revered predecessors, and the like—Trump shows that he bows to no one. He takes on every base of power without fear or hesitation.

The key insight about how Donald Trump leads is that he is the sun around which all else must revolve in the Trump solar system. Power must not reside in institutions, collectives, or equals; all power must radiate from Trump himself. If he is not at the center of an event, then in his retelling it is not important, or it did not happen.

Trump does not like dealing with equals. If he cannot humble the other party, he will likely not engage with them at all. Negotiation, compromise, even friendship must reaffirm his dominance. Subordinates compete for his blessing, and those who drift too far or shine too brightly are cast out.

Because power cannot flow from elsewhere, there is a reliance on dividing and conquering. Unified coalitions are threats to his authority, collective action intolerable. Rivals must be set against each other, drawn into draining, internecine squabbles so that Trump, and Trump alone, can rise above the chaos, pivoting deftly between warring parties fighting for his attention and blessing. He becomes the all-powerful arbiter; and all genuine power is consolidated in the central force that is Trump, never another center of gravity.

In Trump's idealized narrative, there are no ups and downs in his journey anymore. The life of Trump consists not of wins and losses; it is win upon win, regardless of the facts. Failed ventures are spun as successes; bankruptcies spun as strategic savvy; electoral defeats recast as election fraud. Admitting loss in any context would mean diminishing his own grandiose myth of Trump, who is always succeeding, always climbing upward, never falling, let alone—dare anyone even say—failing.

While Trump has many cronies and followers, when it comes to picking friends, he cares almost exclusively about whether you bring him something he needs or serve some purpose for him. Once you cannot, you are prone to being discarded. With his world divided into winners and losers, there is little middle ground to get by with. Failure is not situational but contagious, a viral disease that taints all who associate with it. Yet with losers who are down-and-out, yet retain some constituency that Trump finds useful, he won't hesitate to "help" if he sees something in it for himself. This worldview produces the fluidity of friends: insiders one week, enemies the next. Allies must constantly re-prove themselves and demonstrate their value to avoid outliving their usefulness. Gratitude for past help is a quality in short supply, while enemies are enemies only so long as Trump thinks it's a fight he can win. Contrary to the myth that Trump is all vindictiveness all the time, he will pick a fight only if he thinks he has the clear upper hand against a weaker, intransigent foe and if he believes his target to be broadly unsympathetic. Just as often, he tries to drown the squeaky wheel in oil rather than try to replace it or throw it out completely.

Trump drowns out failure, and any other bad news, with the Trump Perpetual Noise Machine. Like Phil Spector's production, the "Wall of Sound," it overwhelms with sheer volume—slogans, tweets, headlines, outrages. The cacophony completely drowns any murmurs of failure or any cycle of bad news, for Trump is continually defining and owning the news cycle on his own terms through perpetually tossing out new distractions and diversions.

Some of these diversions will seem ludicrous at first, but the sleeper effect is one of Trump's most potent tools. He repeats his assertions so many times that even the most dubious gradually become conventionally accepted facts. This tactic blurs reality. Repeatedly, insistently, Trump claims singular vision: *I, and I alone, can fix things.*

All roads lead back to the world as seen by Donald Trump—Donald the Great. The consistency of this worldview makes him less a conventional leader than the axis around which followers, institutions, and critics all revolve. That is the fundamental dynamic that Trump is constantly trying to create around him, whether it is in engaging with his inner circle, how he runs his businesses, or, as he puts it, how he runs the country and the world.

This framework matters because most observers—critics and allies alike—react to Trump. They do not anticipate him. They are tied in knots, surprised again and again by his "unprecedented" actions, believing him to be unpredictable and capricious. By grasping his Ten Commandments, one can predict rather than merely respond. One can seek to understand not only what Trump does but why he does it, and what the underlying logic is, by seeing the world as Trump sees it and thinking as Trump thinks. Everybody from world leaders to business titans, political rivals, loyal lieutenants, foreign heads of state, and everyday citizens need to understand these Ten Commandments to comprehend Trump's leadership and try to influence his rule.

Regardless of how a reader of this book leans politically, if they seek to influence the actions of Trump and any charismatic leader who attempts to follow in his path from across the political spectrum, they must get past the paralysis of surprise, frustration, and hopeless resignation to understand the levers of influence revealed in each of these Ten Commandments. Within each of these Ten

Commandments, there are lessons in how to work with and against strong leaders such as Trump as well as lessons in how to lead and how not to lead.

1. The Hub-and-Spokes Model: Centralizing All Power in Your Own Hands

Theorists such as Max Weber celebrated bureaucracy as a system of structure to allocate resources fairly and wisely, undercutting the capriciousness of bosses and bullies. Trump is in the business of undermining bureaucratic structures, to the delight of some and the horror of others. His natural state is not to delegate any real authority or to be transparent about his next moves unless they serve his interests at that moment. Allies and adversaries alike should take care in considering whether to grant him the unconstrained leeway to make his governance structure as fluid as he intends for himself.

2. The Real Art of Trump's Deal: Start with a Punch in the Face Versus Building Trust

If you go into a negotiation with Trump or a similar strong leader, wear a helmet, prepare to be struck, and don't be surprised by the trauma he inflicts on you to start with. That is merely his opening bid, intended to throw you off course before negotiations even really begin. If you lose your balance or composure, you've lost the negotiation already.

3. Divide and Conquer: Build Walls, Not Bridges

When up against a leader who relies on divide and conquer, you will not succeed on your own even if you are one of the wealthiest people in the world. You need alliances across parties and diverse constituencies. These alliances not only provide air cover and strength in numbers but, more importantly, can centralize resources and constituencies that a strong leader cannot afford to alienate simultaneously. Only collective action can neutralize a bully.

4. How Trump Makes Money: The Art of Stealing the Deal—Heads I Win, Tails You Lose

Your negotiations have to begin with you privately knowing the worst case deal you could possibly accept. And be prepared to walk promptly when it goes below that threshold, or else, before you know it, you'll be stuck holding the bag, left with only downside risk and little to no participation in any upside.

5. Trump Behind Closed Doors One-On-One: The Fluidity of Friends, Foils, and Foes

It costs you nothing to show respect for Trump privately and to acknowledge his flashes of warmth and authentic charm. You should seek to build on his positive qualities through positive reinforcement, but also subtly remind him of your rock-solid foundations of authority and that your standing does not depend on his blessing. Otherwise you are already cornered.

6. The Wall of Sound: Trump's Perpetual Noise Machine of Constant, Overwhelming Distractions

Focus, focus, focus. Trump is a master distraction artist, and if you take his bait and go down diversionary paths, you have virtually conceded to his framing of the world. You should stay relentlessly focused on your own objectives and message no matter how many diversions are tossed out.

7. Trump's World of Winners and Losers: Class for the Masses, Avoiding Losers like the Plague, and Selective Retribution

If you seek to persuade constructively, you have to approach from a position of strength. Coming in with grievances and complaints, begging for help, looks weak and undercuts your own credibility and standing. And if it isn't constructive, you have to make sure you have more force than he has. As the adage goes, "If you throw a stone at the emperor, don't miss." It is not advisable to attack unless you are certain that you have the upper hand, you are confident you will win, and you are willing to stick to it through a complete, prompt closure.

8. Rewriting History Through the Sleeper Effect

Unless you wish to submit to the strong leader's view of the world, false information has to be challenged, corrected, and pounded back with equal vigor. No matter how outlandish the message—which the proponent may or may not even believe—narratives can be shaped through frequency of repetition rather than factual basis as the foundation of truth.

9. Sultan of Insult: Reducing Complexity to Simplicity

Insults are no laughing matter. They wound the victim, and the humor of the audience rarely conveys acceptance as much as their relief of stress at abusive rhetoric. Although insults can be effective, it is not a strategy for all. Responding to insults with insults puts both parties into the proverbial admonition about trying to wrestle a pig in mud. This doesn't mean taking the high road of not being confrontational at all; rather, it means picking fights selectively and pushing back against heated rhetoric with tactics that make sense for you rather than mirroring anyone else's. You pick the battlefield; it doesn't have to be on the home turf of the Sultan of Insult.

10. Donald the Great: The Role of Grandeur, Image, and Heroic Aura

Some of our greatest world leaders, including many former US presidents, turn to grandiosity; but the quest for heroic stature cannot overwhelm the quest for heroic mission, and heroic self-image cannot overpower the drive for genuine accomplishments and lasting contributions. Not all accomplished leaders need grandiosity for widespread acclaim and lasting impact.

These are the laws of leadership that Trump implicitly follows and that come closer to capturing his leadership style than anything else—more than Moses's Ten Commandments, the US Constitution, the Magna Carta, Benjamin Franklin's *Poor Richard's Almanack*, Norman Vincent Peale's *Power of Positive Thinking*, Dale Carnegie's *How to Win Friends and Influence People*, Stephen Covey's *7 Habits of Highly Effective People*, Trump's own *The Art of the Deal*, or even Shepherd Mead's *How to Succeed in Business Without Really Trying*, a satirical 1952 spoof of the self-help literature that Frank Loesser and Abe Burrows made into a hilarious musical, which critics might argue is an uncanny parallel to Trump's methods.

Trump is not known for public piety or private spiritual devotion, but he does adhere to these Ten Commandments as his personal rules of thumb for gaining, wielding, and keeping power. Some have quipped that his guiding principle could be a warped version of the biblical Golden Rule—not "Do unto others" but rather "Those who have the gold make the rules."

If that line sounds familiar, it's because it comes from *The Wizard of Id*, a wildly popular syndicated comic strip of the 1960s. In it, a tiny, insecure king—himself elected through a rigged vote—declares the same cynical maxim. The strip's creators, Brant Parker and Johnny Hart, intentionally set the story in the "Kingdom of Id," a tongue-in-cheek reference to Freud's concept of the "id," the primal, impulsive drive for power and gratification. The joke worked because it distilled how easily moral ideals can be replaced by something more self-serving.

But Trump's worldview cannot be reduced to a single comic-strip punchline. His strategic playbook is far more elaborate—a full set of stratagems that function as his own Ten Commandments, each one a distinctly Trumpian reinterpretation of the ethical traditions it echoes.

In 1597, when Francis Bacon advised in *Meditationes Sacrae and Human Philosophy* that "knowledge itself is power," he did not mean just scientific knowledge or technological prowess but also human insight. That human insight is crucial to understanding Trump, and a leader like Trump can be supported, criticized, learned from, leveraged, persuaded, and restrained only by grasping the levers he has made apparent to us.

NOTES

INTRODUCTION

1. Abraham Kaplan, *The Conduct of Inquiry: Methodology for Behavioral Science* (Chandler Publishing Company, 1964), 28. The concept, also known as "Kaplan's Law of the Instrument" or "Maslow's Hammer," has become a fundamental principle in understanding cognitive bias and decision-making.
2. For additional insights into Trump's transformation from businessman to reality TV star to politician, see Ramin Setoodeh, *Apprentice in Wonderland: How Donald Trump and Mark Burnett Took America Through the Looking Glass* (Harper, 2024).
3. Maryanne Trump Barry died on November 13, 2023, at age eighty-six. See "Maryanne Trump Barry, Former President's Sister and a Retired Federal Judge, Dies," NPR, November 13, 2023, https://www.npr.org/2023/11/13/1212767277/maryanne-trump-barry-dead; Michael D. Shear and Maggie Haberman, "Maryanne Trump Barry, Donald Trump Sister and Federal Judge, Dies," *The Washington Post*, November 14, 2023. Barry had served as a federal judge on the Third Circuit Court of Appeals and was known for being one of the few people Trump genuinely feared, per author interviews. Secret recordings made by Mary Trump revealed Barry's harsh criticism of her brother, calling him "cruel" and saying he "has no principles."

4. Donald Trump announced his presidential campaign at Trump Tower on June 16, 2015. See "Donald Trump Presidential Campaign Announcement," C-SPAN, June 16, 2015, https://www.c-span.org/video/?326473-1/donald-trump-presidential-campaign-announcement.

5. According to Mary Trump's allegations in her book and recordings, Trump had someone take his SAT exam for him. Mary L. Trump, *Too Much and Never Enough: How My Family Created the World's Most Dangerous Man* (Simon & Schuster, 2020). See also recordings reported in "Maryanne Trump Barry, the Oldest Sister of Former President Trump, Dies at 86," CNN, November 13, 2023.

6. Theodore H. White, *The Making of the President 1968* (Atheneum Publishers, 1969); Rick Perlstein, *Nixonland: The Rise of a President and the Fracturing of America* (Scribner, 2008).

7. On May 30, 2024, Trump was convicted on thirty-four felony counts of falsifying business records. "Donald Trump Convicted on All 34 Counts in Hush Money Trial," Boston University Today, June 3, 2024, https://www.bu.edu/articles/2024/donald-trump-convicted-on-all-34-counts-in-hush-money-trial/. On January 10, 2025, Trump received an unconditional discharge with no penalty. "Trump Is Sentenced in Hush Money Case—but Gets No Penalty or Fine," NPR, January 10, 2025, https://www.npr.org/2025/01/10/nx-s1-5253927/trump-sentencing-new-york.

8. Jack Smith, "Report of the Special Counsel on the Investigation of Donald J. Trump," US Department of Justice, January 2025. Smith dropped federal charges after Trump's reelection but concluded there was sufficient evidence "to obtain and sustain a conviction."

9. Multiple Trump cabinet members and senior officials broke with Trump after January 6, 2021, including Vice President Mike Pence, Attorney General William Barr, Defense Secretary Mark Esper, and others.

10. Author's personal conversation with Donald Trump, Trump Tower, July 2015. This meeting took place shortly after Trump's June 16, 2015, presidential campaign announcement.

11. Jared Kushner, remarks at Yale CEO Summit, organized by the author.

CHAPTER 1

1. Wayne Barrett, *Trump: The Deals and the Downfall* (HarperCollins, 1992); Harry Hurt III, *Lost Tycoon: The Many Lives of Donald J. Trump* (W. W. Norton, 1993).
2. Bob Woodward, *Fear: Trump in the White House* (Simon & Schuster, 2018), 175–80.
3. "15 Times Donald Trump Praised Authoritarian Rulers," CNN Politics, July 2, 2019; "Trump Praises Authoritarian Leaders Putin, Xi, Kim at Bronx Rally," *The Washington Post*, May 24, 2024.
4. "Donald Trump Just Held the Weirdest Cabinet Meeting Ever," CNN Politics, June 13, 2017; "Cabinet Members Heap Praise on Trump," NPR, June 13, 2017.
5. "Trump's Absurdly Obsequious Cabinet Meeting," Outside the Beltway, June 13, 2017.
6. Maggie Haberman, *Confidence Man: The Making of Donald Trump and the Breaking of America* (Penguin Press, 2022), 421.
7. Third Presidential Debate, University of Nevada, Las Vegas, October 19, 2016, Commission on Presidential Debates transcript.
8. Chris Whipple, *The Gatekeepers: How the White House Chiefs of Staff Define Every Presidency* (Crown, 2017), 312–20.
9. Michael Wolff, *Fire and Fury: Inside the Trump White House* (New York: Henry Holt, 2018), 95.
10. Doris Kearns Goodwin, *Team of Rivals: The Political Genius of Abraham Lincoln* (Simon & Schuster, 2005), for historical comparison of leadership styles.
11. F. Scott Fitzgerald, "The Crack-Up," *Esquire*, February 1936.
12. Peter Baker and Susan Glasser, *The Divider: Trump in the White House, 2017–2021* (Doubleday, 2022), 188.
13. Various Trump campaign rallies, 2024–2025, C-SPAN coverage.
14. George W. Bush, Press Conference, April 18, 2006, White House Archives.
15. Stephanie Grisham, *I'll Take Your Questions Now: What I Saw at the Trump White House* (Harper, 2021).

16. "Trump Cabinet Nominations," US Senate, 2025; "Tracking Trump's Cabinet and Administration Nominations," *The Washington Post*, September 2025.
17. "Marco Rubio's Four Jobs in the Trump Administration," *The Atlantic*, May 2025.
18. Jim Mattis, *Call Sign Chaos: Learning to Lead* (Random House, 2019).
19. "Mattis Resignation Letter," December 20, 2018, Department of Defense.
20. "Pete Hegseth Confirmation Hearing," Senate Armed Services Committee, January 2025.
21. "Tulsi Gabbard Named Director of National Intelligence," White House Press Release, January 2025.
22. "Robert F. Kennedy Jr. Confirmed as HHS Secretary," US Senate, February 2025.
23. "Trump's Use of Acting Officials," Congressional Research Service, Report R46556, 2020.
24. Michael Cohen, *Disloyal: A Memoir* (Skyhorse, 2020), 87–92.
25. The murder of Thomas Becket, archbishop of Canterbury, December 29, 1170. See Frank Barlow, *Thomas Becket* (University of California Press, 1986).
26. "Giuliani Sues Trump for $1.4 Million in Unpaid Legal Fees," *The New York Times*, September 2023.
27. Peter Navarro, *Taking Back Trump's America: Why We Lost the White House and How We'll Win It Back* (Bombardier Books, 2022); "Navarro Reports to Prison," CNN, March 19, 2024.
28. "Hang Mike Pence: January 6 Rioters Chanted," House Select Committee Report, December 2022.
29. "Trump Strips Security Details from Former Officials," Politico, February 2025.
30. "McCarthy Ousted as Speaker," *The Washington Post*, October 3, 2023.
31. Anthony Scaramucci, *Trump, the Blue-Collar President* (Center Street, 2018).

32. "Sessions Loses Alabama Senate Primary," Associated Press, July 14, 2020.
33. "Trump Fires Election Security Chief Chris Krebs," Reuters, November 17, 2020.
34. Jeffrey Goldberg, "Trump: 'Americans Who Died in War Are Losers and Suckers,'" *The Atlantic*, September 3, 2020.
35. John Bolton, *The Room Where It Happened: A White House Memoir* (Simon & Schuster, 2020).
36. "Trump's 'Central Casting' Approach to Hiring," Politico, February 23, 2017.
37. Nina Burleigh, *Golden Handcuffs: The Secret History of Trump's Women* (Gallery Books, 2018).
38. Gabriel Sherman, *The Loudest Voice in the Room: How the Brilliant, Bombastic Roger Ailes Built Fox News* (Random House, 2014).
39. Cassidy Hutchinson, *Enough* (Simon & Schuster, 2023), 147.
40. Michael Wolff, *All or Nothing* (Henry Holt, 2025).
41. "Kristi Noem's Teeth and the Trump Vice Presidency Buzz," *The New York Times*, March 20, 2024, https://www.nytimes.com/2024/03/20/style/kristi-noem-teeth-trump-vice-president.html.
42. "Plastic Surgeon Analyzes Kristi Noem's Face Transformation," *Glam Magazine*, 2024, https://www.glam.com/1833933/plastic-surgeon-kristi-noem-face-transformation/.
43. "Mike Pence: Donald Trump's Vice President," *Politico Magazine*, September 11, 2019, https://www.politico.com/magazine/story/2019/09/11/mike-pence-donald-trump-vp-228059/.
44. "How Trump Chose His Vice Presidential Pick, Vance," CNN Politics, July 16, 2024, https://www.cnn.com/2024/07/16/politics/how-trump-chose-vp-pick-vance.
45. "Donald Trump Speech on Economic Tariffs, Rose Garden," Roll Call, April 2, 2025, https://rollcall.com/factbase/trump/transcript/donald-trump-speech-economic-tariffs-rose-garden-april-2-2025/.
46. "Corey Lewandowski's Growing Power at the Department of Homeland Security," CNN Politics, August 5, 2025, https://www.cnn.com

/2025/08/05/politics/corey-lewandowski-growing-power-dhs#:~:text
=Lewandowski%20has%20directed%20the%20firings,run%20for
%20the%20White%20House.
47. Michael Wolff, *All or Nothing* (Henry Holt, 2025).

CHAPTER 2

1. Roger Fisher, William Ury, and Bruce Patton, *Getting to Yes: Negotiating Agreement Without Giving In* (Penguin Books, 2011).
2. Michael Cohen, *Revenge: How Donald Trump Weaponized the U.S. Department of Justice Against His Critics* (Simon & Schuster, 2022).
3. "Trump Buys Former Kluge-Owned Winery," *The Washington Post*, April 7, 2011, https://www.washingtonpost.com/trump-buys-former-kluge-owned-winery/2011/04/07/AF8hn7wC_story.html.
4. Cohen, *Revenge*.
5. "The History of Mar-a-Lago," *Town & Country*, January 20, 2025, https://www.townandcountrymag.com/style/home-decor/a7144/mar-a-lago-history/.
6. "Trump and North Korea: Nuclear Threats and Diplomacy," CNN Politics, June 13, 2018, https://www.cnn.com/2018/06/13/politics/trump-north-korea-nuclear-threat.
7. "How Trump's Gaza Ceasefire Deal Happened," CNN, October 9, 2025, https://www.cnn.com/2025/10/09/politics/how-trump-gaza-ceasefire-deal-happened.
8. Maggie Haberman, *Confidence Man: The Making of Donald Trump and the Breaking of America* (Penguin Press, 2022).
9. "Donald Trump, Roy Cohn, and the Race Discrimination Lawsuit," *PBS Frontline*, https://www.pbs.org/wgbh/frontline/article/donald-trump-roy-cohn-race-discrimination-lawsuit-fight-documentary-excerpt/.
10. "Liberation Day in Retrospect: Six Things That Surprised Investors," J.P. Morgan Insights, October 10, 2025, https://www.jpmorgan.com/insights/markets-and-economy/top-market-takeaways/tmt-liberation-day-in-retrospect-6-things-that-surprised-investors.

11. "Tariffs, Tacos, and Dollars: A Year in Trump's Global Markets," Reuters, November 3, 2025, https://www.reuters.com/business/autos-transportation/tariffs-tacos-dollars-global-markets-year-trump-20-2025-11-03/.
12. "Trump Responds: 'Trump Always Chickens Out on Tariff Threats,'" *Variety*, 2025, https://variety.com/2025/biz/news/trump-responds-taco-trade-trump-always-chickens-out-tariff-threats-1236412080/.
13. "Trump's Middle East Policy: Saudi Arabia Investments," *The New York Times*, May 12, 2025, https://www.nytimes.com/2025/05/12/world/middleeast/trump-saudi-arabia-investment.html.
14. "Foxconn Mostly Abandons $10 Billion Wisconsin Project Touted by Trump," CNBC, April 21, 2021, https://www.cnbc.com/2021/04/21/foxconn-mostly-abandons-10-billion-wisconsin-project-touted-by-trump.html.
15. "Trump and Ukraine: 2025 Developments," *The New York Times*, September 24, 2025, https://www.nytimes.com/2025/09/24/us/politics/trump-ukraine.html.
16. "Tracking Trump's Lawsuits," *USA Today*, https://www.usatoday.com/pages/interactives/trump-lawsuits/.
17. "That Time Trump Sued over the Size of His Wallet," *The Washington Post*, March 8, 2016, https://www.washingtonpost.com/lifestyle/style/that-time-trump-sued-over-the-size-of-hiswallet/2016/03/08/785dee3e-e4c2-11e5-b0fd-073d5930a7b7_story.html.
18. "That Time Trump Sued Over the Size of His Wallet."
19. Michael Cohen, *Disloyal: A Memoir* (Skyhorse Publishing, 2020).
20. "Trump Sues Deutsche Bank over $40 Million Debt on Chicago Property," *New York Daily News*, May 24, 2016, https://www.nydailynews.com/2016/05/24/donald-trump-sued-deutsche-bank-to-get-out-of-40-million-debt-over-chicago-property-two-years-after-rooting-for-housing-collapse/.
21. "Donald Trump Sues Doral Golf Course Neighbors, Claims They Cut Down Trees," NBC Miami, https://www.nbcmiami.com/news/local/donald-trump-sues-doral-golf-course-neighbors-claims-they-cut-down-trees/139630/.

22. "Paint Shop Owner Juan Carlos Enriquez Took Trump to Court and Won," NBC News, https://www.nbcnews.com/news/us-news/paint-shop-owner-juan-carlos-enriquez-took-trump-won-n747756.
23. Michael Wolff, *All or Nothing* (Henry Holt, 2025).
24. "Trump's Justice Department Compensation Controversy," *The New York Times*, October 21, 2025, https://www.nytimes.com/2025/10/21/us/politics/trump-justice-department-compensation.html.

CHAPTER 3

1. "Leaders Who Defined 2025: Donald Trump," *Time*, 2025, https://time.com/7300674/leaders-donald-trump/.
2. "Paul Weiss Responds to Trump Reaction," *The New York Times*, March 21, 2025, https://www.nytimes.com/2025/03/21/business/paul-weiss-trump-reaction.html.
3. "Stop Blaming Law Firms Attacked by President Donald Trump," *Time*, 2025, https://time.com/7273100/stop-blaming-law-firms-attacked-by-president-donald-trump/.
4. "Harvard Teaches Leaders a Valuable Lesson," *Time*, 2025, https://time.com/7278903/harvard-teaches-leaders-valuable-lesson/.
5. "How Dartmouth Became the Ivy League's Switzerland," *The New Yorker*, July 18, 2025, https://www.newyorker.com/news/the-lede/how-dartmouth-became-the-ivy-leagues-switzerland.
6. "Harvard Defiance: The Trump-Supported College Presidents," *Fortune*, April 15, 2025, https://fortune.com/2025/04/15/harvard-defiance-trump-supported-college-university-presidents/.
7. "Who Is Larry Ellison, the Billionaire Trump Friend Who's Part of the TikTok Takeover?," NPR, October 6, 2025, https://www.npr.org/2025/10/06/nx-s1-5560216/who-is-larry-ellison-the-billionaire-trump-friend-whos-part-of-the-tiktok-takeover.
8. "Antitrust Chief Blocking AT&T–Time Warner Deal Didn't See a Problem," CNBC, November 21, 2017, https://www.cnbc.com/2017/11/21/antitrust-chief-blocking-att-time-warner-deal-didnt-see-a-problem.html.

9. "Why CEOs Continue to Support Trump," *The New York Times*, June 23, 2024, https://www.nytimes.com/2024/06/23/opinion/ceo-trump-republican-support.html.
10. "Ken Frazier: The Strongest Man in the World," *Yale Insights*, https://insights.som.yale.edu/insights/ken-frazier-the-strongest-man-in-the-world.
11. "When CEOs Revolted Against Trump," *The New York Times*, August 18, 2017, https://www.nytimes.com/2017/08/18/opinion/ceos-revolted-trump-business.html.
12. "Jeffrey Sonnenfeld, the CEO Whisperer," *Business Insider*, November 2021, https://www.businessinsider.com/jeffrey-sonnenfeld-the-ceo-whisperer-2021-11.
13. "Top CEOs Met to Plan Response to Trump's Election Denial," CNBC, November 13, 2020, https://www.cnbc.com/2020/11/13/top-ceos-met-to-plan-response-to-trumps-election-denial.html.
14. "CEOs Urge Respect for Election Integrity," *Yale Insights*, 2020, https://insights.som.yale.edu/insights/ceos-urge-respect-for-election-integrity.
15. "Woke Big Business Dumps Trump," *Time*, 2021, https://time.com/6111845/woke-big-business-dumps-trump/.
16. "Big Business Mulls Approach to Trump Bid After Opposing Him," ABC News, 2025, https://abcnews.go.com/Business/big-business-mulls-approach-trump-bid-after-opposing/story?id=102367196.
17. "Business Roundtable Missing in Action Amid Trump's Attacks," *Time*, 2025, https://time.com/7286691/business-roundtable-mia-trumps-attacks/.
18. "Trump Tariff Attacks Amazon," Politico, April 29, 2025, https://www.politico.com/news/2025/04/29/tariff-amazon-donald-trump-00315053.
19. "Mexico and Canada Respond to Trump Tariff Deals," *The New York Times*, February 4, 2025, https://www.nytimes.com/2025/02/04/world/canada/mexico-canada-trump-tariff-deals.html.
20. "Trump's History of Lying: From John Barron to @realDonald Trump," *The New Yorker*, 2025, https://www.newyorker.com/news

/our-columnists/trumps-history-of-lying-from-john-barron-to-real
donaldtrump.
21. "Reporter off the Trump Beat," *The New York Times*, July 3, 1991, https://www.nytimes.com/1991/07/03/business/reporter-off-trump-beat.html.
22. "MAGA, Marxist, Maoist? Trump's Assault on Free-Market Capitalism," *Fortune*, August 12, 2025, https://fortune.com/2025/08/12/maga-marxist-maoist-trump-assault-free-market-capitalism-socialism/.
23. "Trump's Role in the Eddie Gallagher Case," *Fortune*, November 26, 2019, https://fortune.com/2019/11/26/eddie-gallagher-richard-spencer-trump/.
24. "Trump and the Federalist Society: Conservative Legal Network," *The Guardian*, June 8, 2025, https://www.theguardian.com/us-news/2025/jun/08/trump-federalist-society-conservative-legal.
25. "Trump's Conservative Courtship," BBC News, 2025, https://www.bbc.com/news/articles/cdrg8zkz8d0o.
26. Michael Cohen, *Disloyal: A Memoir* (Skyhorse Publishing, 2020).
27. Michael Wolff, *All or Nothing* (Henry Holt, 2025).
28. "Bahrain Summit: Middle East Talks," *Fortune*, June 30, 2019, https://fortune.com/2019/06/30/bahrain-summit-middle-east/.
29. "Kushner's Conference 'A Positive Step to Move Forward,' Sonnenfeld Says," CNBC, June 26, 2019, https://www.cnbc.com/video/2019/06/26/kushners-conference-a-positive-step-to-move-forward-academic-says.html.

CHAPTER 4

1. Barack Obama, "Fired Up and Ready to Go," Medium, https://barackobama.medium.com/fired-up-and-ready-to-go-6e65adf0fe54.
2. "Trump University's Gold Elite Program: Nothing but Fool's Gold," NPR, June 6, 2016, https://www.npr.org/2016/06/06/480948631/trump-university-customer-gold-elite-program-nothing-but-fools-gold.
3. Jeffrey Sonnenfeld, *The Hero's Farewell: What Happens When CEOs Retire* (Oxford University Press, 1988).

4. Mary Trump, *Too Much and Never Enough: How My Family Created the World's Most Dangerous Man* (Simon & Schuster, 2020).
5. "Donald Trump, Real Estate Promoter, Builds Image as He Buys Buildings," *The New York Times*, November 1, 1976, https://www.nytimes.com/1976/11/01/archives/donald-trump-real-estate-promoter-builds-image-as-he-buys-buildings.html.
6. Michael D'Antonio, *Never Enough: Donald Trump and the Pursuit of Success* (Thomas Dunne Books, 2015).
7. "Donald Trump and His Real Estate Tax Breaks," *The New York Times*, September 18, 2016, https://www.nytimes.com/2016/09/18/nyregion/donald-trump-tax-breaks-real-estate.html.
8. "Trump Pushed for a Sweetheart Tax Deal on His First Hotel—It's Cost New York City $410,068,399 and Counting," ProPublica, https://www.propublica.org/article/trump-pushed-for-a-sweetheart-tax-deal-on-his-first-hotel-its-cost-new-york-city-410-068-399-and-counting.
9. "How Donald Trump Helped Save New York City," *New York Post*, February 7, 2016, https://nypost.com/2016/02/07/how-donald-trump-helped-save-new-york-city/.
10. "Trump, Robert Moses, and the Battle over Television City," *Politico Magazine*, June 29, 2018, https://www.politico.com/magazine/story/2018/06/29/trump-robert-moses-new-york-television-city-urban-development-1980s-218836/.
11. "Donald Trump and Mayor Ed Koch," *The New York Times*, April 20, 2016, https://www.nytimes.com/2016/04/20/us/politics/donald-trump-edward-koch.html.
12. "Donald Trump: Saving NYC Millions or Making Millions off Taxpayers?," WNYC, https://www.wnyc.org/story/donald-trump-saving-nyc-millions-or-making-millions-taxpayers/.
13. "Trump Organization Loses Bid to Reclaim Operation of Wollman Rink," *New York Post*, September 10, 2025, https://nypost.com/2025/09/10/us-news/trump-organization-loses-bid-to-reclaim-operation-of-wollman-rink/.

14. "Donald Trump, Activist Investor," CNN, August 22, 2016, https://www.cnn.com/2016/08/22/politics/donald-trump-activist-investor.
15. Daniel Reed, "No Art in These Bad Deals: Why Trump Doesn't Talk About Late-'80s Deals for the Plaza, Two Airlines," *Forbes*, October 7, 2015, https://www.forbes.com/sites/danielreed/2015/10/07/no-art-in-these-bad-deals-why-trump-doesnt-talk-about-late-80s-deals-for-the-plaza-two-airlines/.
16. "Donald Trump Really Not Invested in Stock Market," PolitiFact, September 15, 2016, https://www.politifact.com/article/2016/sep/15/donald-trump-really-not-invested-stock-market/.
17. "The Ups—and Mostly Downs—of Trump Shuttle: The President's Long-Defunct Airline," *The Washington Post*, January 2, 2018, https://www.washingtonpost.com/news/retropolis/wp/2018/01/02/the-ups-and-mostly-downs-of-trump-shuttle-the-presidents-long-defunct-airline/.
18. "Arms, Harems, and a Trump-Owned Yacht: How the Khashoggi Family Helped Mold the U.S.–Saudi Relationship," Yahoo News, 2018, https://www.yahoo.com/news/arms-harems-and-a-trump-owned-yacht-how-the-khashoggi-family-helped-mold-the-us-saudi-relationship-090007017.html.
19. "Donald Trump's Taxes and Debt," *The New York Times*, October 4, 2016, https://www.nytimes.com/2016/10/04/nyregion/donald-trump-taxes-debt.html.
20. "How Donald Trump Escaped Crisis: Bankruptcy to Coronavirus," *Politico Magazine*, April 17, 2020, https://www.politico.com/news/magazine/2020/04/17/donald-trump-escape-crisis-bankruptcy-coronavirus-casino-trumpology-183513.
21. "Trump Pays 15.5% in Junk Bond Sale," *Los Angeles Times*, January 22, 1991, https://www.latimes.com/archives/la-xpm-1991-01-22-fi-750-story.html.
22. "Deutsche Bank Cuts Ties with Trump," CNN, January 12, 2021, https://www.cnn.com/2021/01/12/investing/deutsche-bank-trump.
23. "Trump $47 Million Short—Gives Investors 50% of His Prize Casino," *The New York Times*, November 17, 1990, https://www.nytimes.com

/1990/11/17/business/trump-47-million-short-gives-investors-50-of-his-prize-casino.html.

24. "Trump Pays 15.5% in Junk Bond Sale," *Australian Financial Review*, June 9, 1995, https://www.afr.com/politics/trump-pays-15-5pc-in-junk-bond-sale-19950609-k6g68.
25. Donald J. Trump and Kate Bohner, *Trump: The Art of the Comeback* (Random House, 1997).
26. "Trump Tax Schemes: How Fred Trump Helped His Son," *The New York Times*, October 2, 2018, https://www.nytimes.com/interactive/2018/10/02/us/politics/donald-trump-tax-schemes-fred-trump.html.
27. "Trump Tax Schemes: How Fred Trump Helped His Son."
28. "Trump Tax Schemes: How Fred Trump Helped His Son."
29. Michael Cohen, *Disloyal: A Memoir* (Skyhorse Publishing, 2020).
30. Ramin Setoodeh, *Apprentice in Wonderland: How Donald Trump and Mark Burnett Took America Through the Looking Glass* (HarperCollins, 2024).
31. "Trump Products That Disappeared: A List," *Business Insider*, April 2018, https://www.businessinsider.com/trump-products-that-disappeared-list-2018-4.
32. "Trump T1 Mobile Phone Will Likely Be Made in China, Experts Say," CNBC, June 17, 2025, https://www.cnbc.com/2025/06/17/trump-t1-mobile-phone-will-likely-be-made-in-china-experts.html.
33. "Trump Profited from Sales of 'God Bless the USA' Bible," *Business Insider*, August 2024, https://www.businessinsider.com/trump-profited-from-sales-of-god-bless-the-usa-bible-2024-8.
34. "Trump, ZTE, and Indonesia's Lido City," *Vox*, May 15, 2018, https://www.vox.com/policy-and-politics/2018/5/15/17355202/trump-zte-indonesia-lido-city.
35. "Air Force and Trump's Scottish Retreat," Politico, September 6, 2019, https://www.politico.com/story/2019/09/06/air-force-trump-scottish-retreat-1484337.
36. "Trump Hotel's Empty Rooms," Politico, October 2, 2019, https://www.politico.com/news/2019/10/02/trump-hotel-empty-rooms-016763.

37. "Trump Jet, Crypto, Qatar, and Corruption," *Mother Jones*, May 2025, https://www.motherjones.com/politics/2025/05/trump-jet-crypto-qatar-corruption-ethics/.
38. "Trump Media's $400 Million Loss," CBS News, 2025, https://www.cbsnews.com/news/trump-media-truth-social-400-million-loss-sales-revenue-decline/.
39. "Inside Trump Family's Global Crypto Cash Machine," Reuters, October 28, 2025, https://www.reuters.com/investigations/inside-trump-familys-global-crypto-cash-machine-2025-10-28/.
40. "Here's How Much the Trump Kids Have Made Because of the Presidency," *Forbes*, September 22, 2025, https://www.forbes.com/sites/danalexander/2025/09/22/heres-how-much-the-trump-kids-have-made-because-of-the-presidency/.
41. "Melania Trump Documentary," *New York Magazine (Intelligencer)*, 2025, https://nymag.com/intelligencer/article/melania-trump-documentary-amazon.html.
42. "Donald Trump Jr. Is Making Money from the Presidency," *Business Insider*, May 2025, https://www.businessinsider.com/donald-trump-jr-making-money-trump-presidency-1789-capital-2025-5.
43. "Trump Accepts Qatar Plane as Air Force One Replacement," NPR, May 21, 2025, https://www.npr.org/2025/05/21/nx-s1-5406420/trump-accepts-qatar-plane-air-force-one.
44. "Trump 2.0 and the Foreign Emoluments Clause," American Enterprise Institute, 2025, https://www.aei.org/op-eds/trump-2-0-and-the-foreign-emoluments-clause/.
45. "Senate Republicans and the Qatar Jet," Politico, May 13, 2025, https://www.politico.com/news/2025/05/13/senate-republicans-qatar-trump-jet-00345435.
46. "Trump's Miami Resort Wins Approval for $3 Billion Condo Project," Bloomberg, January 16, 2025, https://www.bloomberg.com/news/articles/2025-01-16/trump-s-miami-resort-wins-approval-for-3-billion-condo-project.

CHAPTER 5

1. "Obama's 2011 White House Correspondents' Dinner Roast of Trump Foreshadowed Bin Laden Raid," *Newsweek*, 2025, https://www.newsweek.com/obama-trump-white-house-correspondents-dinner-2011-roast-bin-laden-raid-2063833.
2. "Trump Faces Holdout Republicans on Key Bill," *The New York Times*, July 2, 2025, https://www.nytimes.com/2025/07/02/us/politics/trump-bill-holdout-republicans.html.
3. "Bill Maher Praises 'Gracious, Measured' Trump," Deadline, April 2025, https://deadline.com/2025/04/real-time-bill-maher-praises-gracious-measured-trump-1236367060/.
4. "MSNBC Host Says Trump Told Me to 'F--- Myself' After Reaching Out for Interview—'At Least He Took the Call,'" Fox News, 2025, https://www.foxnews.com/media/msnbc-host-says-trump-told-me-f-myself-after-reaching-out-interview-least-he-took-call.
5. "Megyn Kelly Reveals Why She Regained Love for Trump Despite Strained Past That Included Prez-Bashing," *New York Post*, April 24, 2025, https://nypost.com/2025/04/24/media/megyn-kelly-reveals-why-she-regained-love-for-trump-despite-strained-past-that-included-prez-bashing-ex-fox-news-anchor/.
6. "A Black Mark for Fiorina Campaign in Criticizing Yale Dean," *The New York Times*, September 24, 2015, https://www.nytimes.com/2015/09/24/upshot/black-mark-for-fiorina-campaign-in-criticizing-yale-dean.html.

CHAPTER 6

1. "The Life of a Song: 'Be My Baby,'" *Financial Times*, February 22, 2021, https://ig.ft.com/life-of-a-song/be-my-baby.html.
2. "Trump, Kim, Cohen, and the Limits of the President's Power," *The New Yorker*, March 11, 2019, https://www.newyorker.com/magazine/2019/03/11/trump-kim-cohen-and-the-limits-of-the-presidents-power.

3. "The White House Just Released a Log of Trump's First Call with Zelenskiy," NPR, November 15, 2019, https://www.npr.org/2019/11/15/778497217/the-white-house-just-released-a-log-of-trumps-first-call-with-zelenskiy.
4. "Donald Trump's Attack Tactics," *Fortune*, August 22, 2015, https://fortune.com/2015/08/22/donald-trump-attack-tactics/.
5. "Dan Bongino and the Epstein Connection," CNN, July 14, 2025, https://www.cnn.com/2025/07/14/politics/dan-bongino-epstein.
6. "Trump Seeks to Proceed with $10 Billion Lawsuit over *Wall Street Journal* Story on Epstein," ABC News, 2025, https://abcnews.go.com/US/trump-seeks-proceed-10b-lawsuit-wsj-story-epsteins/story?id=126717491.
7. "Todd Blanche, Epstein, Ghislaine Maxwell, and Trump," NPR, July 29, 2025, https://www.npr.org/2025/07/29/nx-s1-5484129/todd-blanche-epstein-ghislaine-maxwell-trump.
8. "Trump Is Plotting This Desperate Move to Distract from Epstein," The Daily Beast, 2025, https://www.thedailybeast.com/trump-is-plotting-this-desperate-move-to-distract-from-epstein-wolff/.
9. "Bill Clinton's Accusers Resurface," *The New York Times*, October 10, 2016, https://www.nytimes.com/2016/10/10/us/politics/bill-clinton-accusers.html.

CHAPTER 7

1. "Trump Drops Giuliani After Cohen Warning," *The Independent*, 2021, https://www.the-independent.com/news/world/americas/us-politics/trump-drops-giuliani-cohen-warn-b1803294.html.
2. "Trump Trial: Stormy Daniels, Michael Cohen, and Hush Money Allegations," Associated Press (AP), 2025, https://apnews.com/article/trump-trial-stormy-daniels-michael-cohen-hush-money-f96dd7289cf952145cdd6737b29add3d.
3. "I'm in Ruins: Teary Mike Lindell Tells Judge About Smartmatic Lawsuit," ABC News, 2025, https://abcnews.go.com/Politics/im-ruins-teary-mike-lindell-tells-judge-smartmatic/story?id=120887538.

4. "Trump Distances Himself from Sidney Powell After Plea Deal," NBC News, 2025, https://www.nbcnews.com/politics/donald-trump/trump-distances-sidney-powell-plea-deal-rcna121695.
5. "Has Palin Hit Bottom? Describes Feeling Rejected After Being Denied Credentials to GOP National Convention," Must Read Alaska, 2025, https://mustreadalaska.com/has-palin-hit-bottom-describes-feeling-rejected-being-denied-credentials-to-gop-national-convention/.
6. "J.D. Vance Once Compared Trump to Hitler—Now They Are Running Mates," Reuters, July 15, 2024, https://www.reuters.com/world/us/jd-vance-once-compared-trump-hitler-now-they-are-running-mates-2024-07-15/.
7. "Donald Trump Explains Elon Musk Reunion at Charlie Kirk Memorial," *People*, 2025, https://people.com/donald-trump-explains-elon-musk-reunion-at-charlie-kirk-memorial-11814465.
8. Val Demings (@valdemings), "We Will Not Be Intimidated," X (Twitter), post dated 2025, https://x.com/valdemings/status/1958930916564508768.
9. "Trump, Lisa Cook, and the Federal Reserve: Why Every CEO Should Care," *Fortune*, August 26, 2025, https://fortune.com/2025/08/26/trump-lisa-cook-federal-reserve-every-ceo-should-care/.
10. "Donald Trump's Casino Lawsuit with Marvin Roffman," *Politico Magazine*, April 2016, https://www.politico.com/magazine/story/2016/04/donald-trump-marvin-roffman-casino-lawsuit-213855/.
11. Jonathan Karl, *Tired of Winning: Donald Trump and the End of the Grand Old Party* (Dutton, 2023).

CHAPTER 8

1. "The Term 'Sleeper Effect,'" National Center for Biotechnology Information (NCBI), https://pmc.ncbi.nlm.nih.gov/articles/PMC3100161/#:~:text=The%20term%20sleeper%20effect%20has,%2C%20%26%20Sheffield%2C%201949).
2. "Trump's False or Misleading Claims Total 30,573 over Four Years," *The Washington Post*, January 24, 2021, https://www.washingtonpost

.com/politics/2021/01/24/trumps-false-or-misleading-claims-total-30573-over-four-years/.
3. "AI, Trump, and the Future of Facts and Lies," *The Washington Post*, 2025, https://www.washingtonpost.com/opinions/interactive/2025/ai-trump-facts-lies/.
4. "Harris Must Awaken the Nation from the Sleeper Effect at the Debate with Trump," *Fortune*, September 6, 2024, https://fortune.com/2024/09/06/harris-must-awaken-the-nation-from-the-sleeper-effect-at-the-debate-with-trump-and-dispel-the-oft-repeated-falsehood-that-the-booming-u-s-economy-isnt-doing-so-well/.
5. "Trump Sues Writer and Book Publisher," *The New York Times*, January 25, 2006, https://www.nytimes.com/2006/01/25/business/media/trump-sues-writer-and-book-publisher.html.
6. "Voting Restrictions Analysis," CNN, April 11, 2021, https://www.cnn.com/2021/04/11/politics/voting-restrictions-analysis.
7. "Putin and Trump: Who's Playing Whom?," *Fortune*, August 31, 2025, https://fortune.com/2025/08/31/putin-trump-whos-playing-who-russia-ukraine-ceasefire/.
8. "Trump and the Media: A Decade of Coverage," BBC News, November 25, 2015, https://www.bbc.com/news/world-us-canada-34902748.
9. "Kellyanne Conway and the Rise of 'Alternative Facts,'" CNN, January 22, 2017, https://www.cnn.com/2017/01/22/politics/kellyanne-conway-alternative-facts.
10. Alan Brinkley, *Voices of Protest: Huey Long, Father Coughlin, and the Great Depression* (Alfred A. Knopf, 1982).

CHAPTER 9

1. Tim Wu, *The Attention Merchants: The Epic Scramble to Get Inside Our Heads* (Knopf, 2016).
2. "The Neural Basis of the Attention Economy," *Social Neuroscience*, 2016, https://www.tandfonline.com/doi/full/10.1080/17470919.2016.1162194.

3. Thomas Davenport and John Beck, *The Attention Economy: Understanding the New Currency of Business* (Harvard Business School Press, 2001).
4. Harold Garfinkel, *Studies in Ethnomethodology* (Prentice-Hall, 1967).
5. "Donald Trump's Attack Tactics," *Fortune*, August 22, 2015, https://fortune.com/2015/08/22/donald-trump-attack-tactics/.
6. "Candidates Attack Trump in Debate," *The Hill*, 2015, https://thehill.com/blogs/ballot-box/presidential-races/253838-candidates-attack-trump-in-debate/.
7. "All About the Rosie O'Donnell–Donald Trump Feud," *People*, 2025, https://people.com/all-about-rosie-odonnell-donald-trump-feud-11702390/.
8. "Trump Dancing in Salsa-Themed Ads Shows Battle for Latino Vote," Bloomberg Government, 2025, https://news.bgov.com/bloomberg-government-news/trump-dancing-in-salsa-themed-ads-shows-battle-for-latino-vote.

CHAPTER 10

1. "Trump on Trackdown: 1958 TV Series 'The End of the World' Episode Predicted a Wall," CBS News, https://www.cbsnews.com/news/trump-trackdown-1958-tv-series-the-end-of-the-world-episode-build-wall/.
2. Bob Woodward, *Fear: Trump in the White House* (Simon & Schuster, 2018).
3. Joseph Campbell, *The Hero with a Thousand Faces* (Princeton University Press, 1949).
4. Jeffrey Sonnenfeld, *The Hero's Farewell: What Happens When CEOs Retire* (Oxford University Press, 1988).
5. "How Jimmy Carter Lost His Job but Found His Mission: A Personal Remembrance," *Newsweek*, 2025, https://www.newsweek.com/how-jimmy-carter-lost-his-job-found-his-mission-personal-remembrance-2007685.

6. Ron Chernow, *Washington: A Life* (Penguin Press, 2010).
7. Joseph Ellis, *His Excellency: George Washington* (Alfred A. Knopf, 2004).
8. Doris Kearns Goodwin, *Team of Rivals: The Political Genius of Abraham Lincoln* (Simon & Schuster, 2005).
9. Jeffrey Sonnenfeld, *The Hero's Farewell: What Happens When CEOs Retire* (Oxford University Press, 1988).
10. "The Horatio Alger Myth and the American Dream," *Time*, August 2023, https://time.com/6305543/horatio-alger-myth-american-dream/.
11. Thorstein Veblen, *The Theory of the Leisure Class* (Macmillan, 1899).
12. Michael Wolff, *All or Nothing* (Henry Holt, 2025).
13. Leo Braudy, *The Frenzy of Renown: Fame and Its History* (Vintage, 1986).
14. Chris Whipple, "Susie Wiles, JD Vance, and the 'Junkyard Dogs': The White House Chief of Staff on Trump's Second Term (Part 1 of 2)," *Vanity Fair*, December 16, 2025, https://www.vanityfair.com/news/story/trump-susie-wiles-interview-exclusive-part-1?srsltid=AfmBOopKUL5EbS5uDOB9HoI_lrbeo4YRmgii2MtLUM7ZJyqOoCgKNFDL.
15. "Trump's Ego and the Thin Skin Beneath It," Vox, October 25, 2016, https://www.vox.com/2016/10/25/13405270/trump-ego-thin-skinned.
16. "Inside Trump's Gold Luxury Imperial Ballroom," *The Washington Post*, November 3, 2025, https://www.washingtonpost.com/politics/2025/11/03/trump-gold-luxury-imperial-ballroom/.
17. "Trump's White House Ballroom Construction," *The Wall Street Journal*, 2025, https://www.wsj.com/politics/policy/trump-white-house-ballroom-construction-d1616a3e.
18. "Trump's History of Lying: From John Barron to @realDonald Trump," *The New Yorker*, 2025, https://www.newyorker.com/news/our-columnists/trumps-history-of-lying-from-john-barron-to-realdonaldtrump.

ACKNOWLEDGMENTS

I would like to thank my family, friends, colleagues, students, and all the CEOs I've worked with who made this book possible.

First, my loyal, hardworking little team of the Yale Chief Executive Leadership Institute must top the list, including current and former team members Joe DeLillo, Donna DeLillo, Cyndy Oswald Morris, Stephen Henriques, Isabella Giansanti, Georgia Hirsty, Tina Grimes, Erica Fersch, Dan Mullins, Bob Mendlesohn, Xiuling Li, Col. Vito Errico, Major Alex Thew, Alex Bigler, Cathy Hong, Andrew Ward, Brad Agle, Erin Weinstein, Tara Whitehead Stotland, Karon Jolna, Kate Ellis, Paddy Spence, and Cassidy Rhodes. They are a constant source of ideas, extending my reach and my days to make me look far more formidable, knowledgeable, and professional than I often may truly be! They are fortified with a team of fifty Yale School of Management and Yale College students who join in noble causes.

Next, I must salute Yale University and the Yale School of Management for encouraging me to ask large questions about leadership, governance, strategic change, and societal impact cutting across disciplines and sectors. Presidents Maurie McInnis, Peter Salovey, and Rick Levin have inspired me and protected me, as have our "SOM" Deans Kerwin Charles, Sharon Oster, Joel Podolny, and Jeff Garten as well as my Yale CELI board members and other Yale colleagues, including Barry Nalebuff, Andrew Metrick, Judy Chevalier, Edi Pinker, Doug Rae, Stan Garstka, Rick Antle, Ravi Dhar, Jim Baron, Harlan Krumholz, Heather Tookes, Howard Forman, Albert Ko, Fiona Scott Morton, Mushfiq Mobarak, Ben Polak, Kavitha Bindra, Ben Mattison, Nathan Williams, Courtney Lightfoot, Jonathan Weisberg, Jiwoong Shin, Beverly Gage, Jing Tsu, Geert Rouwenhorst, Will Goetzmann, Gary Gorton, K. Sudhir, Amy Wisniewski, Kyle Jensen, Joel Getz, Steve Latham, Peggy Kalb, Bridget Gillich, Nancy Brown, Heather Gerken, and Megan Ranney, along with the late Sigal Barsade, the late Victor Vroom, and the late Bill Donaldson.

Plus, I have a large number of humble, quiet donors who have supported my work, such as Jeff Bewkes, Indra Nooyi, Stuart Miller, Leslie Miller Saiontz, Lynn Tilton, Maurice (Hank) Greenberg, the late Albert H. Gordon, Al Goldstein, the late Bernie Marcus, Rick Goings, Nick Pinchuk, Reuben Mark, Glenn Fogel, Farooq Kathwari, Bill Anderson, Roger Barnett and Sloan Lindemann Barnett, Lester Crown, Susan Crown, the late Jim Crown, Jeffrey Solomon, Joel Myers, Leonard Levie, Ken Schulman, Alan Slatas, John Lapides, Joe Ucuzoglu, Arvind Krishna, Jim Kelly, Kay Koplovitz, Eddie Tam, Courtney O'Malley, Hamdi Ulukaya, Don Layden, and the late Oz Nelson, among many others.

My diligent legal team and legal counselors have provided me with a 24/7 safety net and include Alex Dreier, Dorothy Robinson, Marc Sonnenfeld, Ann Laupheimer Sonnenfeld, Ted Killory, Brad Karp, Courtland Reichman, Tom Glocer, Ken Frazier, Steve Brill, Rick Pildes, Tom Rogers, Bill Brown, Warren Sams, John Witt, John Porter, Josh Archer, Keegan Federal, Michael Bowers, Akhil Reed Amar, Jon Macey, Roberta Romano, Asha Rangappa, Joe Fay, Judge Charles Tiernan, Judge Michael Luttig, Judge Jed Rakoff, Judge Douglas Ginsburg, David Zornow, the late Joel Reidenberg, the late Jonathan Blake, and the late Paul Tagliabue.

ACKNOWLEDGMENTS

I continue to benefit from the wise public relations guidance, policy insight, political knowledge, spiritual guidance, media savvy, and/or firsthand experiences with President Trump of (in alphabetical order) Adam Aron, Joel Babbit, Mary Barra, Michael Beer, Marc Benioff, Arvind Bhambri, President Joseph Biden, Lloyd Blankfein, Senator Richard Blumenthal, Nancy Boghossian, Albert Bourla, Morgan Brennan, the late President George H. W. Bush, the late President Jimmy Carter, Elaine Chao, Michael Dell, Mickey Drexler, Mary Duffy, Richard Edelman, Mark Fields, Karen Firestone, Greg Fleming, Joele Frank, Diane Hessan, George and Joan Hornig, Jared Kushner and Ivanka Trump, Governor Ned Lamont and Annie Lamont, John Lechner, Steve Lipin, Patty Marx, Jim McCann, Bethany McLean, Marshall Meyer, Quinn Mills, Anne Mulcahy, Jeff Pfeffer, Anthony Scaramucci, Steve Schwarzman, David Solomon, Clarky Sonnenfeld, Andrew Ross Sorkin, Vivek Wadhwa, Elise Walton, and the late Ash Carter.

I would also like to thank (in alphabetical order) Vikram Agrawal, Ambassador Yousef Al Otaiba, Mike Allen, Kurt Andersen, Joe Badaracco, Molly Ball, Senator John Barrasso, Norm Bartczak, Kyle Bass, Senator Michael Bennet, Helen Bennett, Mayor RJ Berry, Dan Bigman, President Joseph Biden, David and Ursula Blumenthal, Adam Boehler, the late Jack Bogle, Tom Bossert, Contessa Brewer, Rabbi Herbert Brockman, Greg Brown, Bill Browder, Mika Brzezinski, Erin Burnett, Wayne Cascio, Steve Case, Rui Chenggang, Fu Chengyu, Nichole Cipriani, General James Clapper, Jay Clayton, Sandy Climan, John Clippinger, Olivia-Anne Cleary, Hillary Clinton, President Bill Clinton, Michael Cohen, Kaitlan Collins, Geoff Colvin, Barbara Comstock, Cesar Conde, Anderson Cooper, Marshall Cooper, Wayne Cooper, Senator Bob Corker, Anne Coyle, Jim Cramer, Mark Cuban, Tom Cummings, Jennifer Cunningham, Chip Cutter, the Dalai Lama, Kim Davis, Charlie Dent, Nik Deogun, Bob Diamond, Jamie Dimon, Kyle Dropp, Tom Dudchik, Jimmy Dunne,

Andrew Edgecliffe-Johnson, Mohamed El Aassar, Jim Edwards, Matt Egan, Blair Effron, Sara Eisen, Admiral Marcia Evans, Kelly Evans, David Faber, Michael Feder, Mayor Greg Fischer, Alice Fishburn, Fred Foulkes, Christina Freeland, Scott Galloway, Jamie Gangel, Bart Garrett, Jo Ann Garrett, Ted Garrett, Charlie Gasparino, Bill George, Jason Gewirtz, Paul Gigot, Jerry Giordano, Shane Goldmacher, Larry Golub, Alex Gorsky, Rhona Graff, Senator Lindsey Graham, Steve Greyser, Amy Gutmann, Phil Hanlon, Rabbi Shmully Hecht, Ambassador John Herbst, AJ Hess, Marillyn Hewson, Hope Hicks, Congressman Jim Himes, Mark Hoffman, Reid Hoffman, Ambassador Robert Hormats, Glenn Hutchins, Suein Hwang, Bob Iger, Walter Isaacson, Robert Isom, Sam Jacobs, Ankur Jain, Tom James, Philip Jeffrey, Tracy Jen, Hugh Johnston, Stacy Jolna, Brad Katsuyama, Margaret Keane, Joe Kernen, Congressman Ro Khanna, Rakesh Khurana, Mary Kissel, Klaus Kleinfeld, Amy Klobuchar, General Tom Kolditz, Benn Konsynski, Alex Korson, Chris Krebs, Larry Kudlow, Ellen Kullman, Senator Jon Kyl, Ambassador Philip Lader, Ken Langone, Mike Larabee, Mark Lasswell, Almar Latour, the late Paul and Martha Lawrence, Richard LeFrak, Father Ryan Lerner, Rich Lesser, Matt Levatich, Max Levchin, Mike and Andrea Leven, Nick Lichtenberg, Joanne Lipman, Robert Lighthizer, Joanne Lublin, Terry Lundgren, Frank Luntz, Omeed Malik, Paras Malik, Jonathan Mariner, Judy Marks, General Barry McCaffrey, the late Senator John McCain, General Stan McChrystal, Matt McCooe, Senator David McCormick, Dina Powell McCormick, Bruce McKinnon, Doug McMillon, Jim McNerney, Meredith Lazo McPherron, Danny Meyer, David Miller, Steve Miller, Susan Molinari, Steve Mollman, Tony and Jackie Montag, Steve Moore, Virginia Moseley, Peter Navarro, Chris Nedza, Mark Nedza, Ambassador John Negroponte, Anne Neuberger, Steve Newton, Xu Niansa, Indra Nooyi, Erik Nordstrom, Grover Norquist, Adam Norwitt, John O'Connor, Lawrence O'Donnell, Fiyin Oladiran, Cathy Olian, Judy Olian, Peter Orszag,

Asutosh Padhi, Joe Papa, Steve Papa, Doug Parker, Alan Patricof, the late Danny Pearl, Jen Pellet, Speaker Nancy Pelosi, Mark Penn, John Pepper, Abby Phillip, Rabbi Meir Posner, Jennifer Prosek, Becky Quick, Carl Quintanilla, Vivek Ramaswamy, Imam Feisal Abdul Rauf, Ralph Reed, Emily Reichman, Brian Roberts, George Rohr, Ginni Rometty, Matthew Rose, Wilbur Ross, Michael Roth, David Rubenstein, Prime Minister Kevin Rudd, Stephanie Ruhle, the late Morley Safer, David Salzman, Joe Scarborough, Keith Schiller, Len Schleifer, Senator Charles Schumer, Alan Schwartz, Jim Sciutto, Ivan Seidenberg, Mike Sexton, Ron Shaich, Congressman Chris Shays, Alyson Shontell, Jessica Sibley, Bob Simonds, John Slocum, Michael Smerconish, Jim Smith, Kevin Sneader, Tim Snyder, Jonny Sonnenfeld, Richard Spencer, Jason Stanley, Jeff Stein, Brian Sullivan, Senator Dan Sullivan, Charlie Sykes, Mayor Tom Tait, Denise O'Leary Thiry, Kent Thiry, Jay Timmons, Anne Tironi, Michael Tomasky, Nigel Travis, Olivia Troye, President Donald Trump, Emma Tucker, Laura Tyson, Ali Velshi, Andrew Ward, Senator Mark Warner, Faye Wattleton, Phillip Weiss, Stuart Weitzman, the late John Whitehead, Rick and Joanne Williams, Bob Woodward, George Yancopoulos, Ambassador Andrew Young, David Yoffie, Amy Zegart, and Jeff Zucker.

Lastly, but surely of top priority, I want to thank my coauthor, Steven Tian, the smartest, hardest-working person I know. Friends and colleagues have long figured out that he is the secret weapon behind my quantum leap in productivity the last few years. While I was hardly dormant before, Steven is very humble but is a genuine polymath—great at qualitative, creative leaps of insight and diligent flawless quantitative analysis for a mind that travels laterally and vertically with equal dexterity. Plus, he rarely sleeps. This book would not exist without him.

ABOUT THE AUTHOR

Jeffrey Sonnenfeld is the Senior Associate Dean for Leadership Studies and Lester Crown Professor in Management Practice at the Yale School of Management as well as founder and president of the Chief Executive Leadership Institute, a nonprofit educational and research institute focused on CEO leadership and corporate governance. He has authored eight books, including *The Hero's Farewell*, an award-winning study of CEO succession, and *Firing Back*, a study on leadership resilience from adversity. His work is regularly cited by the general media such as *BusinessWeek*, *Forbes*, *The Wall Street Journal*, *The New York Times*, *Newsweek*, *Time*, *The Economist*, *The Financial Times*, *The Washington Post*, CBS, MSNBC, CNN, FOX, NBC, ABC, and PBS, and he is a staff contributor for CNBC and a staff columnist for *Fortune*, *Time*, *Chief Executive*, and *Corporate Board Member*. Sonnenfeld has informally advised five US presidents across parties and helped Jared Kushner launch the Abraham Accords in the Mideast. Sonnenfeld earned his AB, MBA, and PhD degrees from Harvard University, where he taught for a decade, and has an honorary doctorate from Sacred Heart University. Sonnenfeld was recognized by *Poets & Quants Magazine* as the 2022 Professor of the Year in recognition of his high-profile efforts to catalyze the historic exits from Russia of over one thousand global businesses after the invasion of Ukraine, and named to *Worth Magazine*'s "Worthy 100 Leaders," an annual global listing of the most influential leaders across society. Sonnenfeld has rung the opening bell of the NYSE and NASDAQ a record twelve times, and he has received the Ellis Island Medal of Honor, the 2023 Greatest Impact on Corporate Boards award by *Corporate Board Member* magazine, and the *Academy of Management*'s 2023 Distinguished Scholar Practitioner Award.